Nobody's Son

THE MILLION COPY BESTSELLING AUTHOR

CATHY GLASS

Nobody's Son

**All Alex ever wanted
was a family of his own...**

Certain details in this story, including names, places and dates,
have been changed to protect the family's privacy.

HarperElement
An imprint of HarperCollins*Publishers*
1 London Bridge Street
London SE1 9GF

www.harpercollins.co.uk

First published by HarperElement 2017

1 3 5 7 9 10 8 6 4 2

A catalogue record of this book is
available from the British Library

ISBN 978-0-00-818756-9

Printed and bound in Great Britain by
Clays Ltd, St Ives plc

MIX
Paper from
responsible sources
FSC™ C007454

FSC™ is a non-profit international organisation established to promote
the responsible management of the world's forests. Products carrying the
FSC label are independently certified to assure consumers that they come
from forests that are managed to meet the social, economic and
ecological needs of present or future generations,
and other controlled sources.

Find out more about HarperCollins and the environment at
www.harpercollins.co.uk/green

ACKNOWLEDGEMENTS

A big thank you to my family; my editors, Carolyn and Holly; my literary agent, Andrew; my UK publishers, HarperCollins, and my overseas publishers, who are now too numerous to list by name. Last, but definitely not least, a big thank you to my readers for your unfailing support and kind words.

PROLOGUE

We immediately fell silent as the noise sounded again. The children stared at me anxiously before our eyes went towards the curtains drawn across the patio doors. It was cold and dark outside, but something was out there scratching and trying to get in. Not our cat; she was asleep by the warm radiator, and it didn't sound like a cat anyway. I stood and gingerly crossed the room, my heart pounding and my senses on full alert. There were just the children and me in the house, and I tried to hide my fear from them as I eased one curtain aside and peered into the dark. Nothing. Whatever it was had vanished again like a phantom into the night.

CHAPTER ONE

A NEW YEAR, A NEW CHILD

I'd taken six months off from fostering after my husband had left me. There, I said it – my husband left me. It had been a difficult time, adjusting, supporting my children and reassuring them that it wasn't their fault and their father still loved them. But the fact that I was now able to say out loud that my husband had left me meant I was coming to terms with it and moving on, just as my counsellor had said I would. I only saw her four times and she was also the vicar of our local church. Not that we'd been regular church-goers – Christmas, Easter, Mothering Sunday and the occasional family service – but I knew she was approachable, down to earth and offered counselling. She wouldn't ask me to pray for my husband's salvation or even forgive him, which I couldn't do yet. Get over his cheating and lies and the rejection, yes, but not forgive him, not for making my children fatherless. She'd listened sympathetically, but more importantly she'd told me it was time to acknowledge that my marriage was at an end, that I'd done my best to salvage it and that I should now move on with my life.

In the six months I'd been away from fostering many changes had taken place, developments in procedure and practice that remain part of fostering today. I now had a link worker, Jill, also known as a support or supervising social worker, whose role, as her title suggested, was to support and monitor my fostering to make sure it was to a good standard, to check my log notes were up to date and that my training needs were met. Ongoing training and report writing were now part of fostering for carers and I had to keep a daily record of the child I was looking after, which included appointments the child had, their health and wellbeing, education, significant events and any disclosures the child made about their past. There were also regular reviews for the child and an annual review for the foster carer, and fostering was provided through agencies. I worked for Homefinders, an independent fostering agency with charity status. But of course the heart, the essence of fostering, remained the same. The foster family looked after a child or children, short or long term, who, for any number of reasons, couldn't be looked after by their own parents, and their stories and past experiences were still heart-rending and varied. One change I didn't like was that the children now had to call me their foster carer rather than their foster mum, as it was felt it might be confusing for them. It seemed a bit cold to me, but I had to abide by this as I did all the other fostering practices and regulations.

When I asked my son Adrian, then aged seven, if he thought we were ready to start fostering again, he replied with a resounding, 'Yes.' Then added, 'It's time we got back to normal.' An old head on young shoulders. I didn't point out that we'd never get completely 'back to normal' because his father wouldn't be there, but I knew what he meant. It was time to pick up the threads of our old life. My three-year-old daughter Paula was at an age when she agreed with her older brother, so she was happy to resume fostering too. They'd both grown up with fostering, so having another 'brother' or 'sister' living with them was the norm. Adrian was especially pleased when I told him that we would be looking after a boy, Alex, almost the same age as him, for while he obviously loved his sister their play was at different stages, and nothing beats having a playmate of your own age.

I'd warmed to Jill, my support worker, as soon as I'd met her. She was straight-talking, with lots of social-worker experience, kind and empathetic too. So when she told me a little about Alex and that he wouldn't give me any trouble and was just what we needed to ease us back into fostering, I believed her.

'A New Year, a new start,' I said. It was Saturday 10 January and I was feeling very positive.

Alex, like most of the children we'd fostered, had had a very unsettled early life but was going to be adopted so, to use a term social workers use, his case would have a 'good outcome'. What wasn't so good, however, and worried Jill as it did me, was that Alex was having to move foster homes again now, not long before the move to his adoptive parents. He'd already had three previous foster homes since coming into care, and now he was having to move from his present carers', where he'd been for five months. The couple had two children of their own and the woman was pregnant again and had found it all too much, which I suppose was understandable. But there was only a month before Alex would be moving to his adoptive home.

'And they can't be persuaded to keep him for the last month?' I asked Jill on the phone. 'Moving is so unsettling and Alex has had more than his fair share of moves.'

'Apparently not,' Jill said with a small tut of disapproval, 'although if I was their supervising social worker I'd have tried to persuade them. Some extra support could have been put in to keep Alex there. But the carers are adamant he has to go.'

I was therefore providing what is known as a 'bridging placement' – an interim home in between his present foster home and his permanent adoptive one. I hadn't been given much notice of Alex's arrival, but that was often the case in fostering. Jill had telephoned the day before to tell me a little about Alex. Once I'd agreed to take him, Debbie, his social worker, whom I hadn't met yet, telephoned and said she'd asked Alex's present carers to bring him for a visit on Saturday afternoon, then he could move in on Sunday morning. It was good that Alex was having the chance to meet us and look around the house first so it wouldn't be so strange and unfamiliar when he moved in. As it was the weekend, neither Jill nor Debbie would be present when Alex visited or moved in. His present carers and I were experienced foster carers, so it was felt we could manage this between us, which was fine. Debbie and Jill would phone on Monday to make sure the move had gone well.

In preparation for Alex's visit, Adrian had arranged some of his favourite toys in the living room. He was quietly excited and looking forward to meeting Alex. Paula had brought down one of her favourite dolls from her bedroom.

4

'He won't want to play with dolls,' Adrian said a little disparagingly. Paula looked hurt.

'He might,' I said. 'You do sometimes. And less of the stereotyping, please.'

When the front doorbell rang a little after two o'clock Adrian and Paula came with me to answer it. Paula brought her doll.

'Cathy?' the man standing on my doorstep said. 'I'm Graham, Alex's carer.'

'Hello.' We shook hands. 'And you must be Alex? Nice to meet you. Come on in. It's freezing out there.'

Alex was a slightly built child with brown hair and a sallow complexion, and was huddled deep inside his navy parka. He looked up at me, wide-eyed and nervous.

'It's just me,' Graham said as they came in. 'My wife, Sandy, is having a rest.'

'OK,' I said. 'This is Adrian, my son; he's nearly the same age as Alex.'

'Hi,' Adrian said, taking a small step forward.

'And this is Paula, my daughter, who is three and a half.' Paula grinned shyly and clutched her doll protectively to her chest.

'Nice to meet you both,' Graham said. He was of average height and build with fashionable chin stubble, and I guessed he was in his late thirties. 'Say hello, Alex,' he told him.

Alex managed a small, very timid 'Hello'.

'Take off your coat then, mate,' Graham said to Alex.

Alex did as he was told and I hung his coat on the hall stand. He also took off his trainers. He'd brought a toy car transporter with him and I admired it.

'Adrian likes cars too,' I said. 'He's set some out in the living room for you both to play with.' I led the way down the hall and into the living room.

'Come and play with my cars,' Adrian said to Alex.

Alex left his carer's side and went over and squatted down beside Adrian. Paula watched them shyly from a little distance.

'Would you like a drink?' I offered Graham.

'No, thanks.'

'What about you, Alex?'

He shook his head.

'We won't stay long,' Graham said. 'It's just a short visit to familiarize Alex with his new home.' This was true, but it was also important that Alex spent a little time playing, as it would put him at ease.

'Have a seat,' I said to Graham. 'I'll show you around shortly.'

He sat in one of the easy-chairs and I sat on the sofa. Paula stood beside me, clutching her doll and watching the boys, not brave enough yet to join in.

'You were told why Alex is having to move?' Graham asked me, slightly guiltily, I thought.

'Yes, your wife is expecting. Congratulations.'

'Thanks. She's been very sick with this pregnancy and it's all become too much. Debbie, Alex's social worker, isn't happy with us. She suggested we put Alex in after-school club so we could see him through to permanency, as it's just a month. He already goes to breakfast club. But you know how it is in fostering – one month stretches to two and so on. We couldn't take the risk.'

I nodded. I did know how it was. Carers have to be very flexible, as plans can and do change in fostering, sometimes with very little notice.

'He should only be here a month though,' Graham added. 'Sandy and I have met the adoptive parents. I guess you'll take over where we left off?'

'I would think so.'

'There's a meeting on Wednesday to plan the introduction and the move to his new parents,' Graham said. Alex looked up. 'You're looking forward to meeting your new parents, aren't you, mate?'

Alex gave a small, shy nod and then, lowering his gaze again, continued to play with the cars.

'I haven't been told about the meeting yet,' I said. 'I guess Jill or Debbie will tell me on Monday when they phone. But I'll make a note of it in my diary. What time is it?'

'Not sure. I'll bring all the paperwork with me tomorrow when I move him. I suppose they might postpone the introduction because of this move,' he added. 'I know it's not the best timing, but you have to put your own first, don't you?'

Difficult one, I thought. My experience of fostering had taught me that sometimes the needs of the foster child had to be placed first and your own family did on occasions have to take second place. Toscha, our rather lazy cat, sauntered out from behind the sofa where she'd been curled up in her favourite place beside the radiator. Alex looked startled.

'She won't hurt you,' I said. 'She's just come to say hello. Do you like cats?'

Alex nodded cautiously. My first impression of him was that he was a slightly nervous child, unsure of himself or situations.

Hardly surprising given his unsettled past. Children show anxiety in different ways; some run in loud and assertive while others, like Alex, recede into their shell until they feel safe.

'He's fine with animals,' Graham said. 'We've got a cat and a dog.'

'That's good,' I said, relieved. 'Toscha likes you, Alex.' She was purring loudly and sniffing his jumper. He didn't seem to mind.

I let Alex play for another ten minutes while Graham and I talked – about the weather, fostering and life in general. It was important for Alex to see me getting along with his current carer, as it would give the move and me the stamp of approval, but I was aware that Graham needed to get back so I suggested showing them around the house.

'I'll show you my room,' Adrian said proudly. Taking hold of Alex's hand, he drew him to his feet.

Graham saw this. 'It'll be nice having someone your own age to play with, won't it?'

Alex managed a small smile and picked up his toy trans-porter to take with him.

'So, this is our living room,' I said, beginning the tour. 'We're often in here, playing games or watching the television. You can see the garden through the patio windows. It's lovely to play out there in summer but a bit cold at present, unless of course we have snow.'

'I hope we have snow,' Adrian said.

'Me too,' Alex quietly agreed.

I led the way through to our kitchen-cum-diner.

'That's my place,' Adrian said, pointing to his chair at the table. 'You can sit next me if you like. Can't he, Mum?'

'Yes, of course,' I said.

'That'll be nice, won't it?' Graham said encouragingly.

Alex nodded again.

Toscha had followed us out and Paula bent down to stroke her. Alex did likewise. 'I like your doll,' he said shyly to Paula.

She smiled equally shyly. 'I like your car.'

Great first step, I thought: all three children were talking to each other and Alex was starting to relax a little. I continued the tour downstairs into the front room and then upstairs. Alex wasn't really interested in the other bedrooms or the bathroom – what seven-year-old boy would be? – but it was important that he saw them, as he would be able take away an image of the inside of our house so it wouldn't feel so strange when he moved in tomorrow. However, when we went into his bedroom he looked lost and bewildered. I'd made it as homely as I could, with posters of action heroes on the walls and a Batman duvet cover on the bed, but it still looked rather empty compared to the other rooms.

'It will be much better once you have all your things in here,' I told Alex.

'We'll pack everything when we get home, mate,' Graham said to Alex. Then to me, 'We bought him a bike for Christmas; have you got a shed it can go in?'

'Yes.' Alex looked anxious. 'Don't worry,' I said to him. 'We have room for all your belongings. Nothing will get left behind.' It is often an anxiety for children who come into care or those who've had a number of moves that their possessions will be lost or left behind. And of course in a month's time we'd be packing up all Alex's possessions again and moving him to his permanent home. From what I'd seen of Alex so far he was coping with all of this very well.

'Do you like your room?' Graham asked him.

Alex gave a small nod.

'Good, and remember Adrian's room is just next door,' I said.

We'd seen the other rooms upstairs, so Graham led the way out of Alex's room and downstairs. He didn't return to the living room; instead he stopped at the coat stand and unhooked Alex's coat. 'Get your trainers on then, mate,' he said. 'You'll see Cathy again tomorrow.'

I appreciated Graham wanted to get back to his wife and pack. 'We'll see you in the morning,' I said to Alex with an encouraging smile.

He nodded.

'At eleven o'clock,' Graham said to me. 'Is that what you were told?'

'Yes.'

Alex had put on his trainers and Graham passed him his coat. 'Will I still be able to go to my old school?' he quietly asked Graham.

'I think so, mate,' he replied.

'Yes, you will,' I confirmed. 'I'll take you there in my car. You go to breakfast club so we'll take you there first and then Adrian to his school and Paula to nursery.'

Alex looked relieved and managed another small smile. School is often the only constant factor in a foster child's life if they have to move home; it's familiar, safe and reliable, so it's important that they remain at the same school if at all possible. There was a chance that Alex would have to change schools when he went to his adoptive parents, as the matching process – children with prospective parents – stretches across the country, but if so that would be unavoidable, and it would be the last move he'd have to make.

'See you tomorrow then,' Graham said as they headed down the front path.

We watched them go and then I closed the front door.

'I like Alex, he's nice,' Adrian said.

'I like him too,' Paula agreed.

'He's a lovely little boy, but remember he'll only be staying with us for a few weeks,' I cautioned, as much for my benefit as the children's. I knew how easily we became attached to the children we looked after, especially a child like Alex, unassuming and vulnerable. You felt like you wanted to give him a big hug and never let him go, but he'd only be with us a short while.

We played some card and board games that afternoon and then in the evening, after dinner, the three of us watched some television. The house phone rang at six o'clock and I was slightly surprised to hear John, their father. He usually telephoned on a Sunday evening, but he quickly explained that he was away for a few days so he was phoning now while he had the chance, as he didn't like to let the children down. I bit back the retort at the tip of my tongue about letting the children down in a much bigger way and passed the handset to Adrian, who usually spoke to him first. Adrian told him about school and football and what he'd been doing generally – a life that John had once been part of and familiar with but now needed to be told about. When Adrian had finished his news he passed the phone to Paula who, not understanding about divorce, asked as she had done before, 'When are you coming home, Daddy?' It stung my heart now as it always did.

'He's not,' Adrian said under his breath.

'It's OK,' I said quietly to him. Then to Paula I said, 'Daddy is coming to see you next Sunday.'

John must have said something similar for she repeated, 'Seeing Daddy next weekend.' Then, satisfied that she'd spoken to him, she said, 'Goodbye, Daddy,' and passed the phone to Adrian to say goodbye and hang up.

John would now return to his life as we returned to ours, and while it was getting a little easier for us to accept, I would never understand how a father could leave his family for another woman. Had John's life with me really been so bad? He'd admitted once that it hadn't, that it was just one of those things, beyond his control, that he'd fallen in love with another woman. As though it wasn't his fault!

CHAPTER TWO

UNSETTLED EARLY LIFE

The following morning Adrian was up earlier than usual for a Sunday, eagerly awaiting the arrival of Alex. We'd had our Sunday-morning fry-up for breakfast and I'd cleared up so that I was ready to give Alex my full attention. It's always strange when a new child first arrives – for us as well as the child – as we all adjust to each other's likes and dislikes, habits and mannerisms, but by the end of a few days we're all usually jogging along together in our new routine.

The front doorbell rang a little after eleven o'clock and the children came with me to answer it.

'I'll play with Alex while you help Mum unpack,' Adrian told Paula.

'I want to play too,' Paula said with a whine.

'You can both play with him,' I said diplomatically.

As I opened the front door the cold January air rushed in. Alex and Graham stood side by side in the porch, loaded with bags. 'Good morning,' Graham said cheerfully. 'I'll bring these in and then unpack the rest of the car.'

I held the door wide open so Graham could manoeuvre in the two large suitcases he was carrying. 'Are they all right there?' he asked, setting them down to one side of the hall.

'Yes, fine. I'll sort them all out later.'

'That case has Alex's school uniform in and his winter clothes,' he said, tapping one. 'You may not need to unpack the other. It's his summer gear.'

'OK, thanks.'

Alex, holding his school bag and a carrier bag of toys, with a bulging rucksack on his back, was now standing in the hall looking very lost.

'Here, let me help you with that,' I said, and eased the rucksack off his back.

'You stay here with Cathy,' Graham told Alex, 'while I unload the rest of the car.'

Adrian took the bags Alex was holding from him so he could take off his coat. The poor lad looked even more bewildered now than he had done yesterday. 'Are you OK, love?' I asked him as he stood immobile, making no attempt to take off his coat or trainers. He nodded. 'You'll soon feel at home,' I reassured him with a smile.

'Is this my new home?' he asked.

'For now, yes.'

'But you're not my new mummy?'

'No, love. I'm your new foster carer. You should be meeting your new mummy and daddy in a week or so.'

He nodded again and then began unzipping his parka. Slipping it off, he handed it to me and I hung it on the hall stand with our coats. Graham returned with more bags and set them in the hall beside the suitcases. He also handed me a folder containing the paperwork I needed.

'Do you want his bike in here or shall I take it round the back?' Graham asked me.

'In here, please. Alex can help me put it in the shed later.' It was important Alex saw where his new bike was going so he knew it was safe.

'Shall we play with some of your toys?' Adrian asked, peering into the carrier bag.

Alex gave a small nod and, picking up the bag, followed Adrian down the hall and into the living room. Paula ran after them. Graham returned with Alex's bike and some more bags, which we stacked in the hall. There was hardly any room to move. Children who've been in care a while tend to acquire many possessions – as much if not more than the average child – as carers try to compensate for the depravation of their early years before coming into care. Graham brought in the last of the bags and I was pleased to be able to close the front door against the cold winter air.

'I'll just say goodbye to Alex and then I'll be off,' Graham said, aware that it was advisable to keep his leave-taking short.

I went with him to the living room, where the children were sitting in a small circle on the floor playing with Alex's toys. Toscha was asleep on the sofa.

'Bye then, mate,' Graham said from just inside the door. 'Be good.'

Alex didn't turn or speak. 'Say goodbye to Graham,' I said.

'Bye,' Alex said, but he kept his back to Graham and I knew he was feeling rejected.

I could see Graham was a little surprised, even hurt, by Alex's reaction, perhaps expecting a hug or even tears, but it's a trauma for a child to have to move home when they're settled and Alex was stating how he felt. 'Don't worry,' I said quietly to Graham. 'He'll be fine soon.'

'Bye then, mate,' Graham said again, and then, with no response from Alex, he returned down the hall.

I went with him to see him out. 'I hope everything goes well with the pregnancy,' I said.

'Yes, thanks.' And he was gone, although I knew that the memory of Alex would stay with Graham for a long time, probably forever, just as Alex would remember them, hopefully in a positive light.

Today was all about settling Alex in and unpacking his belongings, so I hadn't planned an outing. After Graham left I checked that the children were still playing happily in the living room, then I carried Alex's suitcases up to his bedroom one at a time. I returned downstairs again for some of his bags of toys and took those up too. I would suggest to Alex that he kept some of his toys in his bedroom and some downstairs to play with, as Adrian, Paula and the other children I'd fostered did. With the hall much clearer I went into the living room and sat with the children for a while and watched them play, then Alex said he needed to use the bathroom so I went with him upstairs to show him where it was, and waited on the landing until he'd finished. As he passed his bedroom he looked in.

'Will I be sleeping in there tonight?' he asked.

'Yes, love. I'll unpack your cases soon.'

We returned downstairs and I made the children a drink and a snack, which we had at the table, with Alex sitting in his place next to Adrian. Everyone was very quiet and on their best behaviour, but I knew from experience that it wouldn't take long before they felt more comfortable with each other. Once we'd finished eating the children wanted to continue playing in the living room. As they were playing nicely – Adrian was sharing his toys with Alex and Alex was sharing his with Adrian and Paula – I said I'd go and unpack Alex's bags and they should call for me if they needed me. I wouldn't have left all the children I'd fostered unattended on their first day, but Alex didn't have any behavioural issues and appeared responsible, as was Adrian, so I felt OK leaving them with Paula. Adrian knew to fetch me if there was a problem.

With school in the morning I wanted to be organized, so I began by unpacking the case that Graham had said contained Alex's school uniform and his casual clothes for winter. I hung them in the wardrobe and then arranged his underwear and socks in a drawer. I placed a pair of his pyjamas on his bed ready for later and hung his dressing gown on the hook on the back of his door. I took his towel and wash bag into the bathroom, where I placed his towel next to ours on the rail and set his wash bag on the shelf within his reach. I listened on the landing for the children and could hear them still playing, so I returned to Alex's bedroom. With the first case empty I opened the second but, as Graham had said, it contained Alex's summer clothes so I closed it again and then put both cases out of the way on top of the wardrobe.

One of the bags I'd brought up contained soft toys and I arranged these on Alex's bed and on one of the shelves. Another bag contained more toys and I emptied it into the toy box. There were another couple of new toy boxes downstairs ready for the toys Alex might want to keep in the living room. Although Alex was only staying for a few weeks, it was important he felt comfortable and 'at home' and wasn't living out of cases. Satisfied his bedroom was now looking more welcoming and lived in, I took his slippers downstairs. Alex and Adrian were just coming out of the living room to take another of Alex's bags of toys through to play with.

'Before you do that let's put your bike away,' I suggested. 'It's a lovely bike – you are lucky.'

'Father Christmas bought it for me,' Alex said with a small smile.

Adrian wanted to come and help put the bike in the shed, and then of course Paula, not wanting to be left out, arrived in the hall and said she did too. We all put on our coats and shoes and Alex carefully wheeled his bike down the hall, through the kitchen, and then Adrian helped him out with it through the back door. Our garden is long and narrow, with a patio at the top and then mainly grass to the shed at the very bottom. 'Shall I ride my bike to the shed?' Alex asked, clearly wanting to.

'Yes.'

He carefully mounted the bike and then rode confidently to the bottom of the garden, where he dismounted. We caught up. 'If the weather is good next weekend we could take the bikes to the park,' I suggested.

'Yes!' Adrian said, and Alex nodded enthusiastically.

I unlocked the shed door and Adrian helped Alex in with his bike and rested it carefully next to his and Paula's. There were other garden toys here too, stored for winter.

'My bike's got more wheels,' Paula said, referring to the stabilizers.

'Otherwise she falls off,' Adrian said with a giggle to Alex.

'Your bike had stabilizers too when you were very little and were learning to ride,' I reminded Adrian. 'I expect Alex used them as well. Many children do.'

We returned indoors and the children continued playing in the living room and sharing their toys nicely. At present, playing together and discovering each other's toys was a novelty, but I knew it was quite possible that after a while the novelty might wear off and squabbles could break out, just as in any sibling or friendship group. Experience had taught me that this was more likely with similar-aged children of the same sex, as Alex and Adrian were. They were either inseparable and best buddies or arguing over the same toy. Generally, if there is a choice of carers then foster children are placed with carers where there aren't already children of the same age, especially if they are staying long term. But often there isn't a choice, as there is always a shortage of foster carers, and as this wasn't long term I didn't envisage too many problems.

The rest of the afternoon passed happily, and when I called everyone to dinner Alex went straight to his place at the table, far more relaxed and confident, as indeed Adrian and Paula were; everyone was thawing out. We talked as we ate and it was only natural that at some point Alex was going to mention his adoptive family, whom he had been told a bit about and was looking forward to meeting for the first time.

'I'm going to have a forever mummy and daddy,' he said. 'I used to just have a mummy, but she can't look after me.' I nodded. 'Graham says my daddy will do lots of things with me, like playing football. Do you have a daddy?' he asked Adrian.

I saw Adrian's face fall. 'Yes,' he said quietly.

'But he doesn't live with us,' I added, saving Adrian the embarrassment of having to say it.

'Daddy takes us out and buys us sweets,' Paula put in.

'That's nice,' Alex said, and began talking about the sweets he'd had for Christmas. Although Alex's question was entirely innocent, I knew Adrian struggled at moments like this. It had taken him months to admit to his best friend that his father wasn't living with us any more, and many of his friends at school still didn't know. Adrian perceived a stigma where others did not, and while it greatly saddened me that he had been placed in this position, there was nothing I could do about it beyond supporting him as he adjusted to having an absent father, as many children now have to do.

After dinner I checked I had everything ready for the following morning. Alex's school bag was in the hall beside Adrian's, his school coat was on the hall stand with our coats, and his school shoes were paired beneath the stand with our shoes. Alex had school dinners, as did Adrian, so I didn't have to make any packed lunches. As we would need to rise early in the morning for our new school run I began the children's bath and bedtime routine just before seven o'clock that Sunday. I read Paula some stories and then, leaving the boys playing, I took her up for her bath and settled her into bed with her favourite cuddly – a velvety soft furry rabbit, which her father had bought as one of her Christmas presents.

I returned downstairs for Alex. He was used to a similar bath and bedtime routine at his previous foster carers'. 'What shall I do with all my toys?' he asked. They were strewn across the living-room floor and Adrian had begun to pack his away into the new toy boxes.

'I have just what you need,' I said with a smile, and I brought in the new toy boxes. 'You can put your toys in these and then you'll be able to take them with you when you leave us.' Which is what I usually did so the children I fostered left me with their toys in boxes and their clothes neatly packed in cases. I only use plastic bags as a very last resort as I feel it's degrading for a child to move home with their belongings in carrier bags and bin liners.

Once the boys had packed away Alex said goodnight to Adrian and I took him upstairs, firstly to his bedroom to fetch his pyjamas. He liked the way I'd arranged his soft toys on his bed and shelf and the toys in the toy box.

'Can I take that toy box with me as well?' he asked.

'Yes.'

He was pleased. Plastic toy boxes aren't expensive but the children love having their own, and of course they help to keep the rooms tidy. I showed him where I'd put his pyjamas and dressing gown and he carried them round to the bath-room, where I ran his bath to the right temperature. I pointed out the laundry basket where he could put his dirty clothes and then, to give him some privacy, I waited on the landing while he washed and dried himself. Once he was in his pyja-mas I waited while he cleaned his teeth. I wouldn't leave a child of his age to just get on with it, especially on their first night, although his self-care skills were very good. We returned round the landing to his bedroom, where I asked him, as I always do when a child first arrives, if he liked to sleep with his curtains open or closed. He said closed. Similarly I asked him if he slept with the light on or off. He said off, and with his bedroom door left open a little. Small details, but their familiarity and the comfort they give to the child help them settle in a strange room. I told Alex that I always left a night light on the landing so he could see where he was going if he needed the toilet, but to call out to me if he woke in the night, as I didn't want him wandering around by himself. Before climbing into bed he chose one of his soft toys to sleep with – Simba from the Walt Disney film *The Lion King*. I asked him if that was his favourite, but he said he didn't have a favourite and just chose a different one each night. Once he was snuggled beneath the duvet with Simba beside him, I said goodnight and then asked him if he'd like a kiss and a hug. He shook his head shyly.

'It's OK. You don't have to,' I said with a smile. I always ask the child, otherwise it's an invasion of their personal space to suddenly be kissed or hugged by an adult if they're not comfortable with it. Some children are very tactile and want hugs and kisses as soon as they arrive, while others wait until they know me better.

'Sandy used to kiss me goodnight,' Alex said quietly. 'But I'll wait for my proper mummy to do it.' Which was very revealing. Alex had been close to his previous carers and felt their rejection. He wasn't going to risk making an emotional investment in me straight away; he was saving it for his adoptive parents, whom he could rely on. 'When will I meet her?' he asked.

'I'm not sure yet. I'll know more when I've spoken to your social worker tomorrow.'

He smiled wistfully, his little face peeping over the duvet. 'I hope it's soon.'

'It shouldn't be long.' My heart went out to him. He was so looking forward to having a family of his own forever, which, of course, most of us take for granted.

Having said goodnight I came out, leaving the door slightly open, and checked on Paula. She was fast asleep, on her side and cuddled up to her soft toy rabbit. I called Adrian up for his bath, and once he was in bed I lay propped beside him on the pillow and we had our usual bedtime chat before we hugged and kissed goodnight. I came out, closing his door as he preferred, and went downstairs. I took the folder Graham had given me from the front room, made a cup of tea and then settled on the sofa in the living room next to Toscha.

With my tea within reach I opened the folder, which contained the information Graham and Sandy – as Alex's carers – had received on Alex. On top was a handwritten note: 'The planning meeting on Wednesday is at 11 a.m. at the council offices. Good luck. Sandy.' I immediately fetched my diary and wrote in the time and venue. I'd have to ask a friend to collect Paula from nursery, as she finished at twelve. I knew the meeting would last at least an hour and then I had the twenty-minute or so drive from the council offices to the nursery. Setting my diary to one side, I began going through Alex's paperwork. The most recent was on top: the minutes of Alex's last review. Children in care have regular reviews to make sure that everything is being done as it should to help the child, and that their care plan is up to date. I glanced through the pages. They were more or less what I would have expected, just an update on his previous review three months before. Sandy had been present at his last review, together with her support social worker, Alex's social worker, his teacher and the independent reviewing officer who chaired and minuted the meeting. Alex's care plan at the time had been to remain with Graham and Sandy until he moved to his adoptive parents', but it had all changed since then, culminating in him being placed temporarily with me. I wondered if there'd be a review while Alex was with me; it's usual when a child moves.

I turned the pages and scanned down the copy of Alex's school report – he was making good progress – then the medical and health checks, a copy of the court order that had brought him into care and miscellaneous paper work. Going further back I found a copy of the minutes of the previous review, from which I learned that Alex had had supervised contact once a week with his mother at the contact centre, but it had been stopped (three months ago) in preparation for Alex being adopted. While this was usual practice for a child who was going to be adopted – to sever any existing bond with his birth family before introducing him to his adoptive parents – it stung my heart as it always did. I could picture that traumatic and distressing scene as Alex's mother said goodbye to her son for the very last time and then had to watch him walk away, never to see him again. While I appreciated that everything would have been done to try to enable his mother to keep Alex, and that the judge would not have made the order without very good reason, it was nevertheless still heartbreaking. How any mother ever comes to terms with losing her child or children I'll never know. Possibly many don't and are never able to rebuild their lives and move on. It made me go cold just thinking about it. Losing a child for any reason is truly the stuff of nightmares.

I continued turning the pages – more reviews and school reports. Alex had been in care a long time, so there was a lot of paperwork. Then nearer the back I found the essential information form, which included a résumé of Alex's early life and the circumstances that had brought him into care. I read that he had been badly neglected as a baby. His mother had mental-health problems and was drug dependent. Alex had never known his father – little wonder he was so looking forward to meeting his adoptive father, I thought. Alex had been in and out of care for the first three years of his life and had remained in care since then, but that wasn't the end of his unsettled life, for since being in care permanently he'd had to move home a number of times. I couldn't find the exact number or the reasons for the moves, but the foster carers' names on the minutes of the reviews kept changing, and reference was made at the review to the most recent move. Sometimes children in care have to move and it's unavoidable – for example, a child with very challenging behaviour may be placed with inexperienced carers who simply can't cope – but Alex didn't have challenging behaviour as far as I knew.

Since publishing my fostering memoirs I've received many emails from young adults who were in care and had repeated moves. Some have lost count of the number of different foster homes they lived in, and are now trying to deal with the fallout of such an unsettled childhood: insecurity, anger, panic attacks, depression, irrational fears, lack of confidence and low self-worth are a few of the issues. True, some care leavers email me to say their experience in care was a very good one and they're grateful to their carers who loved and looked after them as their own, but not all. In a developed society like ours, which prides itself on being caring, we tend to think that if a child can't live with their natural parents then our social-care system will step in and look after them, giving them the love, care and security that their parents failed to, but sadly sometimes they are failed by the care system too. And to make matters worse for little Alex, I now read that he'd been born in prison and had spent the first six months of his life there while his mother completed her sentence. It didn't say what crime she had committed. It was all so very sad.

CHAPTER THREE

ALEX'S PARENTS

My heart ached for Alex. Thank goodness he'd been found a loving adoptive family who would help right the wrongs of his past and nurture him towards a bright and positive future, where he would feel loved and valued and thrive as a child should. I drained the last of my now-cold tea, closed the folder and went into the front room, where I placed it in the lockable drawer. I took out my fostering folder so that I could write up my log notes – the daily record foster carers are required to keep of the child or children they are looking after. When the child leaves this record is usually placed on file at the social services. Returning to the living room, I took a pen and a fresh sheet of paper and headed it with today's date, then I wrote a couple of paragraphs on how Alex was settling in and what we'd done that day. Closing the folder, I placed that in the drawer in the front room too.

Before I went to bed I looked in on Alex. He was sleeping peacefully, although Simba had fallen out and lay on the floor. I quietly picked him up and set him on the pillow again, and then crept out. I never sleep well when there is a new child in the house. I'm half listening out in case they wake frightened, not knowing where they are and needing reassurance, but Alex slept like a log. He was still sound asleep when I checked on him at 6.15, just before I showered and dressed. At seven o'clock I woke all three children and said it was time for them to wash and dress ready for school, and that I needed everyone downstairs for breakfast by 7.20 so we could leave the house at 7.45. I was a little apprehensive about the timing of this new school run; I always am at the start. I obviously didn't want anyone to be late so I was allowing plenty of time, although I knew that by the end of the week it would all be second nature.

I waited on the landing, checking everyone was getting washed and dressed. There was a clock in each of their bedrooms, although Paula couldn't tell the time yet. We all went downstairs together and the children sat at the table while I made breakfast. Alex wanted porridge, the same as Adrian and Paula, and said he was looking forward to seeing his friends at school again. As Alex's school started earlier than Adrian's it also finished earlier, which would allow me time to collect Alex and then return for Adrian. If I was a few minutes late Adrian knew to wait with his teacher until I arrived. The logistics of this school run were a lot easier than some I'd had to organize.

We left the house on time and arrived at Alex's school as I intended, just after eight o'clock. As it was the first day I wanted to go into reception and check the school office had my contact details, as very often they didn't. It relied on the social worker advising the school of the foster carer's details, and with so much going on when a child comes into care or has to move carers, it can easily be overlooked. As we entered the school Alex said goodbye and went off to join his friends in breakfast club, while Adrian and Paula came with me to the reception desk and then waited to one side as I explained to the school secretary that I was Alex's new foster carer. She hadn't been given my contact details and reached for a form for me to complete.

'I've lost count of the number of times that poor kid's address has had to be updated,' she said, unimpressed.

'I know he's had a lot of moves,' I agreed. I filled in Alex's name on the form and then my name, address and telephone number.

'I assume he's staying with you permanently?' she said as I returned the completed from to her. Clearly she was unaware that shortly Alex would be moving to his adopted home, and it wasn't for me to tell her.

'He'll be with me for the time being,' I said.

She tutted, slid the form into a file and then handed me a copy of the school's prospectus, as I'd guessed she'd done to other carers before. 'The term dates are in there, assuming he's still with you then.'

'Thank you,' I said, ignoring the slight. Caring primary-school staff are often very protective of their pupils, with everyone – including the office staff, teachers and the caretakers – knowing the children and looking out for them, but it wasn't my fault Alex had had so many moves.

We arrived in Adrian's school playground with two minutes to spare. Paula and I said goodbye to Adrian, and I waited until he'd lined up with his class ready to go in before I took

Paula to nursery, which was on the same site. She attended nursery three mornings a week and was always a little clingy on Monday, after the weekend, but one of the nursery assistants came over and took her to the sandpit where a friend of hers was playing, so I was able to kiss her goodbye and leave.

When I arrived home the green light on the answerphone was blinking with a message. It was from Jill. 'Good morning, Cathy, I guess you're on the school run. When you have a moment can you give me a ring, please, to confirm Alex's move yesterday went well. Thank you.'

I took off my coat and shoes and returned the call straight away. Jill was always very efficient and I tried to be too. I told her that Graham had brought Alex as arranged and that Alex appeared fine and was settling in, and was in school now.

'Excellent,' she said. 'Well done.' Jill often praised her carers and it was appreciated by us. She was responsible for twelve foster carers and made sure she kept up to date and knew as much about the children we fostered as we did.

'Has there been any mention of a LAC review?' she asked. LAC stands for 'looked-after children'.

I'd read the minutes of his previous reviews. 'No. Just the planning meeting on Wednesday,' I said.

'I've got that in the diary. I'll be there. Usually a child has a review after a change in carers, but I'll check with Debbie. As Alex is only with you for a month she may not feel it's worth it. I'll let you know. I'll see you on Wednesday, but obviously phone if you need to.'

'Thanks, Jill. I will.'

We said goodbye. It was reassuring to know that the fostering agency offered twenty-four-hour support, seven days a week, although I didn't think I'd be needing any help with Alex. He was a dear little boy and was only with me for a very short while.

An hour later Debbie, Alex's social worker, telephoned for an update and I told her more or less what I'd told Jill, including that Alex was in school and the school now had my contact details.

'Thanks, Cathy. The school have been very good with Alex. Has he got all his belongings with him?'

'Yes. I think so.'

'Is there anything he needs?'

'No. Well, apart from his new parents. He's so looking forward to meeting them.'

'I know. Bring your diary with you on Wednesday. We'll be planning the introductions and the move. It's a good match. His adoptive parents already have the experience of bringing up their son, so Alex will have a sibling.'

'Great. How old is he?'

'Nine. Two years older than Alex. He can't wait to have a brother.'

'Fantastic. I do so like happy endings.'

'So do I, Cathy, so do I.'

The morning flew by and it wasn't long before I was collecting Paula from nursery. While I was there I took the opportunity to ask Kay, a good friend of mine who had children of a similar age to Adrian and Paula, if she could collect Paula from nursery on Wednesday, as I had to go to a meeting at the social services. She knew I fostered and said straight away that she could. 'I'll give the girls lunch and I can also collect Adrian if you're not back in time,' she offered.

'Thanks, Kay, that's kind of you, although the meeting should finish long before the end of school.' But it was reassuring to have that safety net. Kay knew a little of what was involved in fostering and we'd helped each other out in the past. She'd been very supportive when my husband had left me and I greatly valued her friendship, as I hoped she did mine. As a foster carer it's essential to have a good support network of friends and relatives who can be relied upon to help out if necessary, just as it is in everyday life. We left the nursery together and then went our separate ways. Paula was delighted she was going to play with her friend on Wednesday. I would need to inform the nursery of the arrangement, in line with their 'keeping children safe' policy.

I find the days fly by, especially during term time with the nursery and school runs. I'd also started working part time, mainly from home – administration work for a small local firm – and I did the work in the evenings or when Paula was at nursery.

After lunch I played with Paula and then read her some stories. Before long it was time to put on our coats and shoes to collect Alex from school. That morning, when I'd taken him, I'd arranged to meet him at a specific place in the play-ground – over to the right – so he could easily find me. It's difficult enough for a child to be met from school by a foster carer – the other kids know they're in care – so it helps them if they can go straight to the carer and not have to search a sea of faces for a half-familiar outline.

Alex spotted me and Paula straight away as soon as his class came out, and his teacher came with him to introduce herself and confirm who I was. Foster carers have identity cards they can show if necessary. She said that Alex had had a good day and had some spelling and reading homework in his bag, and then, wishing us a pleasant evening, went to talk to another parent.

Alex seemed happy and relaxed, and in the car on the way home he talked sweetly to Paula, asking her what she'd been doing while he'd been in school. Not all children know how to talk to little ones, but I guessed he'd had to fit in with so many different families (with different-aged children) that he knew how to interact with younger as well as older children. It was nice to see, and Paula appreciated it.

We arrived in Adrian's playground just as the klaxon was sounding and I stood in my usual spot with the other mothers. Adrian came out and ran over to us and I asked him as I normally did if he'd had a good day. He said he had, but that he had maths homework to do. I suggested to the boys that they did their homework as soon as we were home so that it was out of the way. This was what Adrian usually did and Alex said he'd done the same at his previous foster carers'. I guess most families have a similar routine.

Once home I made the children a drink and then Adrian and Alex fetched their school bags and settled at the table to do their homework. Seeing the boys working, Paula wanted to do some homework too, so I gave her a sheet of paper, wrote her name at the top in big letters and asked her to copy them beneath and then draw a picture. I'd begun teaching her the letters in her name and it was good practice holding a pencil. Once she'd finished she left the table and watched some pre-school television until the boys had finished.

After dinner all three children played nicely together in the living room, sharing their toys, until it was time for Paula's bath and bedtime. I left the boys playing while I took her upstairs and once she was settled I brought Alex up and then Adrian. I usually put the children to bed in age-ascending order – it seemed fair that way and worked well – so the youngest went first and the eldest last, although Alex was only six months younger than Adrian. Alex chose his soft toy giraffe to take into bed with him, and as I said goodnight he asked me, 'Do you know when I'll see my new mummy and daddy?'

'I'll know on Wednesday,' I said. 'I have to go to a very special meeting. Your new mummy and daddy will be there, so will your social worker. We will all have our diaries so we can write in the important dates: the days when you will meet your parents and get to know them, and then the most impor-tant date of all – when you move in.' This was life-changing for Alex, so it was essential I maintained the momentum of excited expectation that would have been started by Graham, Sandy and Debbie when they'd talked to him about being adopted and his new parents. I was also genuinely pleased for him. He'd waited a long time for a family of his own and finally it was happening.

Alex smiled broadly and clasped his giraffe in joy. 'Not long now!' he said, his eyes sparkling.

'Not long at all. Do you have any questions?'

He thought for a moment. 'Not really a question, but can

you tell my new mummy and daddy that I'm so happy and I love them already.'

'I will.'

Alex said similar things to me the next evening – Tuesday – when I saw him into bed. 'Not long now!' he said excitedly. And he gave the soft toy elephant he'd chosen for the night a big squeeze.

'Not long,' I agreed. 'The meeting is tomorrow. Any questions?'

'Will you tell my mummy and daddy that I'm very happy and I can't wait to be their son?'

'I will,' I said, tears pricking the backs of my eyes. 'I'll make sure of it.'

On Wednesday morning Alex told us all individually that I was going to a very important meeting today where I would meet his new mummy and daddy and write important dates in my diary. Then in the car as I drove to take him to school he told us all again collectively that I was going to meet his new mummy and daddy.

'I know, that's great,' Adrian said.

But later, after I'd seen Alex into breakfast club and Adrian, Paula and I were in the car again, Adrian said, 'Can we still see Alex once he's moved? He's my friend.'

'I hope so, but it will depend on his new parents.'

'If they're nice, they'll let us see him, won't they?' Adrian asked.

'Yes, but remember he will only have been with us a few weeks when he leaves, so they might feel it isn't worth it.'

Harsh, but in my experience true, and it was something the children of foster carers had to accept, difficult though it was.

I saw Adrian into school, and then Paula into the nursery. I checked with Kay that she was still able to collect Paula at lunchtime and then I informed the nursery staff of the arrangement. Having thanked Kay, I kissed Paula goodbye and returned home, where I changed out of my jeans and into a smart skirt and jumper, ready for the meeting at eleven o'clock. I slipped on my coat and with my diary in my handbag I left the house and drove to the council offices, arriving with ten minutes to spare. I signed in at the reception desk and then sat in the waiting area until Jill arrived. My stomach had started to jitter with pre-important-meeting nerves, and by the time Jill appeared it was churning.

'All set?' she said, with her usual welcoming smile.

'Yes, ready to go.'

She signed in at reception and also checked which room the meeting was being held in. 'So how has Alex been?' she asked as we made our way up the spiral staircase to the first floor.

'Really good. No problem. He's a lovely boy and is so excited about having a mummy and daddy of his own.'

'Great. He deserves it. And from what Debbie has told me this sounds an excellent match.'

'Good.'

We arrived outside the room, Jill gave a perfunctory knock on the door, pushed it open and stepped in. 'Hello, I'm Jill, Cathy's support social worker.' I followed her in. 'And this is Cathy, Alex's foster carer.'

'Hello,' I said, smiling at the four people grouped around the table. Jill and I took the two free chairs.

'I'm Debbie,' Alex's social worker said to me. 'We've spoken on the phone.'

'Yes, hello.' Normally I would have met the child's social worker by now, but the move had happened quickly and at the weekend, so this was the first opportunity. Debbie turned to the others at the table. 'Would you like to introduce yourselves now everyone is here.'

It was obvious they knew each other, so this was for Jill's and my benefit. 'I'm Lin from the Adoption and Permanency Team,' the woman beside Debbie said.

Jill and I both smiled and said hello. Lin would be the social worker who had matched Alex with his adoptive parents and given them his background details, and would now see them through the adoption process, when her role would end.

'I'm Rosemary, soon to be Alex's mother,' the woman on Lin's left said confidently and without being asked. 'And this is my husband.' She looked to the man seated beside her.

'Good morning. I'm Edward, soon to be Alex's father,' he said with a disarmingly charming smile.

Clearly a very confident couple, well spoken and smartly dressed, who I guessed to be about aged forty. Edward was wearing a light-grey tailored suit with an open-neck shirt, and Rosemary a sophisticated slim-fitting long-sleeve cream dress. We smiled and said hello.

'Great. Let's begin then,' Debbie said with a big grin. 'We all know why we're here, and I see everyone has brought their diaries. I do so love these adoption planning meetings.' We all agreed. Each of us was sitting ready with a diary and pen in front of us and the atmosphere was light and gay. Unlike some meetings I'd attended in respect of the children I fostered, this was a joyous occasion – planning Alex's move to his forever family. 'Lin will take a few notes,' Debbie said, 'but before we begin, does anyone have any questions?'

Edward cleared his throat to speak. 'My wife and I were talking on the way here in the car and we think it would be useful if Cathy could tell us how Alex has been with her since the move. It will give us an idea of what to expect.'

'Yes, absolutely,' Debbie agreed enthusiastically. Lin nodded. 'Cathy, I appreciate Alex has only been with you a few days, but if you could tell us how he's settled in, it would be helpful.'

'Yes, of course.' I was half expecting this. Foster carers are often asked to speak near the start of a meeting about the child they are looking after, as they usually have the most up-to-date information on the child.

'Rosemary and Edward have already been made aware of what Alex's previous carer said about him,' Lin added.

I nodded and looked at Rosemary and Edward as I spoke. 'Alex is a delightful child who appears to be coping very well with all the changes in his life. I could see he felt rejected at having to leave his previous carers, but it hasn't come out in his behaviour. He's eating well – he likes a range of foods. He's sleeping well and is in a good routine. His self-care skills are good. He likes all things that the average boy of seven does: playing games, riding his bike – he had a new one for Christmas – and watching television. He's getting on well with my son, who is the same age, and also my daughter, who is four years younger.'

'That's reassuring,' Edward said. 'Our son is just eighteen months older than Alex. One of the reasons we chose him.'

'It was a matching consideration,' Lin corrected. The way Edward had phrased it made it sound as though they'd gone to a store and chosen Alex.

'Thanks, Cathy. Anything else you can add?' Debbie said to me.

'Alex is healthy, up to date with his dental and opticians check-ups and is doing well at school.'

'Yes, he is,' Rosemary put in. 'We have a copy of his last school report. Our son, James, is doing well at school too. We have a tutor who comes to help James, and Alex will have the benefit of that too.'

'My wife and I consider education very important,' Edward added. 'We both went to university and we expect our sons to do the same.'

I smiled politely.

'Anything else?' Debbie asked me.

'I don't think so, other than Alex is looking forward to meeting you both,' I said to Rosemary and Edward. 'He said to tell you he's so pleased you will be his mummy and daddy and that he loves you already.'

'That's sweet,' Rosemary said, while Edward looked slightly uncomfortable.

'He hasn't met us yet,' he said pragmatically.

'No, but it's fantastic he's so willing to accept you,' Lin pointed out.

Jill and I nodded. 'He can't wait to have a family of his own,' I added.

'I know,' Rosemary said quietly, and I saw her eyes mist.

CHAPTER FOUR

A JOYFUL MEETING

'OK. Now to the actual planning,' Debbie said, and we all opened our diaries. 'I suggest we start the introductions this weekend and, if all goes well, Alex will move in two weeks' time.'

'The sooner the better,' Rosemary said, glancing at her husband. He returned her smile.

'Lin and I will be phoning the three of you [Rosemary, Edward and me] for regular updates in between the visits,' Debbie said. 'If we feel we need to slow the pace we can do so, but I don't foresee any problems.'

'Neither do I,' Lin agreed. 'We started preparing Alex for this when he was at his previous carers', and it was positive from the start. He's more than ready for his own family and knows a little about Rosemary, Edward and James, but hasn't seen a photograph of them yet. Did you remember to bring the album with you?' she now asked Rosemary and Edward.

'Yes, of course.' Rosemary dipped her hand into her bag on the floor beside her. She and Edward would have been asked to prepare a little photograph album with pictures of themselves and their home for Alex, so that when he met them they and their home were already partly familiar. It's standard practice when any child is moved to permanency.

'Could you talk Cathy through the photographs, please, so she can tell Alex,' Debbie said to Rosemary and Edward.

Rosemary slid the album across the table to me and I opened it at the first page, positioning it between Jill and myself. Lin and Debbie had already seen the album; indeed, Lin would have advised Rosemary and Edward on what to include.

The first photograph was of the outside of their house – the first view Alex would see when he stepped from the car. 'Very nice,' I said. 'Where do you live?' I would have known this and other details about them if I'd been the foster carer involved at the start of the adoption process.

'We live in Churchwell,' Rosemary said. 'It's a small village about an hour's drive from here.' The picture showed a large detached modern house on the edge of countryside.

'We have five bedrooms,' Rosemary said, 'so there's plenty of space. James likes to have friends stay over sometimes. I'm guessing Alex will want to do the same.'

'I'm sure he will,' I said. 'That's great.' I turned to the next page: a portrait photo of Edward, Rosemary and James, dressed very smartly and posing for the camera. Even before Rosemary said it, I knew it had been taken by a professional photographer.

'It's our official Christmas photograph,' she said. 'We have one taken every year for our Christmas cards.' I smiled and felt that my Christmas cards with their standard pictures of robins and reindeer might be rather lacking.

'And next Christmas there will be four of you on the card!' Lin exclaimed gaily.

'Yes, indeed,' Rosemary said, smiling. 'Alex will love it. We always have some fun posing for the photo, don't we?'

'Absolutely,' Edward agreed, and glanced at his watch. I wondered if he was pressed for time.

James looked as self-assured as his parents in the photograph, and although he was taller and broader than Alex, his colouring wasn't dissimilar – brown hair and pale skin – so he could easily pass for his brother. Another matching consideration is that ideally the adoptive family should be physically similar to the child and preferably of the same ethnicity so the child blends in, although given the multiculturalism of most large towns and cities now, this was becoming less important.

I turned the page and the next photograph showed the inside of their house – the lounge hall, so spacious it comfortably held a chaise longue and an oval mahogany table, on which stood a magnificent china vase of fresh flowers. A brief image of it going flying as the boys chased each other up and down the hall while playing crossed my mind, but I kept that thought to myself.

Rosemary continued to talk me through the photographs: the dining room with a long, highly polished table and a dozen upholstered dining chairs around it; an exquisitely furnished living room with cream sofas; a morning room with a smaller table and matching oak chairs. 'That is where we usually take our meals,' Rosemary explained. 'Unless we're entertaining, and then we use the dining room.'

I nodded, smiled and turned the page to a luxurious modern kitchen. 'Very nice indeed,' I said. Then there were pictures of the bedrooms and the two family bathrooms.

'We've just had both boys' bedrooms redecorated,' Edward said. 'James's room was only done last year, but we wanted to decorate Alex's room and we couldn't leave James out.'

'No, indeed,' I said. 'I like the blue. I'm sure Alex will love it.'

'I hope so,' Rosemary said. 'There's a big walk-in cupboard for his toys.'

'Where will he keep his new bike?' I asked. 'He's sure to ask me.'

'In the outbuilding behind the garage, with ours,' Edward said. 'We didn't take pictures of that.'

'They all like to go for bike rides together,' Lin said. She would know the family well as a result of the matching and adoption process.

I smiled, impressed.

'James goes for a ride with his father most weekends,' Rosemary said. 'I join them if the weather is good.'

'They go sailing as well,' Lin added. 'And horse riding.'

'Wonderful,' I said, even more impressed.

'I don't suppose Alex has been riding before, coming from a deprived background.' Rosemary said.

'No, I don't suppose he has,' I replied.

'We'll arrange lessons for him at the stables, then we can all ride together,' Rosemary said. 'James also has violin and cello lessons in the evening after school. Alex can choose which instruments he wants to learn.'

'Wonderful,' I said. 'I see Alex is going to be a very accomplished young man.'

'It's lovely that he'll be having so many opportunities,' Lin said.

'Although he will need time to settle in first,' Jill put in. 'There'll be a lot of changes for him in the first few weeks, so don't overload him.' Which was what I'd been thinking.

'No, I know,' Rosemary said. 'We're just rather excited. We want to give him so much.' Edward nodded.

'He's a lucky boy,' I said, and Debbie, Lin and Jill agreed.

The last photograph was of their beautifully landscaped garden, which Jill and I admired. Although I wondered how the flowerbeds would stand up to the boys' football practice. I closed the album and put it in my bag to show to Alex later.

'Now to arrange the actual dates,' Debbie said. 'Cathy, you'll start the introduction by showing Alex the album this evening and answering any questions he might have. Then on Saturday, Edward and Rosemary, you will visit Alex at Cathy's house for about an hour. Shall we say eleven o'clock? Does that suit everyone?'

We all nodded and noted this in our diaries.

'You've arranged for James to be looked after for this visit?' Lin reminded Rosemary and Edward.

'Yes. My mother will be sitting with him,' Edward said. 'Although James was very disappointed he wouldn't be coming.' Lin and Debbie would have explained to Rosemary and Edward that it is generally considered best if just the adoptive parents come on the first visit, otherwise it can be overwhelming for the child to meet too many new faces all at once. It also allows the parents to give the child their complete attention without the distraction of other family members.

'James has only got to wait until Sunday to meet Alex,' Lin pointed out.

'Yes, so on Sunday,' Debbie said, glancing at her notes. 'Cathy will take Alex to his new home for his first visit. An hour is considered about right when everything is new.'

'Will your parents be able to look after Paula and Adrian on Sunday?' Jill quietly asked me. I, too, would be expected to give Alex my full attention for that first visit to his new home.

'It's not a problem. They are out with their father,' I returned quietly. Then to the rest of the group I said, 'Any time suits me.'

'Shall we say eleven o'clock again?' Debbie said.

'Could we make it twelve?' Edward asked. 'So James and I can go for our bike ride first.'

'Yes, sure.'

We all made a note of the time. 'I'll need the address,' I said.

'Yes, of course, sorry, Cathy,' Lin said. 'The details went to Alex's previous carers.'

'I'll give you our card,' Edward said. He took a business-style card from his wallet showing their home contact details and passed it to me.

'Thank you,' I said, and tucked it into the front of my diary.

We continued planning the timetable of introduction. On Monday evening Rosemary, Edward and James would telephone me to have a chat with Alex. Then on Tuesday they would all visit us after school and stay for tea. They would phone to speak to Alex on Wednesday, then on Thursday evening they would visit us again and take Alex out for something to eat. While they were all getting to know each other they'd be seeing each other every other day and speaking on the telephone on the days they didn't see each other. If all was going well, I would take Alex to their house again on Friday evening and leave him for a while. Then on Saturday he'd stay for the day and overnight, and I'd collect him on Sunday morning. On Monday Lin and Debbie would telephone Rosemary and Edward and me for more feedback. Assuming Alex was still happy and coping well, I'd take him to his new home again on Tuesday evening and he'd stay for dinner. On Wednesday Rosemary would collect him from school and he'd stay overnight, and then she'd take him to school the following morning. She'd collect him from school on Friday and he'd stay with them until Sunday, during which time he'd have a chance to meet his paternal grandparents – Edward's parents who lived in the same village. If everything was still fine, we'd move Alex on Monday. It was agreed that he'd have the day off school for the move rather than try to cram it into the evening, and then Rosemary would take Alex into school on Tuesday.

'So Alex is staying at the same school for now?' Jill asked.

'Yes,' Lin said. 'Although it's an hour's journey in the car each way, we feel it will be less disruptive for Alex to continue at his present school until Easter. Then he can start the new term at his new school.'

'That will work well,' Jill said, and I agreed.

'We already have a place reserved for him at the school James goes to,' Rosemary said.

'Now, have I forgotten anything?' Debbie asked, scanning her notes.

'Moving details,' Lin prompted.

'Thank you. It's generally felt that the move should take place in the morning so the child isn't waiting around with time to grow unsettled or anxious,' Debbie said. 'Cathy, I suggest you have Alex all packed and ready by ten o'clock on that Monday, and then Rosemary and Edward will arrive to collect him at ten-thirty. He'll have the rest of the day to settle in and unpack.'

We all nodded and wrote the details in our diaries.

'I'm assuming that on Monday James will be going to school as usual?' Lin asked Rosemary and Edward.

'Yes,' Edward confirmed.

'Will we be able to see Alex once he's left?' I now asked. 'I know he hasn't been with us for long, but it would be nice if we could see him at least once.'

'Are you happy with that?' Debbie asked Rosemary and Edward.

'Absolutely,' Rosemary said. 'We'll stay in touch.'

'Thank you,' I said.

'I'll leave the three of you to make the arrangements for that,' Debbie said to Rosemary, Edward and me. 'I suggest you wait until three weeks after the move so that Alex is settled.' Which was usual practice.

'Will his previous carers, Graham and Sandy, be keeping in touch with Alex?' Jill asked. 'He was with them for some time.'

'They are supposed to be phoning him at your house at the end of this week,' Lin said, looking at me. 'But don't tell Alex in case it doesn't happen.' I nodded.

'And no visit is planned?' Jill asked. When a child has been with a carer for some time they would normally see them on a few occasions after they'd left.

'No,' Lin said. 'Sandy is heavily pregnant. They have stopped fostering now.'

Jill nodded. 'Are you going to have a LAC review for Alex while he's at Cathy's?' she asked Debbie. 'It hardly seems worth it.'

'No. There isn't time and there's too much going on for Alex. It's not necessary. We'll have one after the move.'

Jill made a note.

'Is there anything else?' Debbie asked, looking around the table.

'I'm sure I should be asking lots of questions,' Rosemary said with a nervous laugh, 'but I can't think of them right now.'

Debbie smiled. 'Don't worry. You can phone Lin or me if you think of anything. Or Cathy if it's about Alex's care.' I threw Rosemary a reassuring smile. 'I'll have this timetable typed up today and I'll send each of you a copy,' Debbie said, winding up. 'Good luck everyone. It's very exciting.'

'It is,' Rosemary said. 'And nerve-wracking.'

'That's only to be expected,' Jill said. 'This is life-changing, so imagine what little Alex must be feeling.'

I saw Edward glance at his watch again.

'Lin and I will be in regular contact with you all,' Debbie said. 'Phone if you need to.'

'Thank you,' Edward said, pushing back his chair. 'You won't mind if my wife and I dash. I'm due in another meeting in an hour.'

'No, you go. We've finished here,' Debbie said.

Rosemary and Edward stood.

'See you Saturday then,' I said.

'Yes.' They smiled, and left the room.

Jill and I put away our diaries. 'If there's nothing else, I'll be off too,' Jill said to Debbie and Lin.

'No, that's it. You go,' Debbie said.

Jill and I stood, said goodbye and left the room together.

Outside, Jill said, 'Well, what do you think?'

'They're a very sophisticated couple,' I said, meeting her gaze with a smile.

'Yes, but will they make good parents for Alex and be able to meet his needs? Obviously the adoption team think so.'

'Yes. I don't see why not. They appear highly committed to doing all they can. They seem to be bringing up James very well. Alex is going to be given fantastic opportunities, more than many of the children we see.'

'He is indeed,' Jill said.

'What does Edward do for a living?' I asked out of interest as we continued down the stairs.

'He and Rosemary are in banking, but Rosemary has taken adoption leave. She left last Friday and will be off work for six months.' Adoption leave is common practice now, although much of the six months would be unpaid.

'So you know what you are doing this evening to start the introductions?' Jill now asked as we crossed reception.

'Yes. Talking Alex through the photograph album and answering any questions he might have. He can keep the album?'

'Yes. It's his.'

Outside the building, Jill said, 'Phone me if you need any help or advice, but I'm sure you'll be fine. And enjoy. It doesn't get much better than this – moving a child to their forever home.'

'No, indeed,' I said. 'I will.'

CHAPTER FIVE

A POSITIVE START

'Did you see them?' Alex asked, arriving breathless at my side. As soon as his class had come out he'd dashed across the school playground to me.

'Yes, I spent two hours with your mummy and daddy,' I said with a big smile. 'They're lovely people and are so looking forward to meeting you. They've made a special photograph album just for you so you know what they look like.'

'Can I have it now?' he asked excitedly.

'It's safely at home. I'll show you and tell you all about it as soon as we get in.'

'Oh. That's a long time,' he moaned.

'Alex, it's about forty minutes, less than an hour.' We left the playground and walked towards the car.

Paula was watching Alex, somewhat bemused. He'd really gained confidence in the last few days and was coming out of his shell.

'When will I meet them?' he now asked.

'Saturday. They're coming to our house on Saturday and then we go to visit your new home on Sunday. But I'll explain all about it once we're home.' This was all too important to rush through on the school run. I wanted to take time, to sit down with Alex and be able to give him my full attention as I talked him through the photographs and explained the time-table of the introductions and move.

'I went to my friend's house today,' Paula told Alex as we got into the car.

'That's nice,' he said.

'I went because Mummy had to go to the meeting,' she said cutely.

'Did you have a nice time?' he asked her. How kind of him, I thought. He was bothering to make conversation with her when his mind must have been far away and on all that was happening to him.

'Yes, I did, thank you,' she said.

'Did you meet my brother too?' Alex now asked me as I started the engine.

'No. He was at school. We will both meet him on Sunday at your new home.'

'Why not Saturday?' Alex asked impatiently.

'Because that first meeting between you and your mummy and daddy is a special time, just for the three of you. Then on Sunday you'll meet James and you'll be able to spend time with him and your mummy and daddy.' From now on I would always be referring to Rosemary and Edward as Mummy and Daddy to Alex, as it would help cement their role and reinforce the new family unit.

We collected Adrian from school, and once home I made the children a drink and a snack, and then settled Adrian and Paula with some activities at the table, explaining that I had to talk to Alex about something important.

'It's about his special photograph albanny,' Paula said, mispronouncing album.

'Yes, album,' I corrected. 'I'm sure he'll show you both later.' The photographs of Alex's new family were very personal to him, so it was important he saw them first and then he could share them later if he wished.

I took Alex into the living room with the photograph album and we sat together on the sofa. I placed the album on his lap. 'Alex,' he read his name from the large, brightly coloured lettering on the front.

'Yes, it's yours to keep,' I said.

He carefully opened the first page and looked at the photograph of the front of their house.

'Wow. Is that my new home?' he asked.

'It is,' I said.

'It's big.'

'Yes. So there's lots of space for you and James to play.'

'Wow,' he said again. Taking his time, he savoured the picture and then turned the page.

I watched his expression change from awe to intrigue as his gaze fell on the photo of his new family and he 'met' them for the first time. It was impossible to know what he was thinking or feeling. Suddenly being presented with your ready-made forever family isn't something many of us ever experience. Wonder, reverence, elation and trepidation must have been a few of the emotions that ran through him as he sat in silence beside me staring at the photograph. He could have as much time as he needed and I wouldn't complicate his thoughts with unnecessary words. This was a moment he would remember forever – the first time he saw his family. It was monumental.

'They look very smart,' he said quietly after a while.

'Yes, they do. They wore their best clothes for the photograph and they posed for it in front of a photographer. Like you do for your school photograph each year.'

Alex continued to study the photograph, gazing into the eyes of his family as they smiled back. 'I think James looks a bit like me,' he said.

'Yes, he does a little. He's only eighteen months older than you and loves to ride his bike, just as you do.'

Alex's eyes lit up. 'Have they got a garden? We can ride our bikes in the garden.'

'Yes, they have, a big garden. There's a picture of it at the end of the album. The whole family like to go for bike rides. They live in a country village so there are lots of good places to ride.'

'Wow. I'm looking forward to riding my bike with my family in the country.' My heart went out to him.

'They do other things as well,' I said. 'They go horse riding, and if you want to learn to ride a horse, your mummy said she will arrange lessons for you.'

'Horses are very big,' Alex said, a little concerned. 'I don't know.'

'You don't have to make a decision now, but not all horses are big. See how you feel once you've moved in and have been to the stables and seen the horses. James is also learning to play a musical instrument. You can too if you wish. Your daddy said you could choose an instrument to learn to play and then he'll arrange lessons for you at home.'

'Great. Can I learn to play the guitar?' he asked excitedly.

'I don't see why not. You'll have to ask your mummy and daddy when you see them. I'm sure they'll be pleased you are interested. James also has a tutor to help him with his school work and he can help you too, although you are doing very well at school.'

He smiled. 'I like my school.'

Best get this piece of news out of the way, I thought. 'Alex, you'll be able to stay at your present school for a few weeks after you move to your family. But then after Easter you will start your new school, which is closer to your home.'

'Why? I like my school,' he asked, perturbed. 'My friends are there.'

'I know, but it's an hour in the car each way, which is a long time. I'm sure you'd rather be at home in the evening playing than sitting in a car travelling. You'll make lots of new friends at your new school and I expect you'll be able to keep in touch with some of your old friends. It's the same school James goes to.' I knew that once Alex was settled with his family the move to his new school wouldn't seem so daunting, especially as James was there already.

'When do I move to my new home?' Alex asked, turning the page of the album.

'In two weeks' time. But we're jumping ahead of ourselves. Let's finish looking at the photographs first, and then I'll explain what is going to happen and when.'

As Alex turned the pages I talked about the different rooms, taking my time and waiting until he'd finished studying each photograph before going on to the next. Through the open living-room door I could hear Adrian and Paula doing the activities I'd arranged on the table. Then as Alex neared the end of the album Adrian called out, 'I'm hungry, Mum. Are you nearly done in there?'

'I won't be too long. Good boy.'

Once Alex had finished looking at the last photograph – of the garden – he flipped through the pictures to the one of his family again and studied it thoughtfully. 'Do you think they will like me?' he asked at last.

'Yes. Definitely. And I'm sure you'll like them. It's bound to feel a bit strange for you all to begin with until you get to know each other. But before long it will be like you've always been there.'

'And they'll love me like you love Adrian and Paula?' he now asked.

My heart clenched. I hadn't given him a hug yet, respecting his personal space, but instinctively I put my arm around him and hugged him. He didn't pull away. 'They will love you lots and lots,' I said. 'Like I love Adrian and Paula and they love James.'

He smiled. 'I'm going to love them lots too. I'm so lucky.'

I swallowed the lump rising in my throat. 'They're lucky to have you, Alex. You're a lovely boy.' He smiled. 'So now let me tell you what is going to happen over the next two weeks when you meet your family, and then I'll make some dinner.' He straightened and, holding the album to his chest, listened intently as I began by telling him about his parents' visit to us on Saturday, and then our visit to them on Sunday when he would meet James. I continued outlining the timetable of introductions – the visits and telephone calls, culminating with the Monday he would move. 'You don't have to remember all of this,' I said. 'I'll be telling you each day and asking you if you have any questions or worries. I've moved children to their forever families before and it all works out perfectly, so don't worry.' The timetable of introduction was always similar and worked well. It was designed to give the child and the adoptive family sufficient time to get to know each other without overburdening them – hence the days when they spoke on the telephone but didn't actually see each other. The pace could be slowed if necessary, but in my experience it was usually speeded up as the adoptive family and the child bonded and were eager to be together permanently.

Alex nodded. 'Can I show Adrian and Paula my pictures now?'

'Yes, of course, if you'd like to.'

'Adrian! Paula!' Alex cried at the top of his voice. 'Come and see what I've got.'

They didn't need telling twice. 'We're coming!' Adrian shouted. Two pairs of feet scuttled from the table and into the living room.

I stood. 'Come and sit beside Alex so you can both see. I'll go and make dinner.'

They leapt onto the sofa and sat either side of Alex. He waited until they were settled like a teacher waits for a class to silence, before quietly but confidently reading his name from the front. 'Alex.' Then he said, 'This is a book about my family.'

I went to the patio doors and drew the curtains against the cold night sky as Alex opened the album and announced, 'This is a picture of my house.'

'Cool,' Adrian said admiringly.

'Is that where you are going to live?' Paula asked.

'Yes, with my family.'

'Cool,' Paula said, copying her brother.

Alex gave them a moment to savour the picture and then turned the page. 'This is my family,' he said proudly, pointing. 'That's my mummy. That's my daddy and that's my brother, James. They've got their best clothes on because they had their photograph taken by a photographer, like we do at school.'

I smiled to myself, and I left the room with them huddled around the album.

Alex was inseparable from his photograph album for the rest of that evening. When he wasn't looking at the actual pictures he was holding the album or had it close by. He brought it to the dinner table with him, where he tucked it under his chair while he ate. It was beside him while he did his homework and then on his lap as he watched television. At bedtime he took it upstairs with him, clutching it protectively to his chest. He did leave it outside the toilet but took it with him into the bathroom, where he placed it in one corner, safely out of reach of any splashes of water. Once in his pyjamas he carried it through to his bedroom and then tucked it under his pillow for the night. 'It will be safe there,' he said.

'Yes, it will.' I smiled.

'Have my family got pictures of me?' he asked as he climbed into bed.

'They'll certainly have at least one of you.' A recent photograph of Alex would have been included in the paperwork for the adoption matching process.

'Do you think they're looking at it now?' he asked.

'They might be.'

'I'm going to meet Mummy and Daddy on Saturday and my brother on Sunday.'

'Yes, that's right. They'll come here on Saturday for an hour and then you and I will go there on Sunday.'

He nodded contemplatively and was about to snuggle down when he realized he'd forgotten to choose a soft toy for the night. He climbed out, picked up the polar bear with its gaily striped scarf, then climbed back into bed.

'Do you think James takes a cuddly to bed with him?' he asked.

'Possibly, I don't know. You could ask him on Sunday.'

'I might be too shy to ask,' Alex said, and lay down.

'James is likely to be shy too to begin with,' I said. 'Remember that. But you'll soon get to know each other and relax.' I tucked him in. 'Would you like a goodnight kiss?' I wondered if he might, as he'd been happy to have a hug earlier.

'No, thank you,' he said with a small, embarrassed smile. 'I'm saving all my kisses for my mummy.'

'I understand,' I said, also smiling. 'Night then, love. Sleep tight.'

He turned onto his side, and with one arm around the polar bear slipped the other under his pillow to rest on the album. With a little sigh of contentment he closed his eyes for sleep.

The following day Alex brought the album down to breakfast and then returned it to under his pillow before he went to school. Many children store their treasured possessions under their pillow; sometimes it's the only safe place in their house. Jill, Debbie and Lin all telephoned that morning to see how the previous evening had gone, when I'd shown Alex the album and explained the timetable of introduction. I said it had gone very well indeed and that Alex was looking forward to meeting his adoptive family. I told them he treasured the album and had slept with it under his pillow. They were touched and pleased, as this positive start boded well for when they all met, and indeed for when Alex moved in. If a child is ambivalent or even negative towards their adoptive family at the beginning of the process, the parents can face a very unsettled few months when the child moves in, with challenging behaviour designed to test the parents' love and commitment. Thankfully they are usually prepared for this, and with post-adoption support they can appreciate how difficult it must be for the child, with all the adjustments they have to make.

I telephoned my parents that morning. We usually spoke on the phone a couple of times a week and saw each other on alternate weekends, with either them visiting us or us them. They're the typical loving grandparents who dote on and spoil their grandchildren. They also welcome any child or children I am fostering. We'd been due to see them this weekend, but I now realized that wasn't going to be possible. Adrian and Paula were out with their father on Sunday and I would be taking Alex for his first visit to his new home. They could have come on Saturday afternoon, but I felt that would be too much for Alex. He would have met his parents for the first time that morning, and then to have to meet more new people (whom he probably wouldn't see again) in the afternoon could have been confusing and unsettling. Dad was out, so I explained the situation to Mum. She was understanding and said we'd get together again as soon as possible.

The rest of the day passed much as usual. I did some work,

collected Paula from nursery at lunchtime and the boys from school in the afternoon. The evening disappeared as most school-day evenings do with dinner, homework, stories, bath and bed. Alex had checked that his album was still under the pillow when he'd arrived home and had left it there for safe-keeping, periodically popping up to his room to take a peek. At bedtime he asked me to go through the photographs again and also the timetable of the introductions before I said goodnight, which I was happy to do.

The following day was Friday and Adrian was pleased it was the end of the school week and that he would be seeing his father on Sunday. Contact was something we'd all had to adjust to, and it was now working as well as could be expected, although the feeling that none of this should ever have happened in the first place stayed with me. Yes, I blamed John, but I kept it to myself so it didn't affect the children's relationship with him. Alex was obviously pleased the week-end was nearly here as he would be meeting his parents. In the post that morning was a letter from Debbie enclosing a copy of the timetable, and I put it with my diary.

Alex was quieter than usual that evening and I thought he was probably a little nervous, which was only natural; he had a lot to think about. I asked him a few times if he was all right and he said he was. As we didn't have to be up early for school in the morning I let the boys stay up a little later, although I took Paula up at her usual bedtime as she needed more sleep at her age. At 7.30 the boys and I were in the living room play-ing a game of cards when the house phone rang. Leaving the game, I picked up the handset from the corner table. 'Hello?'

A half-familiar male voice said, 'Cathy?'

'Yes.'

'I hope I haven't disturbed you. Is this a good time to speak to Alex? It's Graham. We were told we should phone at the end of the week.'

'Yes, of course. Debbie mentioned it. I'll put him on. How are you?'

'Fine, thanks. Sandy will speak to him too.'

'OK. Just a minute.' Lowering the phone, I said to Alex, 'It's Graham, he'd like to say hello.'

Alex was concentrating on the cards he held in his hand and, without looking up, shook his head.

'Alex, it's Graham and Sandy, your old foster carers. They'd like to talk to you.' I saw his face set as he shook his head again. 'Are you sure?' He nodded and turned slightly away. 'All right, I'll tell him.'

I returned the phone to my ear, but before I spoke Graham said, 'He doesn't want to talk to us, does he?'

'No. Sorry. There's rather a lot going on for him right now, and he's in the middle of a game. If he changes his mind we'll phone you.'

'OK,' Graham said easily and, I thought, a little relieved. 'Tell him good luck with his adoptive family.'

'I will. Thank you for phoning.'

We said goodbye and I replaced the receiver. 'Graham said good luck,' I said to Alex. 'If you change your mind and want to phone them let me know.' I doubted he would. He was moving on from the past and looking to a brighter future with his forever family.

CHAPTER SIX

ALEX MEETS HIS PARENTS

Unsurprisingly, Alex was awake early the following morning. I heard a noise in his bedroom at six o'clock, just as I was waking. I went round in my dressing gown to find him wide awake, sitting up in bed, surrounded by his soft toys and with the photograph album open on his lap.

'Are you OK?' I asked quietly, going in, and not wanting to wake Adrian and Paula.

'I'm reminding myself of what my family look like,' he said.

'All right. That's fine. I'll tell you when it's time to get dressed.'

Alex wasn't unhappy so I left him to view his photographs in private.

Adrian and Paula woke just before eight o'clock and everyone was dressed and downstairs ready for breakfast by 8.15. It never ceases to amaze me how quickly children can get dressed at the weekends when there is no school and the promise of being able to play all day.

Alex brought his photograph album down to breakfast and placed it under his seat. But then he just toyed with his food and hardly ate a thing. I told him not to worry, that he could make up for it at lunch and that I, too, was feeling nervous and I was sure his mummy and daddy were as well. I then tried to distract him by arranging various toys and board games at the table and in the living room, and, encouraged by Adrian and Paula, he made a brave attempt to play with them. But over the next hour he grew quieter and more withdrawn. At 10.45, fifteen minutes before Edward and Rosemary were due to arrive, Alex went up to his bedroom and closed the door.

His behaviour didn't surprise me. Alex wasn't a confident child and the enormity of meeting his new parents had finally taken its toll. Leaving Adrian and Paula playing in the living room, I went upstairs, knocked on Alex's door and went in. He was in bed, fully clothed.

'Alex, love, it's not bedtime yet,' I said lightly, going to his bedside. He had the duvet pulled up to his chin.

'I know, but I like it in here,' he said quietly. 'It's nice and safe and warm.'

'Yes,' I agreed. 'It's comforting being in bed, but you'll be very hot in there.'

'I don't mind.'

I paused and looked at his little face peeping over the duvet, large eyes watching me cautiously. 'Alex, I know you must be feeling anxious and worried. That's only natural. This is a big day for you all, but is there anything in particular that is worrying you?'

He shook his head, but then said, 'Yes.'

'Can you tell me what it is?'

'They might not like me,' he said, clearly having been thinking about this for a while.

'They'll like you,' I said. 'I'm sure of it.'

'But supposing they like me to begin with and then after a few months they change their minds and stop liking me? Like Graham and Sandy and the others did. I'd have to move all my things again and go to another new school.'

I knelt beside his bed so his face was level with mine. 'Alex, this is very different to what's happened in the past. They are going to adopt you. That is a commitment for life. When a child is adopted it's the same as if the parents had the child. They will love and care for you just as they do James.'

'But how can you be sure?' he asked.

'Because they will have spent a long, long time going through the adoption process, when they will have thought about and talked about what they are going to do. So they would have had plenty of time to change their minds. Also, they would have been seen by a social worker many, many times, and she would have asked them lots of questions to make sure they were right to adopt. It's not easy to adopt and many people who want to can't. Then there would be more time and meetings as the social worker matched them with you. All this can take two years, sometimes longer, so I know they are committed and are not going to change their minds.'

'Oh, I see,' Alex said thoughtfully. 'I didn't know that.'

'It would have been going on without you knowing. But I expect Debbie talked to you about being adopted a while back and asked you if you'd like to be.'

He paused and then said, 'Yes, but that was ages ago. I remember she asked me if I'd like a forever mummy and daddy and I said yes, and we talked about what they would be like.'

I nodded. 'Yes, that's right.' Once the social worker has confirmed with the child that they would like to be adopted, they wouldn't normally be given regular updates on what is a lengthy and laborious process until a suitable match is found. Not only would it be unsettling for the child, but it's a sad fact that many children in care – especially older children – are never found adoptive homes and remain with foster carers until they reach eighteen (making them an adult in the eyes of the law) and have to leave care.

'Well, since that day Debbie talked to you about being adopted she has been looking for suitable parents for you,' I said. 'Then when you were at Graham and Sandy's she told you she'd found them.'

His face brightened a little. 'Yes, I remember. So my new mummy and daddy won't ever want to give me back?'

'No, love, they won't give you back. Adoption is for life.'

'Even if I'm naughty?'

I smiled. 'Even if you're naughty.'

Alex smiled too and then gave a little shudder. 'But I'm still nervous.'

'That's normal. So am I.' I copied his shudder and he laughed.

'Good boy, up you get then. They'll be here soon.' I glanced at the clock on the wall; it was 10.55.

He'd just got out of bed when the front doorbell rang. 'Is that them?' he asked, his eyes widening in alarm.

'I expect so.'

He shot back into bed and pulled the duvet up and over his head.

'Mum! Door!' Adrian shouted unnecessarily from the foot of the stairs. He knew not to answer the door, even if we were expecting someone. It was part of our 'safer caring policy', which all foster carers work to.

'I'll be down!' I called. Then to Alex, who was still under the duvet, 'Can you come down with me?'

'No,' came the muffled reply. 'I'm too scared.'

'OK. Stay there for a few minutes while I go down and let them in. I'll take them into the living room and once they're settled I'll come back up for you. How does that sound?'

'I'll try.'

'Good boy.'

I came out, leaving his bedroom door open – I knew he'd be listening out for his parents' voices – and returned downstairs. Adrian was now peering through the security spy hole in the front door. 'It's them,' he said. 'I recognize them from the photograph in Alex's album. But they're not wearing their best clothes.'

'Adrian, don't tell them that!'

He grinned cheekily and then stood beside me as I opened the front door. 'Hello, lovely to see you again,' I said, welcoming Edward and Rosemary.

'And you, Cathy,' Edward said. Then to Adrian, 'Hello, young man.'

'Hello,' Adrian said politely.

'He's very different from his photographs,' Rosemary said as they came in. 'I wouldn't have recognized him.'

'Oh no, this isn't Alex,' I said. 'This is Adrian, my son.'

'I'm sorry,' Rosemary said with an embarrassed laugh. But it broke the ice.

'Come through and have a seat in the living room,' I said. 'I'll fetch Alex down in a minute. He's in his bedroom.'

'Not still in bed, surely?' Edward exclaimed jocularly. 'James and I have been on a five-mile bike ride already.'

I smiled. 'No, he's not in bed, he's just a bit nervous.'

'Shall I go up and talk to him?' Rosemary kindly offered.

'I think it would be better if I persuaded him to come down,' I said. We went into the living room and I introduced Rosemary and Edward to Paula.

'Hello, dear,' Rosemary said. 'What are you doing? Playing?' She gave a small, shy nod.

'This is Alex's mummy and daddy,' I told Paula.

'That's nice,' she said cutely.

'What a sweet child,' Rosemary said.

'Not always,' Adrian added quietly.

Edward laughed. 'That's girls for you, lad! Give me sons any day.'

'Can I get you a tea or coffee?' I offered as Edward and Rosemary sat on the sofa.

'Not for me, thank you,' Rosemary said.

'What about you, Edward? Would you like a drink?'

'No, thank you. I was rather hoping to meet Alex.'

'There's no rush,' Rosemary said. 'He's bound to be shy to begin with.' But Edward looked at me expectantly.

'I'll see if he's ready to come down,' I said, and left the room. I appreciated that Edward was probably as nervous as the rest of us and that we all showed it in different ways, but I hoped he would soften his manner a little when he spoke to Alex who, unfamiliar with Edward, might find it a little intimidating.

I was about to start up the stairs when Alex appeared, coming down, carrying his photograph album under one arm and his toy Simba under the other.

'Well done, good boy,' I said. I waited for him at the foot of the stairs and as he joined me he slipped his hand into mine. I gave it a reassuring squeeze.

'Can I sit on your lap?' he whispered.

'Yes, of course.'

'This is Alex,' I said to Rosemary and Edward as we entered the living room. I went to the armchair and lifted him onto my lap.

'Hello, Alex,' Edward said. 'I'm Edward and this is my wife, Rosemary.' It was far too formal and distant, but I put it down to nerves.

'This is your new mummy and daddy,' I said to Alex.

Looking up at them from under a lowered head he managed a small, wary smile.

'I see you've got the photograph album I made for you,' Rosemary said. 'Do you like it?'

Alex nodded. 'He did, very much,' I said. 'We've all had a look.' Adrian and Paula were sitting on the floor beside the toy boxes. They'd stopped playing and were now studying Alex's parents.

'We were very impressed by how smart you looked in your photograph,' I said, making conversation.

'Thank you,' Rosemary said, and again smiled at Alex. 'That's kind of you. We saw a picture of you in your school uniform and you looked very smart too.' Her manner was just right and she seemed more at ease than Edward, who clearly didn't know what to say for the best. 'And you like school?'

Alex managed another small nod.

'So, Alex, what hobbies do you like?' Edward asked.

Alex shrugged. Put on the spot, his mind had gone blank. I knew that feeling well.

'You like lots of things, don't you?' I said, giving him a reassuring hug. 'You like riding your bike, playing all sorts of games, drawing and painting, reading and watching some television.'

'Chess?' Edward asked. 'I'm teaching James to play. Do you play chess?' Alex shook his head.

'You'll be able to teach him, won't you, love?' Rosemary said to Edward. Then to Alex, 'Would you like that?'

Alex nodded.

So we – the adults – continued making conversation, contrived and stilted, but no more than I'd expected for this first meeting. Alex sat on my lap, clutching his photograph album and Simba, and managing a small nod where appropriate and stealing glances at his parents. Then, after about ten minutes, he slid from my lap, placed the album and Simba on the floor and went over to join Adrian and Paula – a sign he was feeling more comfortable. The toys they were playing with were a mixture of Alex's, Adrian's and Paula's. They were still sharing nicely, although we always separated them into their respective toy boxes when we cleared up at bedtime.

'You've got some lovely toys, Alex,' Rosemary said. 'Do you have a favourite?'

'This one,' Alex said, finally able to talk to her and holding up the car transporter loaded with cars.

'Wow, that looks good,' Rosemary enthused. 'James has cars too. Can I have a closer look?'

'Show it to your mum,' I encouraged.

Alex stood and went over to the sofa. Standing close to Rosemary but not quite touching, he proudly showed her the transporter. She admired it as any mother appreciated and praised their child's interests. 'Look at all those wheels,' she said, pointing to its underside. 'And all those different makes of car it's carrying. I think that looks like a Jaguar. Wow. How does the back of the transporter lower to take the cars off?'

Alex set the transporter on her lap, unclipped the back and began rolling off the cars.

'I think James had one just like this, didn't he?' Rosemary asked Edward, bringing him into the conversation.

Edward nodded. 'He used to like playing with cars when he was little.'

Rosemary admired each car as Alex carefully 'drove' it off the transporter and onto her lap as Edward looked on. Then she helped Alex load them again. Alex was far more relaxed now he was playing with her. When they'd reloaded the cars Rosemary asked, 'Can you show me what else you have in your toy box?'

'Yes,' Alex said. 'But you'll have to come and sit on the floor with us.' Which she did, admiring not only Alex's toys, but Adrian's and Paula's as well.

After about ten minutes, I became aware that the time was passing and I felt Edward needed to be more included, so I suggested that they might like to play a board game all together. Alex looked hopefully at his parents. 'Yes, please,' Rosemary said, and Edward nodded.

'I'll get my football game. It's in my bedroom,' Alex said

excitedly. Jumping to his feet and smiling broadly, he ran out of the living room and upstairs.

'How are we doing?' Rosemary asked me anxiously.

'Fine, don't worry. He's relaxing. It will be much easier tomorrow now you've met each other.'

'This isn't a long game, is it?' Edward asked, glancing at the clock on the mantelpiece. 'Only I've got a table booked for lunch at two o'clock.'

'No, it won't take long,' I said. 'And it's important we stick to the hour for this visit.'

Alex ran back into the living room clutching his football board game, and I drew the coffee table over to the sofa. 'If you sit on the sofa between your mum and dad you'll all be able to reach the board,' I said.

Rosemary and Edward quickly moved apart to make room for Alex, and he sat between them. It looked so right. Now more confident, he removed the lid from the box and then carefully took out the pieces, explaining what they were for and how the game was played, while his parents watched attentively. I saw Adrian glance over wishfully; he liked playing this game with Alex (it was too advanced for Paula), but he'd have to play another time. This was special for Alex and his parents, and playing together would help them bond. As they began to play I joined Adrian and Paula on the floor with their game.

Now that Edward was no longer obliged to make small talk he too relaxed and was soon enthusiastically playing the game, wanting to win as much as Alex did. As the cheers or sighs went up as a goal was scored or missed I relaxed as well. Sitting together on the sofa and enjoying the game, they already looked like a family. All they needed now was James.

Alex won the game by two points and we all clapped. 'That's a good game,' Rosemary said. 'Can you bring it with you tomorrow so we can all play it?'

'Yes,' Alex said enthusiastically. 'I'll put it by the front door ready. James can play as well.'

Well done, Rosemary, I thought. Just what was needed, and I knew tomorrow would go well.

CHAPTER SEVEN

MEETING JAMES

Although Alex's first meeting with his parents had been a success on Saturday, by the following morning some of his worries had returned. He was awake early again and I found him sitting up in bed poring over his photograph album. 'Supposing James doesn't like me?' he asked anxiously.

'He'll like you,' I said. 'I know you're a bit nervous and he will be too, but it will all be fine, really it will.'

'I hope so,' Alex said wistfully. 'I know I will like James.'

'And he'll like you.'

But that morning Alex wasn't the only one facing the day with a mixture of excitement and apprehension. Adrian, Paula and I were too. While contact with their father was working reasonably well, the situation still felt very uncomfortable, awkward and even upsetting, especially when I had to say goodbye to Adrian and Paula at the door and they went off on a family outing that I could never be part of again. I knew they struggled, and while they always enjoyed their days out with their father, parting from me at the start of the day and then having to say goodbye to their father at the end was as difficult now as it had been when the arrangements began. They dealt with it in their own ways. Adrian said a quick, manly goodbye, while Paula prolonged parting – from both me and her father – with lots of extra hugs and kisses. Whether John found it difficult I didn't know, but given that it was his decision to leave us he could hardly complain, and if he had done he would have received little sympathy from me. *He's made his bed so he'll have to lie in it*, as my mother would have said.

No one wanted a cooked breakfast that morning, which we often enjoyed at the weekend, and once the children were dressed they couldn't settle to much, so I switched on children's television to keep them all occupied. John arrived promptly at 10.30 and I went with Adrian and Paula to see them off at the front door, where I greeted John politely. As usual Paula asked me if I could go out with them, and as usual it hurt to say no.

'This is your special time with your father,' I said.

She hugged and kissed me and then Adrian took her by the hand and followed their father to his car.

There were just twenty minutes before Alex and I had to leave, so I joined him in the living room to watch some television. He asked a couple of times how long it was before we had to leave but didn't say much else. I reassured him again that meeting James would be fine and there was nothing to worry about. At 10.50 I told him it was time to put on our coats and shoes and, without saying anything, he obediently left the sofa and went down the hall, while I switched off the television and then checked the back door was locked. His football game was still in the hall where he'd left it ready to take, but now doubt set in and he began wavering as to whether he should take it or not. 'James might not want to play it,' he said, setting the box on the floor again. 'I don't think I'll take it.'

'It's up to you, love, but if it was me I'd take it just in case. If the two of you decide you don't want to play with it there's nothing lost, but your mum thought James would like it.'

'OK,' he said, picking up the game again. 'Can I leave it in the car?'

'Yes, of course.'

He carried the box to the car and placed it beside him on the back seat. I checked his seat belt was fastened and then got in, with the route instructions and my handbag on the passenger seat beside me. I knew roughly where their village, Churchwell, was and as it was only small I didn't think I'd have any problems finding their house once there. Alex was quiet as I drove. Each time I glanced at him in the rear-view mirror he was gazing pensively out of his side window, clearly deep in thought, and I reassured him that meeting James was nothing to worry about. Then about halfway there he said he felt sick, so I lowered the windows for some fresh air and he soon recovered. I guessed it was nerves.

He sat quietly again, gazing out of the window, and when I turned off the main road I asked him to look out for the signpost for Churchwell, which kept him occupied. We both saw it together and then as I drove through the village I asked him to look out for the road name. He spotted it, and then recognized the house from the photograph in his album. 'Well done,' I said.

I parked the car on their driveway behind the car that was already there and cut the engine. I went round and opened

Alex's car door, which was child-locked, and waited as he climbed out. He looked a little pale. 'I'll leave my game in the car,' he said. 'I can fetch it if James wants to play it.'

'Good idea,' I said.

He slipped his hand into mine and we walked up their front path, which ran beside a neat border of winter pansies and evergreen shrubs. I didn't have to press the doorbell – the door opened as we approached it.

'You must be James,' I said, smiling at the boy standing before us. 'I'm Cathy and this is Alex.'

'Pleased to meet you. Hi, Alex. Come in. Dad said he thought I should answer the door.' Confident and at ease, James appeared older and far more mature than Alex, who was only eighteen months younger, but then of course James was on home territory and his life experiences had been very different from Alex's. Stability and opportunity builds confidence.

'Mum and Dad are going to say hello and then leave us to play,' James said to Alex as we went in. Their spacious lounge-hall with its chaise longue, oval table and vase of fresh flowers was just as we'd seen in the photograph. 'I've arranged toys and games in my bedroom,' James said. 'Take off your coat and then we can play.'

Alex instantly dropped my hand and quickly took off his coat. Rosemary and Edward appeared from the room on our right. 'Good afternoon,' Edward said, taking our coats. 'How are you, Alex?'

'Good,' he said.

'We thought it would be less intimidating for Alex if James answered the door,' Rosemary said to me.

'It seems to have worked,' I agreed. Alex was smiling and relaxed and had lost all signs of his previous apprehension and nervousness.

'Can we go to my room now?' James asked his father excitedly.

'Yes, of course,' Edward said.

'This way,' James said to Alex, and he ran up the stairs with Alex close behind.

'I'll be down here if you need me!' I called after him, but he'd gone.

'James is sensible. He'll take care of him,' Edward said, hanging our coats in the walk-in cloakroom. 'The plan is they'll play for a while in James's room and then James will show Alex around the house, beginning with his bedroom.'

This wasn't the way I would usually introduce a child to their new home – I would be with them as the parents showed us all around – but Alex had appeared happy enough to go with James.

'You can have a seat and relax with Rosemary while I make you a drink,' Edward said. 'What would you like?'

'Tea if you are making it, thank you,' I said.

'And you, love?' he asked Rosemary.

'Coffee, please,' she said.

Edward, now on home ground, was far more at ease than he had been at my house. His manner had lost that abrasive edge and he seemed perfectly charming. Whistling to himself, he headed down the hall to make the drinks while I followed Rosemary into their immaculate living room, with its cream sofas and occasional table centrepiece just as it had appeared in the photograph.

'James has been so excited all morning,' Rosemary said as we sat down. 'He's been counting down the minutes till Alex's arrival since he got up. I'm pleased you weren't late. He didn't want to go for a bike ride, but Edward insisted – to keep him occupied. How was Alex?'

'A little quiet and nervous, but that's only to be expected. He seems fine now.'

'Good. We've explained to James about Alex's background and he understands. But he's been so looking forward to having a brother that it doesn't matter.'

I smiled amicably, although I wasn't exactly sure what Rosemary meant. 'The adoption process can take a long time,' I said. 'The assessment and then all the waiting to be matched with a child.'

Rosemary nodded. 'Although because we said we'd take an older child we were matched quite quickly. Most couples want babies or a toddler, but I couldn't be bothered with all those nappies again. And a baby wouldn't have been much of a playmate for James, would it?' I nodded. 'We couldn't have any more children of our own,' Rosemary confided. 'James was conceived through IVF [in vitro fertilization], but when we tried again, when James was two, it didn't work. We had three goes and our doctor advised us to stop, as the drugs can be harmful to a woman's body. So Edward and I decided to go down the adoption route, which is the next best thing to having your own, isn't it?'

'Yes, although I tend to think an adopted child is a special gift.'

'That's a lovely way of putting it. I must tell James and Edward.'

Rosemary then asked me, as many people do, why I fostered. As we were talking Edward returned with the drinks on a tray, which he placed on occasional tables within our reach.

'The boys are getting on like a house on fire,' he said as he sat down. 'I just had a listen outside James's bedroom door and he's looking after Alex just as we told him to. I don't think they're going to cause us much trouble. James is so accommodating.'

I took a sip of my tea and set the cup in the saucer. 'I expect Debbie or Lin mentioned what we call the honeymoon period?' They looked at me, unsure. 'It's the first few weeks when everyone is on their best behaviour before ...' I didn't need to go any further.

'Before he starts to test us,' Edward put in.

'Yes, but it won't just be Alex,' I said.

'No, we know,' Rosemary said. 'James could start to play up too and demand more attention.'

'Yes. Once the boys feel completely relaxed in each other's company they won't be on their best behaviour the whole time and could both start to test the boundaries.'

'We're prepared for that,' Rosemary said.

'How long does that period usually last?' Edward asked, sipping his coffee.

'It's impossible to tell, but on average I would say a couple of months sees the worst over with. It happens a lot in foster-ing. Then you turn a corner and normality resumes.' They both smiled.

'So how do you deal with it in fostering?' Rosemary asked.

'By reassuring the child that he or she is safe, loved and wanted, and keeping in place the boundaries for good behaviour. It is so easy to feel sorry for the child when they've suffered and have had a rough start in life. But allowing their behaviour to spiral out of control doesn't help them. Boundaries are safe and secure and as important as love.'

'I hope I don't have to tell Alex off too much,' Rosemary said, looking slightly concerned.

'I'm sure you won't. Alex hasn't got challenging behaviour; just take it as it comes. He is so looking forward to having a proper mummy and daddy of his own. Do you know he doesn't want a goodnight kiss from me because he says he's saving all his kisses for you?'

'That's so sweet,' Rosemary said. 'I'll give him all the kisses he wants and more. James stopped wanting a goodnight kiss a long while ago.'

'He's too old for all that soft stuff now,' Edward said, returning his cup and saucer to the tray.

'I'm not sure we're ever too old for a hug and a kiss, are we?' I said lightly.

'No, you're right,' Rosemary agreed. 'Especially with a child like Alex.'

'He does seem very young for his age,' Edward said. 'The social worker said to expect that.'

'When a child has been badly neglected they fail to flourish,' I said. 'It can affect their physical and emotional development. Once the child is in a loving and stable home they can quickly make up for it.'

'I think Lin said something similar,' Rosemary added.

At that moment the living-room door flew open and James and Alex burst in. 'Come and see what we've built,' James cried excitedly.

'We're on our way,' Edward said, immediately standing.

'We've been playing with my Meccano,' James said. 'You said Alex would like it and he does.'

'I like James's Meccano,' Alex told me.

'I can't wait to see what you've made,' Rosemary said.

We followed them upstairs and into James's bedroom where two construction-kit robots stood side by side, the detritus from the rest of the kit scattered across the floor.

'I made this one,' James said proudly, pointing to the larger, more sophisticated robot.

'And I made this one,' Alex said.

'They're both fantastic,' I said, going over for a closer look.

'I helped Alex make his,' James said to his father.

'Good lad,' Edward replied, and I smiled at Alex.

Once we'd finished admiring the boys' robots, Alex was keen to show me his bedroom. It was just as we'd seen in the photograph: freshly decorated in shades of blue, with plenty of cupboard space, a navy carpet and a spaceman patterned duvet and matching curtains. Rosemary then suggested that she show me around the rest of the house while the boys played. They returned to James's bedroom and Edward went with them. Rosemary and I walked in and out of the upstairs rooms, and I said that when Alex visited next time I'd suggest to him that he brought something of his – a game or cuddly toy – to leave in his room, which would help make him feel at home. Then each time we came he could bring something else, so he gradually transferred some of his possessions (and feelings of being home) from my house to here. I added that I would take down some of the posters from his bedroom walls so that he could put them up here.

Rosemary hesitated. 'Edward doesn't usually allow James to stick things on his bedroom walls,' she said. 'It makes such a mess, but I'm sure we can make an exception for Alex.'

I looked at her. 'Do what you would normally do and feel comfortable with. Your house rules are bound to be a bit different from mine, and it's important you treat both boys the same. Although I use Blu-Tack for posters, which doesn't leave much of a mark.'

'Cathy,' Rosemary said with feeling, 'if Alex wants his posters on his walls, he can put them on with cement if it makes him happy.'

We smiled and walked on. Once Rosemary had shown me the upstairs of the house (James and Edward were now showing Alex), we continued downstairs. All the rooms were as I'd seen in the photographs and just as neat and tidy. We returned to the living room while Edward, James and Alex finished their tour, and then it was time for us to leave.

'Can't I stay for a bit longer?' Alex asked plaintively.

'Not this time,' I said. 'We have to keep to Debbie's timetable. You'll be speaking to Mummy, Daddy and James on the phone tomorrow and then they are coming to our house for tea on Tuesday.'

With a small collaborative groan of disappointment the boys accepted this.

'I'm hoping to make it to yours on Tuesday,' Edward said to me. 'But I'm not normally home from work then. Rosemary will bring James if I'm not back – we've reorganized his tutor.'

'I know these introductory periods often upset the family's normal routine,' I said. 'But then it all settles down once the child has moved in.'

'It's not a problem,' Rosemary said.

We all said goodbye in the hall, with the boys giving each other a high five.

'It's gone well, don't you think?' Rosemary said to me.

'Yes, very well.'

Despite the cold they all saw us off at the door, waving until we were out of sight.

'How long until I see them again?' Alex asked as they disappeared from view.

'They're going to phone you tomorrow. Then you'll see them again on Tuesday and Thursday at our house.'

'When can I go to their house again?'

'Friday.'

'We didn't have time to play my football game,' Alex now lamented, resting his hand on the box containing the board game.

'You were too busy,' I said, smiling at him in the rear-view mirror. 'Did you have a nice time playing with James?'

'Yes, it was good. I think James is going to be a very nice brother to me.' And for the rest of the journey Alex talked non-stop about James and all the things they were planning to do. I'd never seen him so animated, and it was fantastic.

What wasn't so good was having to watch Adrian and Paula say goodbye to their father when he returned them from contact at 6 p.m. But as usual I put on a brave face, wished John a safe journey and then, after he'd gone, kept the children occupied to distract them from the fact that they probably wouldn't see their father again for two weeks, possibly longer. The contact arrangements were his; he could see Adrian and Paula when he liked. Thankfully that evening there was plenty to talk about as Alex told Adrian and Paula all about his visit to his parents' house and playing with James. That night when I wrote up my log notes it was all positive and I slept soundly.

CHAPTER EIGHT

PLANS FOR THE FUTURE

Lin and Jill both telephoned on Monday morning for updates on the weekend. I was able to say that the visits had gone very well and I outlined what we'd done. Lin thanked me and said that Debbie was in court on another case for most of the week and she'd be in touch when she had a moment, but in the meantime she'd keep her updated. When I spoke to Jill she said, 'Good luck, Cathy. You've got a busy couple of weeks coming up. You know where I am if you need me.'

'Thanks, Jill.'

I'd written a simplified version of the timetable of introduction for Alex and had pinned it to the cork board on his bedroom wall so that each morning he knew what was happening that day, and he could tick it off at night. The telephone call on Monday from his family was a little laboured to begin with. Alex hadn't had much experience of using a telephone and answered his mother's questions politely, but with one word, so it made conversation a little difficult.

'Have you had a good day at school?' she asked.

'Yes,' Alex replied.

'Have you had your dinner?'

'Yes,' Alex said.

'Did you eat it all?'

'Yes.'

It was similar when Edward spoke to him. Edward asked Alex which subjects he liked best at school and he said, 'Games.' Edward followed it through by asking which games in particular he enjoyed and Alex said, 'Football.' And so it continued. But it didn't matter that the conversation was a little awkward, as this call would still achieve its purpose: to maintain and develop the bond that was starting to form between Alex and his new family, and which would gather momentum towards the date when he moved in.

However, conversation became easier when it was James's turn to talk to Alex. Alex visibly relaxed, and after they'd both said hi Alex asked James if he'd made any more robots. James said no because he had homework to do. I was sitting beside Alex on the sofa during the call, and he replied that he had homework too – reading and science. They then spent some time discussing the ills of homework and how it should be banned so they could play all evening at robots and similar. Eventually James said he had to go and practise his violin, and Rosemary came on the line again to say goodnight to Alex. When they'd finished Alex passed the phone to me and Rose-mary said she was pleased James and Alex had had a good chat, and then confirmed the arrangements for the following evening – that they would be with me at about 5.30 for dinner and would stay approximately two hours. Rosemary apolo-gized that she still couldn't say for definite that Edward would be joining us, but he would do his best to leave work early.

On Tuesday morning Alex was so excited that his mummy, daddy and brother were coming again that it was no surprise he told his teacher. At the end of school she came out to see me in the playground.

'Alice Cork,' she said. 'We met briefly before.'

'Yes.'

'Alex has been telling me all about his new family. He's so excited. His social worker spoke to our Head and I understand he'll be able to stay with us for the rest of the term.'

'Yes, that's right. You'll meet Rosemary, his mum, next week when she collects him from school.'

'I'll look forward to it. Well, I just wanted to say have a good evening. You can tell me about it tomorrow,' she said, smiling at Alex.

We said goodbye and she went over to speak to another parent while Alex, Paula and I began across the playground.

'It was all right to tell her, wasn't it?' Alex asked me.

'Yes, of course, love. It's your news, you can tell who you like.'

'I told one of my friends, but he wasn't really pleased, not like Miss. He said it was sad that I couldn't live with my proper mummy, but he doesn't understand, does he?'

'No, he doesn't,' I agreed, 'but Miss Cork will.' I thought it must be virtually impossible for a young child brought up by loving parents to comprehend why Alex would be excited when he would never see his birth mother again. Whereas his teacher would have some experience of children, like Alex, who'd been neglected or abused by their birth family.

On the way to collect Adrian from school Alex asked me if I thought his dad would be able to come to dinner this evening with his mum and James. I had to say I didn't know but that I hoped so. He asked me again when we arrived home and I could only give him the same reply. He was still very excited and I settled the boys at the table to do their homework while I made dinner, as they wouldn't have time to do it after Alex's family had left. When they'd finished they went to play and I laid the table ready for dinner. As 5.30 approached – the time they were due to arrive – Alex began to grow nervous again, which was understandable. When the doorbell rang he fled upstairs, saying he was going to hide in his bedroom and they could find him. Adrian went up with him, which left Paula and me to answer the front door.

'Great. You've made it,' I said, pleased to see Edward. 'Alex will be glad.'

'It was a rush but this is too important to miss,' Edward said, coming in and kissing my cheek. He was wearing his office suit but had taken off his tie.

'Hello, poppet,' Rosemary said to Paula, patting her head. She grinned shyly.

'Alex and Adrian are hiding,' I said to James. 'Perhaps you'd like to find them? Upstairs, turn right and Alex's room is on the left.'

James ran upstairs while I showed Rosemary and Edward through to the living room. 'How has Alex been?' Rosemary asked.

'Very excited and a little nervous. He's been telling his teacher all about his new family. She's lovely. You'll meet her next week.'

'I'm looking forward to it. Miss Cork, isn't it?'

'That's right.'

'Something smells good,' Edward said, collapsing into an armchair. 'I didn't have time for lunch.'

'Edward!' Rosemary said, lightly chastising him.

'It should be ready soon,' I said. 'It's chicken casserole. I'll check on it.'

'Can I help you?' Rosemary offered.

'It's OK. There's nothing much to do. Make yourself comfortable.' I offered them a drink but they both declined.

Paula came with me into the kitchen, where I kept her away from the oven as I checked the casserole, which was ready. A couple of minutes later I went into the hall and called everyone for dinner. The boys, who were still upstairs, stampeded down like a herd of elephants.

'Hello, love,' Rosemary said to Alex, greeting him in the hall. 'How are you?'

'Hungry,' Alex said.

Edward laughed. 'So am I.'

'Me too,' Adrian and James agreed.

I showed them to the table and then served the meal. To begin with all that could be heard was the sound of cutlery on china.

Sometimes it can be a little awkward eating with people you hardly know, and while the adults might have felt this, the children were relaxed in each other's company and ate and talked without reservation. Edward just ate – he clearly was hungry – while Rosemary and I made polite conversation, and Paula stared at our guests, fascinated, and had to be reminded to eat. Once the boys had finished we excused them from the table and they went into the living room to play while Edward had a second helping. Although this evening was about Alex continuing to get to know and bond with his family, it was important that we kept the atmosphere as relaxed and natural as possible, so it would have been unwise to insist that Alex spent every single minute in the company of his parents.

When Edward had finished eating, Rosemary helped me clear away the dishes and then we returned to the table to talk. Paula was content to sit on my lap listening and watching us. Edward told us a bit about his work and also that they'd just booked a holiday for the spring break to Disney World in Florida.

'James and Alex will love that,' I said.

Rosemary nodded. 'James has been before, but he wants to go again. And I know Alex hasn't been abroad at all.'

'No, he hasn't. What's happening about a passport for him?' I asked, aware that obtaining one can be an issue and takes time for looked-after children.

'Debbie is applying for it,' Rosemary said.

'Good.'

'Do you think it's all right to tell Alex he is going?' Rosemary asked.

'Yes. I don't see why not. It's nice to have something to look forward to. He'll be so excited.'

As it turned out there was no need for Rosemary or Edward to tell Alex about the holiday as James, brimming with the news, had told him. When I called the boys for pudding the first thing Adrian said was, 'Mum! Alex is going to Disney World.'

'I know, isn't he lucky?' But I felt a little sad for Adrian, as a trip to Disney World was something John and I had talked about doing before he left, and there was little chance of that happening now.

Everyone enjoyed the crumble and custard, and once we'd finished we all went into the living room where Alex set out his football board game. He, his parents, James and Adrian played while I kept Paula amused with her toys. It was nearly her bedtime now and she was becoming a little fractious, but, as I'd said to Rosemary, this introductory period would disrupt all our routines.

They had two rounds of the football game and it was just after 7.30 when I saw them to the door. 'We'll phone you tomorrow,' Rosemary told Alex. 'Then on Thursday we're taking you out for dinner.' Alex threw her a really warm, appreciative smile. 'Would you like a hug?' she asked him.

He nodded and, delighted, Rosemary gave him a hug, and then Edward shook his hand. As they left I could tell by their faces that they, too, felt the evening had been a great success. Alex had taken another step closer to his family and before long they would all be together. He would have his forever family and Rosemary and Edward the son they so dearly wanted.

As it was close to Adrian's and Alex's bedtimes I took the boys up to bed at the same time as I took Paula, and then left them to get ready while I put Paula to bed. She fell asleep almost immediately. I was pleased that Edward had managed to come this evening, as I knew it would mean a lot to Alex. As I tucked him into bed that night he said, 'Dad left work early so he could see me. That shows how much he loves me.'

'It does,' I said, smiling.

'I think he's going to be a good dad, don't you?'

'Yes. I'm sure he will be.'

'And Mummy will be a good mummy and James a good brother. I'm so happy.'

'So am I.'

The introductions continued. Alex's family telephoned on Wednesday evening and then took him out to dinner on Thursday. They went to a little bistro I suggested in our high street and had an enjoyable time. On Friday morning Jill and Lin telephoned for updates and I was able to tell them everything was going well and to plan. They were obviously pleased, although this was no more than they'd expected. Alex was ripe for a permanent family and this family was a good match for him. On Friday, following the timetable, I left Alex at his new home for two hours, where he had dinner, and I took Adrian and Paula for something to eat in the neighbouring town, as there wasn't time to go home. We returned as arranged to collect Alex at 7.30 and Paula slept in the car on the way home while Alex told Adrian about his evening. I listened as I drove and it all seemed to be positive. He and James had played and then the family, including Edward, had eaten together – lasagne, which Alex had enjoyed. After dinner Alex had watched James do his violin practice, which he had to do every evening, but he said it sounded a bit 'squeaky'.

Saturday was a really big day for Alex, as he was spending his first night at his new home, so I carefully packed his over-night bag. He wasn't at all apprehensive and was looking forward to sleeping in his new bed. He chose his soft toy,

Simba, to take with him, which he was happy to leave there for next time. As per the timetable we were due to arrive at about 11 a.m. Adrian and Paula came with me, but they understood that we wouldn't stay for long. Alex wanted to show Adrian his bedroom, so we popped in for a quarter of an hour only and then said goodbye. With nothing planned for the afternoon I made an impromptu visit to my parents, who were surprised and pleased to see us. We stayed for tea.

On Sunday we woke to a very light covering of snow – pretty but not deep enough to do anything with other than make footprints. The children and I went out into the garden for a while after breakfast, then had to leave to collect Alex for eleven o'clock. By the time we arrived a wintry sun sat in a cloudless sky and the snow had melted. Churchwell, their village, surrounded by countryside, was idyllic – quintessentially English, as you would see on a picture postcard – but remote. There wasn't even a village shop. Alex was tired and kept yawning, as he and James had stayed up late. Rosemary said she'd made it clear to them that this was a treat and once Alex had moved in they would be keeping to regular bedtimes, apart from weekends, when there was no school in the morning. We all said goodbye, I put Alex's overnight bag in the boot of the car and his family waved us off. In the car Alex told us his dad and James were going cycling now the snow had gone and he was looking forward to going with them once he'd moved in – in a little over a week's time.

'Great,' I said. 'That sounds good. Did you remember to leave Simba on your bed?'

'Yes, but I hid him under the covers. James doesn't have soft toys. He's says they're for little boys.'

I glanced at him in the mirror. 'Alex, there is no need to feel embarrassed about taking a toy to bed with you.' He met my gaze but didn't reply. 'James was nice to you, wasn't he?'

'Yes. We had to play what he wanted all the time, but I didn't mind.'

Alex was used to living with other children (from being in care) and therefore had experience of sharing and taking turns, while James had been an only child, so sharing, especially at home, could be a learning curve for him.

'You don't always have to play what James wants,' I said, glancing at him again in the mirror. 'Shall I mention it to your mum?'

'No. I can tell her if I want,' Alex said easily. 'She's nice. She said if I had any problems I should tell her. But it's not a problem.'

'OK. See how it goes then. But remember to tell her if there is anything at all worrying you.' It was important that Alex knew he could confide in her if necessary.

'Yes, I will,' he said.

School for Alex the following week was just an irritating interruption in between the times he saw his family or spoke to them on the phone. They dominated his thoughts and conversation as he eagerly awaited the next time he could see or speak to them. And when he wasn't talking about the next time he would see them he was reminiscing about the last time. On Monday the telephone conversation with his family was much easier and it flowed; he was talking to them for over half an hour. Then on Tuesday, straight after school, I took him to his new home for dinner. It was when I had to make a journey like this on a cold, dark evening that I really felt being a single parent. Had my husband still been living with us he would have most likely looked after Adrian and Paula so they could stay at home in the warm and have dinner rather than going out again. Thankfully, Adrian's homework didn't have to be given in the following day, and he was good enough not to complain about losing his evening. I think he appreciated there was little alternative.

While Alex was with his family I took Adrian and Paula to eat in the neighbouring town again, and then had to drive back along the poorly lit, unfamiliar country lanes with a frost settling. I was relieved when we were all safely home.

On Wednesday morning Alex took his overnight bag into school with him, as Rosemary would be collecting him that afternoon and taking him home. Adrian and Paula came with me to the school office that morning, as I wanted to check that the school knew of the arrangements. They did, and the school secretary suggested that Alex left his bag in the office for safekeeping. We said goodbye to him and that we would see him the next day, and he ran off happily to breakfast club. The secretary smiled.

Shortly after I'd returned home from taking Adrian to school, Debbie, who had now finished the court case she'd been attending, telephoned for an update. I said that everything was still going well. She confirmed that Rosemary would collect Alex from school again on Friday, when he would spend the weekend at his new home, and then I would collect him on Sunday afternoon. Sunday night would be his last with us, as he moved on Monday. Debbie said she'd spoken to the Head of Alex's school, so his teacher was aware of these arrangements and that Alex would be having Monday off. She thanked me for all I was doing and said to phone if I needed anything.

With Rosemary collecting Alex from school that afternoon there was less rushing around for me as I just had Adrian to collect, although once home Alex's absence was obvious. He hadn't been with us for long but he was such a dear little chap and had fitted so easily into our family that it felt as if he had been with us for much longer. He would be dearly missed.

The following day, Thursday, when I collected Alex from school, he came out with his overnight bag and looked at me, slightly puzzled. 'Where's Mum?' he asked.

'She's at her house. Did you think she was going to meet you?' He nodded. 'I know it's a bit confusing, but not for much longer. You're coming back with me tonight and then your mum will collect you tomorrow and every day after that.'

He smiled, and Paula, pleased to see him, threw her arms around him and gave him a big hug.

Jill telephoned shortly after we arrived home, having spoken to Debbie. She said they'd agreed that it would make sense if Rosemary stopped by my house on her way to collect Alex from school the following day (Friday) and took his overnight bag and also some of his other belongings, including his bike, so they didn't have it all to move on Monday. It would also help Alex to feel more at home, as he was spending the whole weekend there. Debbie had cleared this with Rosemary and I said I'd have Alex's belongings ready. Jill wished us a pleasant weekend, and once I'd finished talking to her I told Alex what was happening. He was very happy that his bike was going. 'I'll be able to ride it at the weekend,' he said. And I felt guilty that he hadn't had a chance to ride his bike while he'd been with me as I'd originally said, but we'd been so busy there really hadn't been an opportunity.

When his family telephoned that evening much of his conversation with James was about riding their bikes and other things they were planning to do at the weekend: two boys on a big adventure. Edward wasn't home from work, so just James and his mother spoke to Alex. Rosemary also spoke to me and confirmed she'd stop by around 2.30 p.m. the next day for some of Alex's belongings.

The following morning Alex was beside himself with excitement at the thought of spending the whole weekend with his family and going for a bike ride. Adrian was looking a bit envious, so I told him that if the weather was good we would take his bike to the park.

'Perhaps my dad could take me bike riding?' Adrian said, which stung me as such comments always did.

'You could ask him,' I said. 'Although he took his bike with him when he moved.' When he went to live with his secretary, I thought but didn't say. 'You do other nice things when he takes you out,' I added. 'And when Paula is older the three of us could go bike riding.' But I doubted this would make up for not going with his father.

We took Alex to school that morning, and as we said goodbye we wished him a nice weekend. The next time we would see him would be Sunday afternoon (before his move on Monday) and I was planning a special goodbye tea. When children have been with the same foster carer for some time it's usual to give them a little goodbye party, but Alex had only been with me a few weeks and had never met my parents, brother or my friends, so it seemed more appropriate that it was just us. I would buy him a leaving present and card the following day and make his last evening with us special. Goodbyes are always difficult, but thankfully Alex, like many of the children I'd fostered, was leaving us to go to a loving forever home, so there was plenty to be happy about.

When Rosemary arrived that afternoon I had Alex's cases, some of his toys – in the boxes – and his bike ready in the hall. Rosemary was surprised he had so much, especially when I said there was as much if not more again, which I would pack ready for Monday.

'I always thought that foster children didn't own many possessions,' she said as we loaded her car. This was a mistake many people made and I explained to her that while this was sometimes true when a child first came into care, once they'd been in care a while they had as much as any other child – sometimes even more, as the carer made up for what they'd missed.

'I see,' Rosemary said. 'I'll have to explain that to James. I told him he'd have to let Alex have some of his toys, but really there's no need.'

'No, but it's still nice to share.'

'Oh yes, I've already told James that.'

Rosemary didn't stay for a coffee, as she wanted to leave in plenty of time to collect Alex from school. Paula and I saw her off at the door and then I had to try to explain to Paula why Rosemary was taking Alex's belongings: that she was his mummy now and Alex was happy he was going to live with his new family on Monday. But of course it was impossible for a small child to understand and she slipped her hand into mine and said, 'My mummy.'

'Yes, I'm your mummy forever and ever.'

CHAPTER NINE

UNWELCOME NEWS

'Can't I stay?' Alex protested when I collected him on Sunday afternoon.

'No, love, you have to go back with Cathy for just one more night,' Rosemary said to him. 'Then you come to stay with us.'

'Forever,' I added, smiling encouragingly at Alex. 'I'm going to make us a special tea with jelly and ice cream, and we've bought you a present.'

'A present!' Rosemary exclaimed, helping Alex into his coat. 'You can't miss that. Enjoy your evening and we'll see you tomorrow morning.'

She kissed the top of his head and Alex came with us, a little reluctantly, while Rosemary and James saw us off. Edward had gone out for a while. As I settled the children into their seats I saw that Adrian was looking a little hurt that Alex hadn't wanted to come with us, and I threw him a reassuring smile. But of course it was a good sign that Alex had wanted to stay with his family, and confirmed that during the introductory period he had successfully transferred his affection and sense of where home was from us to them. By the time we arrived home Adrian was chatting happily to Alex and they were both looking forward to our party tea.

I'd hung balloons and streamers in the living room and had set the table ready with a colourful tablecloth, matching napkins and paper party cups. In our absence Toscha had managed to pull down one of the streamers and was playing with it, chasing it around the room, which made Alex laugh.

'Do you think my mum will let me have a cat?' he asked me.

'I don't know, you'd have to ask her. Not everyone likes pets.'

'I'll ask her tomorrow,' he said.

I organized some party games that worked with just the few of us – hide and seek, hunt the thimble, sleeping lions, pass the parcel (in which I'd hidden a wrapped sweet between each layer of paper and a prize in the centre). Then I set the party food on the table: small sausage rolls, slices of pizza, little samosas, cheese straws, crisps and bowls of finely sliced cucumber and tomatoes, which we ate with fizzy lemonade. Once we'd had our fill of the savouries I brought out the individual jellies and ice cream, and a plate of chocolate biscuits and cupcakes. Then we gave Alex the presents we'd bought him and which I'd previously wrapped – boxed games of Guess Who?, Operation and draughts, which he'd enjoyed playing with us, together with a card signed by us all. There was also a good-luck card from my parents containing a five-pound note, even though they'd never met him, which was kind. There was a card from Jill sent on behalf of the agency wishing Alex luck in his new home. Once he'd finished admiring the cards and gifts, I packed them in one of his cases so they wouldn't be forgotten. Then we settled in the living room to watch a children's movie, popping to the table every so often to help ourselves to another biscuit or savoury. By the end of the evening most of the food had gone.

Although Alex didn't have to be up for school the following morning – it was his moving day – Adrian had to be, so I took the children up to bed at a reasonable time; Paula first and then Alex and Adrian. Alex's room was looking bare now with everything packed apart from his nightwear, one soft toy and a change of clothes for the morning.

'This is my last night here,' he said as, after a wash, he climbed into bed. 'Will I remember it?'

'You may,' I said. 'But I've taken a photograph of your room and put it in your Life Story Book, as well as some of us. It's packed in one of the cases.' Alex knew about his Life Story Book from being with other carers. It is a record of the child's time with the carer and includes photographs and memorabilia – for example, cinema tickets, the child's drawings and merit certificates from school – and is considered part of good fostering practice now. It's an aide-memoire that the child takes with them to supplement their own memories so they can retain a sense of their past. Having to move around so much can blur memories, as they don't have their birth parents to keep a treasure chest of memories alive.

'Will my mum and dad put photographs in my book too?' Alex asked.

'You can decide that with them. They will certainly take photographs, but they may put them in photograph albums. That's what we do here.'

He nodded and snuggled down, and appeared to be taking the end of his stay with us in his stride. 'Well, goodnight then, love,' I said. 'It's a busy day for you tomorrow, so get some sleep. Would you like a goodnight kiss?'

'No, thank you,' he said with a small, embarrassed smile. 'I'm saving all my kisses for my mummy.'

'I know.'

He turned onto his side and with one arm around his polar bear gave a little sigh of contentment as he closed his eyes ready for sleep.

The following morning Alex was up and getting dressed when I went into his room. 'It's all right, you've got plenty of time,' I said. 'They're not coming until ten-thirty, after we've taken Adrian to school.'

'I know, but I want to be ready,' he said excitedly.

'OK. But stay in your room and play while I get Paula up.' Which he did.

For Adrian it was another Monday morning, and because it was the middle of winter the dark and cold outside added to his feeling that he'd rather be in bed than getting ready for school. It took a few reminders before he was up and dressed and downstairs having breakfast.

'This is my last breakfast here,' Alex announced with a child's ability to state the raw truth.

It didn't help, and Adrian nodded glumly while Paula stared at Alex, not sure what to say.

In the playground I discovered that Paula's nursery was closed until further notice due to a burst water pipe, so she would have to come home with me. However, a friend of

Adrian's handed him a party invitation, which brightened his spirits.

'Can I go?' he asked eagerly.

'Yes, I should think so. I'll check in the diary and then we'll return the acceptance slip.' Adrian would have done it there and then.

When the klaxon sounded for the start of school Adrian knew he had to say goodbye to Alex and he did so quickly. It was Adrian's way of dealing with the separation.

'Bye,' he said. 'It was nice having you stay.'

'Bye,' Alex said.

I said goodbye to Adrian, wished him a good day and said I'd see him at the end of school. He gave me a quick hug and then ran off to join his class, but I saw him turn round for one final glance at Alex. We returned home, where Alex played with Paula and her toys while I gathered together the last of Alex's belongings and packed them in the cases. I could hear them laughing and chuckling as they played. Alex was very good with little children and I was pleased we were ending on a happy note.

At ten o'clock I made us all a drink and a snack, which we'd only just finished when the front doorbell rang – at 10.20.

'That's them!' Alex cried. Slipping from his chair, he ran down the hall and then waited for me to open the front door.

'Good morning,' I said brightly to Rosemary and Edward. James was at school.

'Good morning, Cathy,' Edward returned equally brightly. 'How are you?' Rosemary said to Alex as they came in.

'I'm good,' he grinned, and gave her a big hug.

'What a lovely welcome!' Rosemary smiled, clearly pleased.

Edward was in his suit, so I guessed he was going straight to work after the move. We all knew we should keep Alex's departure short, as it was generally felt that to prolong this final goodbye could be upsetting for the child – although Alex was so focused and looking forward to starting his new life that I didn't think leaving us was going to be a problem for him. Not like some children I'd looked after, who for various reasons really didn't want to leave and move on.

I waited with the children indoors while Edward and Rosemary loaded the car. Then, once it was packed, they returned inside and we stood in the hall ready to say goodbye.

'Well, thanks for everything,' Edward said, shaking my hand warmly. 'Look after yourself and say goodbye to Adrian for us.'

'Thank you, I will.' Paula was holding my hand, so I told her to say goodbye to Alex.

'Bye,' she said sweetly and the adults smiled.

'Bye, Paula,' Alex said and gave her a little hug.

'Goodbye then, love,' I said to him. 'It's been great having you stay. Your mummy and daddy are very lucky to have you.'

He smiled.

'That's kind,' Rosemary said.

'Bye, Cathy,' Alex said, and slipped his hand into his mother's.

'Thanks for everything,' Rosemary said to me, kissing my cheek. 'You'll phone us in a couple of weeks?'

'Yes.' This had been agreed at the planning meeting. It was usual for a carer to phone at least once after a child left and to hopefully see them. 'But do phone me if you have any questions or problems,' I added. 'Although I'm sure you won't.'

'Thank you.'

As it was cold outside I slipped Paula into her coat while we saw them off. We stood on the pavement just the other side of our garden gate and waved as the engine started and the car began to slowly pull away, Alex's little face beaming at us through the rear window.

'Bye!' Paula and I called, waving.

We continued waving until the car had disappeared from view and then we returned indoors. Yes, I had a twinge of sadness that Alex had gone, but I knew he was going to the best place ever – a loving adoptive home. I also knew it wouldn't be long before I was fostering another child, for sadly foster carers are always needed for children who can't live with their own families.

I played with Paula for a while and then, as I was reading her a story, she dozed off on the sofa. While she slept, I took the opportunity to telephone Debbie to tell her Alex's move had gone well.

'Excellent,' she said. 'I was going to phone you later. So there weren't any last-minute hiccups?'

'No. It was a textbook move. It went perfectly smoothly.'

'Good. I'll let Lin know. She will be seeing the family regularly until the adoption goes through.' This was normal practice.

Debbie thanked me for all I'd done and we said goodbye. I then telephoned Jill to update her, but she was out of the office, so I left a message with a colleague saying that Alex's move had gone to plan. Jill telephoned back an hour later, by which time Paula was awake and playing with the building bricks on the floor of the living room, where I took the call.

'So you survived your first placement after your break,' Jill said lightly.

'Yes, although it wasn't much of a survival test. Alex was lovely and no problem at all.'

'Even so, he could have become unsettled and angry after all his previous moves. It's down to your good fostering that the transition to his adoptive family was so successful.'

'Thank you, but I think it was the promise of going to his adoptive family that saw him through.'

'Nevertheless, you played your part. And you're ready to foster again?'

'Yes.'

'Good. Because this next lad could be more of a challenge.'

I gave a small laugh. 'Yes, go on.'

'Connor is ten years old and the social services are going to court on Thursday to try to bring him into care. His family are well known to the social services. He has a number of half-brothers and sisters who are already being cared for by relatives, and Connor is the last to go. His father is in prison and his mother obviously doesn't want to lose him, so she is opposing the social services application. Connor has challenging behaviour, but his social worker told me she's sure it's because there are no boundaries at home. His behaviour is reasonably manageable at school.'

'I see,' I said hesitantly. Carers are expected to take any child referred to them within the age range they are approved to foster. It's not a pick-and-choose situation – all these children need a home. I was currently approved to foster newborns to sixteen-year-olds, so I would be expected to take Connor. I could say no, but it would have to be for a very good reason.

'His social worker is aware that you're a single parent and have two young children,' Jill continued. 'Ideally she'd like him to have a male carer but none are free. She said she's sure that if he goes to an experienced carer who can manage his behaviour he will settle down.'

'I see,' I said again. 'Does he have any history of violence?' I asked, mindful of Adrian and Paula.

'At home there have been incidents but not in school. He has no respect for his mother.'

'And you think Adrian and Paula will be safe? I obviously don't want to place them in danger.'

'I think Connor will be hard work to begin with, but with firm and consistent boundaries I'm sure he will soon settle.' Which wasn't exactly what I'd asked, but was probably as much reassurance as Jill could offer.

'All right. When is he arriving?'

'I'll speak to his social worker and call you back. Assuming they're granted the Care Order on Thursday, I expect they'll want to move him on Thursday evening or Friday.'

'OK.'

An hour later Jill phoned back, having spoken to Connor's social worker again. She said that Connor would be brought to me on Friday evening so he had the weekend to settle in before going to school on Monday, and more details would follow. 'His social worker said to say thank you,' Jill said. 'She'll call you on Friday morning, if not before.'

We said goodbye and I replaced the handset and then played with Paula and the building bricks.

When I hear a child has challenging behaviour I do worry, not only for my own children, but about whether I will be able to meet the challenge, and manage and improve the child's behaviour. However, I'd done it before (albeit when I'd been married), so there was no reason to think I couldn't do it again.

That afternoon I told Adrian that we might be having a ten-year-old boy come to stay with us at the end of the week, although I didn't burden him with talk of challenging behaviour. Connor's behaviour would be my responsibility and to tell Adrian – to forewarn him – could have worried him, and may also have become a self-fulfilling prophecy: if you believe something about a person or situation, it is more likely to become true. As it was Adrian would take Connor as he found him and I would be keeping a close watch on him, and practising my 'safer caring policy', which all foster carers now had. This included keeping the door to the room where the child was open and not leaving them unattended. Paula, of course, was at the age when she trusted everyone unless they proved otherwise, in which case she would get very upset.

The week passed. Paula's nursery stayed shut but was hoping to open again the following week. I had Connor's room ready, although I hadn't heard anything further. When the telephone rang late on Friday morning it was Jill. 'About Connor,' she began.

'Connor's social worker hasn't telephoned,' I said.

'No. Sorry, she's been very busy. She won't need the placement right now. An aunt of Connor's who is already looking after one of his half-brothers has come forward and offered to look after Connor as well. The social services are looking into her suitability and carrying out a preliminary assessment. They are back in court the week after next so there won't be a decision until then. The judge agreed that Connor can stay with his mother in the meantime.'

'All right,' I said, a little disappointed. I'd grown used to the idea of Connor and had been looking forward to the challenge.

'We won't keep the placement open,' Jill said, 'so I'm sure it won't be long before you have another child.' She paused and I heard her take a breath as though she was summoning up her courage to say something unpalatable. 'But I need to talk to you about another matter.' Her voice was now flat and serious, and I immediately wondered what I'd done wrong.

'What's the matter?' I asked.

'Am I right in saying that Alex didn't show any signs of disturbed or challenging behaviour while he was with you?'

'No. He coped with everything remarkably well. Why?'

'Debbie phoned me this morning. There are problems.'

'Problems? Already? Not with Alex's behaviour, surely?'

'Perhaps the move has unsettled him or maybe Rosemary is panicking, but when Lin visited her on Thursday she said she wasn't coping.'

'Not coping with Alex?' My voice had risen and Paula, who was playing nearby, looked over. 'What is there not to cope with? He's a lovely little boy and he's only been there a few days.'

'I know,' Jill said evenly. 'We're not sure either exactly what the problem is, but Rosemary told Lin she thought that perhaps they should have had more time to get to know each other.'

'It's a bit late for that now!' I said, emotion getting the better of me. 'What is Alex supposed to have done?'

'Apparently, Rosemary said there have been some instances between James and Alex. Lin said it sounded as though James was jealous.'

'That's hardly Alex's fault,' I snapped.

'I know, and Lin has explained that there will be a period of readjustment for everyone. James is having to share his home and parents with a new brother, and Rosemary is having to share her affection between two sons now. Lin has reassured Rosemary that it's not uncommon, but she thinks it might help if you could visit Rosemary and have a chat with her. You're used to looking after children who aren't your biological children and you could help reassure her.'

'Yes, of course, I'll do what I can, but I'm really not understanding this at all.'

'To be honest, neither am I. Lin did say that it was unusual to have problems this early; it's more likely to happen after the "honeymoon period" is over – in a few months.'

Which did little to dispel my concerns. 'When does she want me to go?' I asked.

'Lin has suggested Tuesday morning, if you are free. The sooner the better.'

'OK. I'll see if my parents can babysit Paula, otherwise I'll have to take her with me.' It was a day Paula didn't go to nursery.

'Thanks. I'm sure that will be fine. I'll let Lin know, and then call you back and confirm. Shall we say about eleven on

Monday? Then you and Rosemary will have done the school runs.'

'Yes, all right.'

We said goodbye and I slowly replaced the handset. My heart was drumming loudly and my mouth was dry. This didn't make sense, and I was worried sick about Alex.

CHAPTER TEN

ANOTHER MATTER ENTIRELY

I telephoned my parents and Mum said she and Dad could come on Tuesday and look after Paula; they'd be delighted to. I said that I didn't know how long I would be and the place I had to go to was an hour's drive away, but I'd leave some lunch ready for them. Mum told me they could meet Adrian from school if necessary. Although I was sure I'd be back in plenty of time, it was reassuring to have this safety net. I just hoped it didn't snow, as the country lanes leading to Churchwell would soon become impassable and I doubted they'd be cleared very quickly.

That weekend Alex was never far from my thoughts. But having got over the initial shock of learning there was a problem, and so early on, I soon convinced myself that, as Jill had suggested, Rosemary had panicked and with some reassurance would be fine. I could identify with that feeling of panic. I'd experienced it on occasions with children I'd fostered when things weren't going as well as I'd anticipated. It's a sudden crash of confidence that I'm not up to the task in hand, so I take a step back, calm myself and then work through the issues – whatever they are. In my experience, once you've overcome these challenges the bond with the child becomes stronger for both of you, and, of course, the longer you know each other the more secure and confident you feel, until you reach the point where you're both completely relaxed and the child is just another family member.

By Monday Rosemary would most probably have overcome her feelings of inadequacy and be positive again, maybe even managing a smile at her previous reaction. Adopting a child is a huge, life-changing commitment and nothing can fully prepare you for when the child actually moves in. Perhaps a longer introduction might have helped, as Rosemary had suggested, and if she or Edward had mentioned it we could have slowed the pace. But from my point of view the timetable had been appropriate for Alex, so there'd been no reason for me to request a longer introductory period. I guessed it was possible that Alex had become unsettled from the move and, if so, as an experienced foster carer I had plenty of strategies that would help Rosemary. So all in all, on Monday morning as I waved goodbye to Paula and my parents I was optimistic.

It was a cold, bright day, the winter sun shining in a cloudless sky. With no children in the car to be kept amused on the journey I didn't have to listen to children's songs and stories, so I switched on the radio and tuned it to a local station that played easy-listening music and gave news bulletins, traffic and weather reports. There'd been a heavy frost during the night, which had produced some treacherous driving conditions early on, but now the route I was taking seemed clear. As I drove my thoughts turned to little Paula, who'd been so pleased to see her grandparents. She'd have a great day with them; all that love and attention. And even if I was back in time to meet Adrian from school, which I hoped to be, Mum and Dad were going to stay on so they could see him. They'd always been loving grandparents, but since my husband had left we'd all become even closer, and my father was a good male role model for the children.

The journey to Churchwell ran smoothly and I pulled onto Rosemary and Edward's drive at 10.55. I'd become familiar with the approach to their house during the introductory period, when I'd brought and collected Alex, although I hadn't expected to see it again so soon. Rosemary answered the door as soon as I pressed the bell, dressed smartly as usual, and with a polite but restrained smile. 'Good morning, Cathy. It was nice of you to come. I'm sure you've got better things to do.'

'It's good to see you,' I said, also a little restrained. I followed her into the living room, neat and tidy as usual.

'Do sit down,' she said, waving to the immaculate cream sofas. 'Would you like a coffee?'

'Yes, please.'

Rosemary went to make the coffee as I sat on one of the sofas. There were no toys littering their living room as there were at my house, as the boys kept their toys in their bedrooms here. The house seemed strangely, unnaturally quiet now. On all my previous visits James, Edward and Alex had been in so there'd been talk and movement, but now, with Rosemary in the kitchen at the rear of the house, there was just the absolute silence of the type that can only be found in the middle of the countryside.

Rosemary returned with the cups of coffee on a tray and passed one to me. 'Thank you, I'm ready for this,' I said with a smile.

'Who's looking after Paula?' she asked, settling on the other sofa. 'Lin said you might have to bring her.'

'My parents have come for the day.'

'That's good of them.'

I nodded and we both sipped our coffee. There was then a short, awkward silence before Rosemary said, 'I feel embarrassed you've been sent. Did Debbie tell you what happened?'

'Jill, my support social worker telephoned me. I don't know all the details. But please don't feel embarrassed. I'd have been more surprised if there hadn't been any problems at all.'

'That's kind of you to say,' Rosemary said and concentrated on her coffee cup. Then she looked up and away before bringing her gaze back to me. 'Perhaps it's asking too much of James to share his life and home with another child after so long alone.'

'What makes you say that?' I asked, immediately concerned.

'They had a fallout over the weekend. It started off small – about James not wanting to share one of his toys – and then it escalated. James got very angry, especially with me. He said I didn't have time for him any more and Alex was my favourite and I loved him more. Which is obviously ridiculous. But Edward took James's side and agreed with him that I was spending too much time with Alex. I got upset. It's true, I have been spending more time with Alex, but that was to help him settle in and make him feel included. I mean, this has always been James's home; he shouldn't need constant reassurance that I love him, should he?'

'Yes,' I said, with a relieved smile. 'James will need lots of reassurance, to begin with at least.' Rosemary looked slightly taken aback. 'It's very similar when a new foster child arrives,' I said. 'My children, who are usually content and happy to amuse themselves, suddenly start demanding attention, even little Paula, who can burst into tears if she doesn't get it. I've heard other carers say the same. Sometimes you feel as though there aren't enough hours in the day and you're being pulled in all directions at once. Then after a few weeks it all starts to settle down.'

'You see, that's the difference between you and me,' Rosemary said fervently. 'You've had that experience. I haven't. James was very good about sharing his toys and me during the introductions, but suddenly he's become possessive. When he was angry he even said he didn't want a brother any more. Thankfully, I don't think Alex heard. But you say that's normal?'

'Yes. James is bound to feel it. He's been an only child for all his life, then suddenly it's all changed and he sees you loving and caring for another son.'

'But what can I do about it?'

'There is quite a bit you can do to help,' I said. 'Put aside some one-to-one time each day just for you and James. That's what I do with Adrian and Paula. You'd be surprised what a difference it makes – even just fifteen minutes a day. It's your precious time together and it will make him feel special.'

'I can see that, but I'm just wondering when. Our days and evenings are full.'

'Alex is younger than James,' I said. 'Does he go up to bed before James?'

'Yes.'

'So once Alex is in bed and you've read him a story and given him his one-to-one, you could then do the same for James.'

'He usually does his violin and cello practice then.'

'Can he do fifteen minutes less or go to bed a bit later?' I asked. 'If not, perhaps you could take Alex up to bed fifteen minutes earlier. I think it's really important to fit in some time with just you and James. Is Edward able to help in the evenings?'

Rosemary shook her head. 'He's rarely home before eight o'clock on weekdays. He's here most weekends though. In fact, he suggested something similar yesterday.'

'Oh yes?'

'We all went out for our Sunday-morning bike ride. It was the first time we'd done it with Alex. But he can't ride as fast as James, and James was becoming frustrated at having to keep waiting for him. So in the end Edward said that he and James would ride on ahead and I could do a shorter ride with Alex at a slower pace.'

'And it worked?'

'Yes, I suppose it did. Although when we got home James kept boasting about how far he and his dad had ridden compared to Alex, so I told him off.' Rosemary looked at me with self-recrimination.

'Don't beat yourself up,' I said. 'Having two children is as new for you as it is for James to have a brother. Give yourself time. Make sure James has one-to-one time with you and

Edward, and obviously give both boys lots of love and attention. Tell James how much you love him and are proud of him.'

'He knows that.'

'But say it. He needs to hear it right now. You've waited so long for another child – with all the build-up, the reality can be a bit of an anti-climax.'

Rosemary's expression finally lost its anxiety. 'So you think I'm expecting too much too soon?'

'Yes.'

'Perhaps that's the answer to my next question. Or rather confession.'

I looked at her questioningly.

'This is difficult. I wasn't going to mention it, but I don't feel the same towards Alex as I do towards James. Alex is so affectionate, he wants lots of hugs and kisses, but it doesn't feel natural to me. It's like I'm hugging a stranger. I didn't feel that with James when he was little and I used to hug and kiss him.'

'You had all the time in the world to bond with James, right from when he was a baby,' I said. 'Of course you won't feel the same towards Alex straight away. Bonding comes gradually from what we do for the child, shared experiences and just spending time together. Each time you do something for Alex – wash his hair, hug him, read him a story, help him with his school work or tuck him into bed – you will grow closer and your bond will strengthen. Love will gradually replace affection and you'll feel a comforting familiarity when you hold him close.'

'Do you really think so?' Rosemary asked.

'Yes. Absolutely. Some of the children I foster throw themselves into my arms as soon as they arrive. I hug them as much as they want, but I'll admit it feels strange to begin with. I'm used to the feel and smell of Adrian and Paula, then suddenly I have this little stranger in my arms wanting lots of affection. But with each hug it becomes easier, more natural, until it's as though I'm hugging another one of my children. It will come, I promise you. Just give yourself time.'

'So you don't think I'm cold for not feeling the same towards Alex as I do towards James?'

'No, not at all. If you said you felt exactly the same towards them both so early on I'd be surprised. But I'm sure you will in time. Just make sure you give James as many hugs as you do Alex.'

'James is too old for all that now and Edward doesn't encourage it, but I'll tell Edward what you said. He's been having difficulties too.'

'Similar to the ones you describe?'

Rosemary briefly hesitated before replying, 'Yes.'

I nodded and finished the last of my coffee. 'Is there anything else worrying either of you?' I returned my cup and saucer to the coffee table.

'Not really. I was concerned by James's behaviour and what he said about Alex, but I suppose we just have to be patient.' I nodded. 'I think it will be easier when Alex starts at James's school. I'm spending so much time in the car with the school run at present.'

'Welcome to my world,' I said with a small laugh. 'Some of the school runs I do see me in the car for more time than I'm at home during the week.'

'I don't know how you fit it all in. We had such a smooth routine before, but now I seem to be all over the place. There's never a moment to spare. I was so organized at work.'

'I think you're doing fine,' I said. 'Just concentrate on what's important and leave the other stuff – like housework. Alex isn't expecting superwoman. Just a mum.'

Rosemary smiled. 'I know. But it's difficult changing what you've been used to for so long. James just fitted in.'

'Alex will too. And Rosemary, all those hugs and kisses Alex wants to give you, it's his way of showing how much he loves you. He didn't want a hug or kiss from me. He was saving them for you.'

She gave a small sigh. 'He's such a dear little chap. I hope we can live up to his expectations.'

'You already have. You have given him a family of his own who will love and care for him forever. That's all he's ever wanted for a long while.'

I drove home with that warm frisson of satisfaction that comes from a job well done – a mission accomplished. The concerns Rosemary had raised were completely natural, and the problems – not really problems at all – were to be expected, and would rectify themselves with time. I thought that she and Edward had perhaps set themselves too high a standard, and as I'd told Rosemary they just needed to relax into their new roles and ensure that both boys had their fair share of attention. As I thought might have happened, Rosemary (and possibly Edward too) had panicked at the first hurdle – when the reality hadn't completely matched up with their ideal of their new family. I hoped my words and sharing my experiences had helped – they seemed to have done.

When I arrived home I found Mum, Dad and Paula snug on the sofa in the living room playing a game. Paula was so involved and enjoying the attention that she just about managed a glance in my direction. Mum said that Paula had been fine and Lin had telephoned and asked that I call her as soon as I returned. Mum also said that she'd left some lunch plated up for me in the kitchen. I thanked her, but went first into the hall to make the call, as I knew Lin would want feedback on my visit to Rosemary as soon as possible.

'They'll be fine,' I reassured Lin as soon as she answered. I then explained Rosemary's worries and told Lin of my responses.

'And that's all?' Lin asked, relieved.

'Yes, assuming Rosemary told me everything. She's going to have a chat with Edward about the suggestions I made.'

'Thank you so much. I'll phone Rosemary shortly, but I wanted to talk to you first. In the preparation course we discussed the impact adoption was likely to have on them all, including James, but I guess the reality is different.'

'Yes. And, of course, their routine has been turned upside down. Rosemary had everything running so smoothly before.'

'If it would help, we could change Alex's school sooner,' Lin suggested. 'He was going to move schools anyway after Easter.'

'You could mention it to Rosemary. It might help if she knows she has the option, although there are only a few weeks left in this term.'

'I'll see what she thinks. Hearing your perspective and the way you adjust to the children you foster must have helped enormously. Thank you so much.'

'You're welcome. I'm sure everything will be all right, but I'm happy to talk to Rosemary again if she wants me to. Then once they're more settled it would be nice if we could visit.'

'Yes, of course. I'll phone Rosemary now.'

We said goodbye and I went into the kitchen for the lunch Mum had plated up for me and took it into the living room to eat. Paula continued playing with Dad as Mum talked to me. Fifteen minutes later Jill telephoned, and I went into the hall to speak to her. I told her what I'd told Lin and she, too, was relieved that the problems were nothing more serious. She thanked me and said she'd be in touch when a new referral came in. As I was no longer on standby for Connor, a new child could arrive at any time, and Jill would telephone me when they received a referral from the local authority. It could happen very quickly. The unpredictable nature of fostering – as well as looking after and helping the child – appeals to me. No two days are ever the same, although I never forget that each child I look after comes to me as a result of a family in crisis.

Mum and Dad took Paula with them when they went to meet Adrian from school, and then once home again Dad helped Adrian with his homework while Mum played with Paula. They stayed for dinner, after which Mum helped me with Paula's bath and bedtime routine, while Dad began teaching Adrian chess. Both children loved the time spent with their beloved nana and grandpa, and Paula was delighted when Mum read her lots of bedtime stories before she fell asleep. They finally left just before nine o'clock, once Adrian was in bed, so what had started out as a day of some uncertainty had ended very happily indeed.

On Wednesday I received a telephone call from Jill advising me that it was likely a five-year-old girl would be brought into care on Friday. She'd telephone again when she had more information. I didn't mention this to Adrian and Paula; I'd wait until it was definite and I had more details, as I knew that arrangements in fostering can and do change at the last minute. It can be unsettling for birth children if there are too many false starts. However, when Jill phoned again it wasn't about the five-year-old girl who might be coming into care but another matter entirely, and it shook me to the core.

CHAPTER ELEVEN

REJECTION

I already knew Jill well enough to recognize when she was about to impart bad news. Usually upbeat and positive in her manner, she now gave a heartfelt sigh and then paused before continuing, as though bracing herself and preparing me for what she was about to say. It was Thursday and Paula and I had had lunch and were in the living room, where I'd been helping her complete an early-years puzzle. I'd perched on the edge of the sofa to take the call as Paula continued playing on the floor. Jill continued, 'Cathy, I'm very sorry to have to tell you that Alex is being returned into care.'

I heard what she was saying but didn't fully grasp her meaning. 'For respite?' I asked, which seemed the only explanation – that Rosemary and Edward were asking for a short break from Alex. Highly unusual in an adoption and so early on, but the only reason I could think of, and Jill was going to ask me to look after Alex for a few days.

Another small pause before Jill said, 'No, not respite. I'm afraid the adoption has failed. Rosemary and Edward are returning Alex into care.'

'No, they can't,' I said. 'That's impossible. It doesn't happen in adoption. Adoption is for life. It's a permanent commitment, like having your own child.' My stomach churned, sick with fear.

'I know. Lin and Debbie are very upset too. They invested a lot in this. I've just finished a long telephone conversation with Lin.'

'But what's happened? Perhaps if I talk to Rosemary again …'

'Lin suggested that, but Rosemary and Edward are adamant it won't help. Edward telephoned Debbie first thing this morning and said that they now realized adopting was the wrong decision. That James was happier as an only child, and it was better that they admitted their mistake now rather than later when Alex had settled in.'

'I can't believe I'm hearing this.'

'I know. Lin discussed James's feelings during the adoption process, and of course he was interviewed and his views included in the assessment on their suitability to adopt. There was nothing to suggest this might happen. Apparently there was a minor fallout last night between the boys. Debbie and Lin have spoken to Rosemary and Edward this morning and tried to persuade them to give it some more time, but they're adamant that Alex should be removed as soon as possible.'

'Removed,' I repeated numbly.

'Lin has told them that the earliest it can be is tomorrow.'

'Where is Alex now?' I asked, trying to come to terms with what I was being told. 'Does he know yet?'

'No. He's at school. Rosemary took him as usual this morning.'

'That'll be a nice surprise when he gets back!' I said caustically. 'I really don't believe this. I just don't. They seemed so committed. And now they're returning Alex like an unwanted product. He's going to be devastated. He believed this was his last move – his forever family. I reassured him it would be.' I stopped as my eyes filled and I choked up. 'Sorry, Jill,' I said, my voice breaking. 'Give me a moment, please.' I reached for a tissue from the box and wiped my eyes. 'It's OK, love,' I said to Paula, who was looking at me very concerned. I wiped my eyes again, took a deep breath and then picked up the handset. 'I'm here, Jill.'

'Are you all right?' she asked kindly.

'I just can't believe this. Poor little Alex. How could they?'

'I know,' Jill said stoically. 'We feel the same. Debbie will call a disruption meeting in a few weeks to see what went wrong and if any lessons can be learned, but for now we need to concentrate on Alex. Debbie or Lin will talk to him about what has happened and reassure him it wasn't his fault, but will you be able to take him back?'

'As long as I don't have to meet Rosemary or Edward again, yes.'

'Thank you. I'll get back to you when I know what the arrangements are for returning him to you.'

'And Rosemary and Edward didn't give any other reasons apart from James being happier as an only child?' I asked. I was still struggling to make sense of it and I was angry.

'Not really. Rosemary said Alex wasn't like James and they didn't believe he'd fit into their family long term. I think they must have had totally unrealistic expectations.'

I bit my bottom lip to quell my anger and thought that was probably the understatement of the year.

Jill repeated that she'd phone again once she'd spoken to Debbie and knew the details for Alex moving back to me, and then we said goodbye. I replaced the handset and sat on the sofa, brimming with anger and sorrow. That poor child. At present ignorant of what awaited him. Had it been better to admit they'd made a mistake now as they'd told the social worker? I didn't know. A mistake shouldn't have been made at all. If their expectations of adoption had been unrealistic then surely that should have come out during the assessment process. Clearly it hadn't or they wouldn't have been accepted to adopt. Had I seen anything that might have suggested this could happen? Not really. Alex was different from James, but that was to be expected given his life experiences. The boys were close in age – that had been one of the factors matching Alex to the family – so some sibling rivalry as well as comradeship was natural and to be expected. But that didn't explain their complete rejection of Alex, for rejection was what it was and how Alex would doubtless see it.

The more I thought about it, the more I felt that Alex had been cruelly deceived and I'd been part of that deception – persuading him to accept and love what was supposed to have been his forever family. Now what would I tell him? I'd no idea. It was beyond my experience, as it would be for most foster carers. I was aware that some adoptions did fail – or 'disrupt' as the social services preferred to call it – but that was usually after many years, often when the child reached puberty. They started acting out all their early suffering and torment, and then the parents, unable to cope with the child's very challenging behaviour, contacted the social services and asked for help. Sometimes, even with support and therapy, the adoption irretrievably broke down and the child had to leave, but that wasn't true in Alex's case. It hadn't had a chance to fail! He had only been there two weeks. It had been more 'try it and see': a brother for James, a playmate – no, thank you, we've changed our minds!

My eyes filled again as I gazed on little Paula, so loved and cherished. How different her life was to Alex's. All the promises that were made to him now lay in pieces. Not only of the love and security of a forever family, but of the outings and activities he was so looking forward to: riding his bike on a Sunday morning, sailing, horse riding, the planned trip to Disney World, learning to play a musical instrument, and the myriad of shared experiences that bond a family and help it to flourish. I thought back to the planning meeting when Lin had said that it was lovely Alex would be having so many opportunities but Jill had warned that he shouldn't be overloaded, as he would need time to settle in first. Overloaded! Settle in! He hadn't had a chance to settle in or become overloaded! I also remembered Alex's worries just before he met his parents for the first time, when he'd run upstairs and hidden in his bed, anxious that his new mummy and daddy wouldn't like him, and I'd reassured him they would. 'Supposing they like me to begin with and then after a few months they change their minds and stop liking me?' he'd asked, fearful of another rejection and move. I'd knelt beside his bed and reassured him that couldn't happen, that adoption was a commitment for life and his new mummy and daddy would love him forever, just as they did James. How bitterly ironic those words seemed now.

I was devastated, and I felt the cruel deception played on Alex personally. I needed someone to talk to, to share the burden; that's when couples who foster have the advantage – there's someone to share the good and bad times. Paula, perhaps sensing my unhappiness, came over and scrambled onto the sofa beside me. I put my arm around her and then picked up the telephone and pressed the key for my parents' number. Although they hadn't met Alex, they knew I'd been looking after him and he'd been adopted. I wasn't going to pour my soul out; I just needed to talk.

'Hello, love, everything all right?' Mum asked. I usually phoned in the evening for a chat, not during the day.

'We're OK,' I said, 'but I've had some bad news. You remember I told you about Alex, the little boy who was going to be adopted?'

'Yes. How is he?'

'His adoptive parents have given up on him. They've changed their minds about adopting and are sending him back into care.'

'What?' Mum gasped. 'I thought adoption was permanent – for life.'

'It should be. But they're saying they made a mistake and that their son is happier as an only child. He's coming to live with me again.'

'I hope they're not allowed to adopt another child,' Mum said.

'No, they won't be. But Alex will be so upset. He doesn't know yet.'

'Oh dear. But probably best he's coming back to you. They don't sound very nice people to me to do that.' Which I'd been thinking too. Since Jill's phone call my opinion of Rosemary and Edward had plummeted dramatically, and apart from their lack of commitment I wondered what else they hadn't told the social services. 'When's he moving to you?' Mum asked.

'I'm not sure yet, I'm waiting to hear from his social worker. Probably tomorrow.'

'How long will he be with you this time?'

'I've no idea. The social services won't have had a chance to consider long-term plans yet. This has all happened so quickly.'

'At least he knows you,' Mum said. 'It would have been even worse for him to have to go to another new home.' Mum's a gem and can always find something positive to say, even in the most awful situations.

'Yes. I was on standby for another child, but she'll be placed with other carers now.'

'Well, love, once Alex has settled in your dad and I must come and visit so we can meet him, or you can visit us. Let us know if you need any help at all.'

'Thanks, Mum.'

'And try not to worry. I'm sure he'll recover staying with you.' Her words helped a little.

During the afternoon Jill, Debbie and Lin all telephoned and I learned of the arrangements for Alex coming back to me. Debbie was going to see Alex once he was home this afternoon and, with Rosemary present, tell him what was happening. 'It's going to be very difficult,' Debbie said. 'Rosemary didn't want to be present, but I told her it was important. I wasn't going to let her off that easily.' Debbie also said she'd spoken to the school and told them the bad news. They were obviously shocked and saddened, but would help support Alex in school. 'At least he didn't have to move schools,' Debbie added. Which was certainly a blessing, as it was now the one constant factor in Alex's otherwise very unsettled life. His teacher had shared his joy at being found an adoptive family and I knew she would share his sorrow and try to help him through this difficult time.

Debbie said that the following day Rosemary would pack Alex's belongings while he was at school, then collect him from school at the end of the day. Once home, she, Edward and James would say goodbye to Alex and then Debbie would collect him and his belongings and bring him to me. 'Rosemary wanted me to collect him from school and bring him straight to you so she didn't have to face school or him again, but I told her that saying goodbye was important, upsetting though it will be.' Debbie then thanked me for looking after Alex again and said she'd see me on Friday evening.

When Jill telephoned she confirmed the arrangements and said I should call their out-of-hours service if I needed help over the weekend, and that she'd visit us the following week. 'I didn't have a chance to meet Alex on the bridging placement,' Jill said. 'It wasn't necessary. But when he's a looked-after child again I'll be seeing him regularly.' Jill, as my support social worker, visited every month while a child was with me. She wished me luck, thanked me and we said goodbye.

When Lin telephoned she was withdrawn and full of self-recrimination. Ultimately the decision to take Rosemary and Edward to the adoption panel as a good match for Alex had been hers. 'What did I miss?' she asked me.

'I don't know. Alex and James are close in age, but that could have worked out. Jill said she thought that Rosemary and Edward probably had unrealistic expectations.'

'Not while they were talking to me they didn't,' Lin said defensively. 'They said all the right things. Ticked all the boxes. But they didn't give it a chance.'

'I know.'

'My husband's a social worker and I phoned him at lunchtime to offload. He said he'd once dealt with an adoption that failed after four days. It was early on in his career and he blamed himself, but I really don't know what else I could have done.'

I wasn't qualified to comment. I knew the types of questions that Rosemary and Edward would have been asked during the adoption assessment, but I had no idea of the discussions that had resulted or whether they should have alerted Lin and raised concerns. Clearly she hadn't thought so at the time.

'Anyway,' Lin said, 'the most important thing now is that Alex doesn't feel any of this is his fault. Debbie is going to talk to him and I know you'll follow that through.'

'Yes, of course.' Although we both knew that many children who came into care believed it was their fault. How much worse would it be for Alex, who had been led to believe he'd been found the perfect family?

It was a bleak day for everyone involved in Alex's case.

* * *

That afternoon, after collecting Adrian from school, I waited until we were home before I told both children the bad news.

'They don't want him?' Adrian exclaimed, although that wasn't how I'd phrased it. I'd been very careful in choosing my words. Paula stared at me wide-eyed, mirroring Adrian's shock.

'Rosemary and Edward feel they have made a mistake in wanting to adopt,' I said, sitting between them on the sofa. 'It's nothing to do with Alex personally. It was very wrong of them to get this far, but at least Alex can come back here, and we'll do our best to help him.'

'But they were supposed to be his mummy and daddy,' Adrian said. 'Forever and ever. They seemed like nice people. I told Alex they were.'

'I know, love. So did I. I don't know what went wrong, but it certainly wasn't Alex's fault.'

'I don't think they are nice people after all to do that to Alex,' Adrian said, his little face sad and downcast. Paula nodded in agreement.

'That's what Nana said,' I offered.

'But they seemed nice,' Adrian said, struggling as I and the social workers had done to understand. 'They promised to take him to Disney World, and sailing and camping. He was so looking forward to doing all that.'

'There have been lots of broken promises, which Alex will have to come to terms with,' I said. 'But the worst broken promise of all is that he no longer has the loving forever family he was promised.' Adrian's face fell further, but to underplay what had happened or cover it with platitudes would have been dismissive of Adrian's feeling. Acknowledging pain, disappointment and suffering is part of the healing process. Aged three, Paula was in some ways protected.

'We'll look after him,' Adrian said.

'We will,' I agreed, and I hugged them both.

I was anxiously watching the clock as I made dinner. Rosemary would have collected Alex from school by now and they would be home, with Debbie telling Alex the dreadful news. How on earth would she phrase it? I couldn't think of an easy way to tell him, but I guessed as a social worker Debbie would have had experience in delivering bad news: telling a child they were leaving their family to live with a foster carer, for instance. Although of course in that situation – removing a child from their birth family – there would usually have been some warning. Probably months of visits and monitoring by the social services before the child was removed. It wouldn't normally be like this – happy families one minute and then 'it's over and you're going to have to leave' the next. I doubted Debbie's previous experience was going to be of much help.

By six o'clock, the time we sat down to dinner, I assumed Alex had been told. What was he doing? How had he taken the news? Was he eating his dinner or had he fled to his bedroom, too upset to eat? Knowing Alex, I guessed he'd probably gone very quiet, and once his social worker had left crept up to his room where he was now lying on his bed, cuddling one of his soft toys for comfort. My heart bled for him. I wished I could be with him now to try to ease his pain.

Adrian and Paula didn't mention Alex again during the evening, although I guessed that, like me, they were probably thinking plenty. After dinner I heard Adrian read his school book and then, once Paula was in bed, we played a couple of games of draughts before it was time for him to go to bed. As I lay with him by the light of the lamp, giving him a good-night hug and having a chat about his day, he said, 'You wouldn't ever send me away, would you?'

'Of course not. You don't get rid of me that easily!' I said, trying to lighten his mood. But the fact that he had asked the question at all showed just how unsettling this experience was for him. Paula, that much younger, didn't perceive the wider implications, so for her Alex would simply reappear.

'What has happened to Alex is shocking and upsetting, but it is unusual,' I emphasized. 'Most children who are adopted have happy and normal family lives, the same as if they were birth children. This should never have happened, and the social workers will be asking themselves lots of questions to see what went wrong and to try to make sure it doesn't happen again.'

'What sort of questions?' Adrian asked, snuggling close.

'Well, for example, did Rosemary or Edward say something that might have given a clue that they weren't suitable to adopt? The social worker would have spent a lot of time talking to them, asking them questions and listening to what they said. Perhaps she missed something.'

'Or perhaps they just changed their minds,' Adrian said.

'But you can't do that with adoption. It's a commitment, and if they weren't absolutely sure then they should never have continued with the adoption.'

'Poor Alex,' Adrian said, and gave me another hug. Then after a moment, 'Would you ever adopt?'

'I have you and Paula and I like fostering, but in the future, who knows?'

'Fostering is different from adoption, isn't it?' he said.

'Yes, with fostering we hope that the child will be able to go home to their own family. Whereas with adoption the child can't go home, so they are found a new forever family.'

'I wouldn't mind if you wanted to adopt,' Adrian said, kissing my cheek.

'That's nice, although it would be something we'd have to all talk about for a long time. Perhaps when Paula is older.'

Satisfied, he gave me another hug and then snuggled down ready for sleep. 'Love you, Mum.'

'Love you too.' I kept my arm around him until he fell asleep.

Before I went to bed that night I headed up a clean sheet of paper in my fostering folder, ready to begin or rather continue my log notes for Alex. He'd been gone such a short length of time that I hadn't passed the first set of notes for his bridging placement to Debbie yet. I wrote today's date and Alex's name at the top and then briefly stated that he would be returning to me the following day as a result of the failed adoption. I didn't go into detail on what had happened, as the social services would cover it in their report. Having done this, I returned the folder to the locked drawer in the front room and then let Toscha out for a run before going to bed.

I didn't sleep well. I spent most of the night lying in the dark thinking about Alex: alone in his bed in that large, freshly decorated and newly furnished bedroom that was supposed to be his. Was he also awake? I wouldn't be surprised. Upset and worrying about his now-uncertain future. Or possibly he'd cried himself to sleep, which broke my heart. My thoughts wandered around that splendid house, which had so impressed us, and the advantageous lifestyle Alex was going to enjoy. Could all those trappings of success have influenced Lin's assessment of Rosemary and Edward? It was possible, I supposed; choosing them for Alex over a family who had little in terms of material possessions and struggled to make ends meet. Yet that other family may have been able to offer the unconditional love and nurturing that Alex needed, for it's not about what a family owns, but their love and commitment. I didn't doubt that Rosemary and Edward loved James, but evidently they didn't have what it took to throw that love wider and extend it to a child who wasn't their own flesh and blood – something that should have been picked up during the assessment.

I tormented myself with all sorts of scenarios and was pleased when the night was over and I could get up and start the new day. In about twelve hours Alex would be with me, and I was determined to do all I could to help him get over his dreadful ordeal and disappointment.

Leaving behind my maudlin nocturnal ruminations, I showered and dressed in a more positive frame of mind, and then woke the children. Adrian was in a better place, too, and was soon planning the games he and Alex could play together 'to take his mind off what has happened', he said. Which was sweet. When I explained to Paula that Alex would be coming to live with us again later today she grinned and then fetched her favourite doll, which she put on Alex's seat at the table and said he could play with.

After I'd taken Adrian to school and Paula to nursery I went to the supermarket and stocked up on Alex's favourite foods. I also bought some new posters for his bedroom, as he'd taken the others with him. On my return home I unpacked the shopping and then stuck the posters on Alex's bedroom walls. It seemed like only yesterday I was taking down the others and packing them, together with all his other belongings. I'd purposely kept the weekend ahead free to give Alex the chance to settle in again. If the weather was fine, we could go out for a walk or take the bikes to the park. I'd just see what Alex wanted to do.

I collected Paula from nursery but found it impossible to settle that afternoon, and my concentration was only half on the games I played with her. Most foster carers are nervous just before a new child arrives, wondering if they will be able to meet their needs and if the child will like them. Once the child arrives I am usually so busy that I don't have time to worry and just deal with any problems as they arise. Now, my anxiety wasn't for a new child but for Alex, and what I could possibly say and do to help him.

CHAPTER TWELVE

WHY DID THEY STOP LOVING ME?

Allowing an hour for Rosemary to collect Alex from school and for Debbie to arrive and load Alex's belongings into her car, then the hour's drive to me, I wasn't expecting to see them before 6.30 p.m. At six o'clock the children and I ate dinner and I plated up Alex's, for I assumed he wouldn't have had time to eat at Rosemary's. As seven o'clock approached and there was still no sign of Alex, Paula was becoming fractious, so I took her up to bed. I'd just returned downstairs at 7.30 when the doorbell rang.

'Is that him?' Adrian asked, rushing into the hall.

'I expect so.'

Adrian stood beside me as I opened the door. It was a cold, wet night. In the light of the porch stood little Alex, holding his social worker's hand, coat zipped up, his face very pale and with dark circles beneath his eyes.

'Hello, love,' I said. He looked back at me, tired and bewildered.

'He fell asleep in the car,' Debbie said as they came in. 'I had to wake him.'

'How are you?' I gently asked him.

He gave a small despondent shrug and dropped Debbie's hand.

'Let's take off your coat then,' I said. I began undoing the zipper as Debbie took off her own coat and hung it on the hall stand.

'Once he's settled, perhaps you could help me unpack the car?' Debbie asked.

'Yes, of course.' Adrian was looking at Alex, not sure what to say and do for the best.

I offered Alex my hand but he didn't take it, so I led the way down the hall and into the living room, where Toscha, curled on the sofa, opened one eye to see who had arrived. Adrian had arranged some toys on the floor for them to play with, but Alex, clearly exhausted, sat on the sofa next to Toscha. Debbie sat beside him and Adrian and I took the easy chairs.

'How are you doing, love?' I asked Alex again. He answered with another despondent shrug.

'He's had a lot to cope with,' Debbie said. 'The school have been good. I've told Alex that what has happened wasn't in any way his fault; that sometimes children go to new families and it doesn't work out.' I thought Debbie was letting Rosemary and Edward off very lightly; I would have been far less generous. 'They've given Alex a good-luck card,' Debbie said, 'which they've all signed. There's a twenty-pound note in it so Alex can treat himself.'

I knew she was expecting me to say something positive. 'That's nice,' I said to Alex. 'We can go shopping and you can buy something you want.'

Alex kept his gaze firmly on the ground, as unimpressed as I was by the gift, which I thought was little recompense for ruining his life.

'I managed to fit everything into my car,' Debbie continued. 'If we left anything behind Rosemary will send it here.' She rubbed her forehead. She also looked very tired from what must have been a long and emotionally exhausting day for her too. 'I've told Alex I'll see him here next week one day after school to make sure he's settled in. I was thinking of Wednesday?'

'I'll put it in the diary,' I said. It was usual practice for the child's social worker and the carer's support social worker to visit soon after a child moved in.

'I've also told Alex that if he has any worries or questions to speak to you.'

'Yes, that's right,' I said, throwing Alex a smile, but he didn't respond. Head hung low, dejected and bewildered, he was a shadow of his former self: the child who'd left me barely two weeks before so full of hope and joy for a bright new future.

'Do you have everything you need?' Debbie asked me.

'Yes.'

'I think Alex will benefit from a good night's sleep,' she said, glancing at him. 'I can't imagine he slept much last night.'

I agreed. 'Adrian will be going up soon as well. I'll take them up once you've gone and they can have a lie-in tomorrow, as it's Saturday.'

Debbie nodded. 'Can I have a word?' Debbie asked me, and then mouthed 'in private'.

'Yes, we can go into the front room,' I said, standing. 'Alex, would you like to play with some of these toys Adrian has put out while I speak to your social worker?'

Adrian immediately slid out of his chair and went over and squatted on the floor beside the toys. Alex, aware of what he was being asked, reluctantly left the sofa and walked slowly to where the toys were and then sat on the floor beside Adrian. As Debbie and I left the room Adrian was taking the lid off the compendium of games as Alex watched, detached and disinterested.

In the front room I switched on the light and drew out two chairs from the table. Debbie collapsed into one of them with a heartfelt sigh.

'Would you like a coffee or tea?' I offered.

'No, thank you. I won't be too long – I need to get home once I've finished here. Just to bring you up to date. I saw Alex yesterday with Rosemary present and I explained to him that he wouldn't be able to live with her and Edward any longer and would be returning here. It came as a complete shock to him. He had no idea. The colour drained from his face and he began to tremble. I thought he was going to pass out or have a fit. We gave him a glass of water and he slowly recovered, but he's remained very quiet since.'

'Hardly surprising,' I said.

'No. Rosemary had the decency to apologize to Alex that it hadn't worked out. I telephoned the school earlier before I collected Alex, and his teacher said he'd been withdrawn all day. She'll keep an eye on him.' I nodded. 'When I collected him this evening only Rosemary was in again.

Edward was at work and James was at a friend's house. Rosemary said they'd both said goodbye this morning before they left.

'Did Rosemary say any more about why they were giving up on Alex?'

'No. Only that they realized once he'd moved in that they'd made a big mistake and adoption wasn't for them. She also said she thought it would be easy to find Alex a new home.' Debbie sighed again, this time from exasperation. 'I told her it didn't work like that and matching a child to suitable adopters was a lengthy, in-depth process, not to mention the effect all this would have on Alex. I just hope his birth mother doesn't get wind of this.'

'Oh?' I asked. Because Alex had come to me for a short bridging placement I didn't have as much background information as I would have had if he'd been staying longer.

'His mother opposed Alex being adopted,' Debbie explained. 'We had to go to court for an order. She's already made one complaint against us. If this gets out there'll be another one.' This was the worst-case scenario – a child placed for adoption against the mother's wishes, only to have it fail. 'I assume he can stay here for as long as necessary?' Debbie asked. 'Jill said he could.'

'Yes.'

'Thank you. I think that's everything. Do you have any questions?'

'I'm guessing it's too early to think about long-term plans for Alex?'

She nodded. 'One of the meetings I'll need to arrange is with the permanency team to look at options, and we'll need to hold a placement disruption meeting. I think you will be asked to that.'

'All right.'

'So you'll be okay over the weekend?'

'Yes.'

'Goodness knows what the little chap is thinking. He hasn't said a word to me. Phone our duty manager if there's a problem, otherwise I'll see you on Wednesday, as close to four as I can. I'm in court all day.'

We returned to the hall where Debbie took her coat from the stand and put it on while I popped into the living room. The boys were as I'd left them: Alex sitting beside Adrian, watching him but not joining in. 'Everything OK?' I asked. 'I'm just going to help Debbie unload her car.'

Adrian looked up and nodded, but Alex kept his gaze down.

I went along the hall, slipped on my coat and then followed Debbie out to her car. It was crammed full of Alex's belongings: bags, boxes and cases in the boot and on the back seat, together with Alex's bike. Having moved Alex to Rosemary and Edward's in stages, I'd forgotten how much he had.

'We'll stack it in the hall and front room for now,' I said to Debbie as she passed me the first box. 'I'll sort it all out tomorrow.'

With the front door open and on the latch to stop it from closing in the wind, we went up and down the front garden path, gradually transferring the contents of Debbie's car into the hall and front room, until all that remained was Alex's bike lodged in the footwells behind the front seat. Together we lifted it out and then I wheeled it up the garden path, into the house, and then through to the kitchen ready to put in the shed when it was light the following morning. Debbie closed the front door and we returned to the living room, where she said goodbye to Alex. He didn't reply or look up.

'Alex, love,' I said gently, 'Debbie is going now. Can you say goodbye to her?'

'Goodbye,' came his small, plaintive voice, but he kept his head down.

'Goodbye, pet,' she said. 'Try to have a good weekend and I'll see you next week. Bye, Adrian.'

'Bye,' Adrian said, glancing up at her.

We left the boys in the living room and returned down the hall. As we passed the bags I asked Debbie if she knew which one contained Alex's nightwear, but she didn't.

'No worries,' I said. 'I've got spares if necessary.' My priority was to get Alex into bed as soon as possible and then unpack tomorrow.

'I'll phone on Monday if I have the chance,' Debbie said as she opened the front door. 'Otherwise I'll see you both on Wednesday.'

We said goodbye, and I was pleased to close the door again against the cold night air. It was now nearly nine o'clock. I returned to the living room, where Alex was still sitting beside Adrian, watching him but not joining in the game. I went over and sat on the chair just in front of them.

'Alex, love, it's very late. I've saved you some dinner. Would you like it before you go to bed?'

He shook his head.

'Not even a little? You could have it in here on a tray.'

'I'm not hungry,' came his small reply.

'OK. Would you like a drink?'

He shook his head again. I wasn't surprised; eating and drinking is often the first casualty of upset and trauma. Hopefully he would make up for it the following day.

'Come on then, time for bed,' I said to both boys.

'Shall I pack away the game first?' Adrian asked.

'No, I'll do it later.'

I offered Alex my hand to hold but he didn't want it, and, standing, he followed Adrian and me out of the living room and down the hall. I paused by his bags. 'Alex, do you know which bag has your night things in it?' He shook his head.

'Shall I help you look for them, Mum?' Adrian offered.

'Thanks. We'll have a quick look but if we can't find them, I've got some spares you can use for tonight,' I told Alex.

The boxes obviously contained his toys so we eliminated those from our search and began opening some of the bags. Alex watched us, dazed and exhausted. Who knew what was going through his mind? Thankfully, the third bag I unzipped contained a pair of his pyjamas and his wash bag. 'Excellent,' I said, smiling at him. 'It's nice to have your own things.' But he just looked at me, lost and confused.

We went upstairs and I left Adrian to wash and change while I went to help Alex. He remembered where the toilet was and I waited on the landing until he'd finished, then I carried his pyjamas and wash bag into the bathroom.

'Just a quick wash and brush your teeth tonight,' I said. 'You can have a bath tomorrow.' I ran the water in the sink, squeezed out his flannel and washed his face. I squirted some toothpaste onto his brush and he gave his teeth a little brush. I waited just outside the bathroom while he changed into his pyjamas and then we went round the landing.

As we passed Paula's bedroom door Alex asked in a very quiet voice, 'Has that little girl gone too?'

'No, love, Paula is asleep in bed. She lives here all the time. She's my daughter.' But how confusing must it be for Alex, with his experience of ever-changing transient families? What most of us take for granted – a loving, stable family – had never been part of his life and remained a distant dream.

We continued round to his bedroom. 'I've bought you some new posters,' I said. He glanced up at the walls and then looked at his bed. 'We've forgotten a cuddly,' I said, realizing the omission as Alex now did. 'You get into bed and I'll pop down and find one. You don't mind which one tonight?' I remembered that he had chosen a different soft toy each night.

He climbed into bed and I went downstairs, hoping that I'd be able to find a cuddly without too much searching. I thought a good place to start looking was in the bag where I'd found his pyjamas. I unzipped it and began delving down beneath some more pyjamas and clothes, and then my fingers alighted on not one but two soft toys. I pulled them out and was relieved to see Simba and the polar bear again. I returned upstairs.

'You've got a choice,' I said to Alex as I went into his room, holding up the two cuddlies. 'Which one would you like tonight or would you like both?'

'Both,' he said quietly from his bed.

I sat on the edge of the bed and tucked them either side of him, their heads on the pillow beside his. 'That looks cosy,' I said, drawing the duvet up to his chin. I'd already closed the curtains, as I knew he liked them shut. Similarly, I knew he liked his bedroom light off and the door left slightly open while he slept. He looked up at me, pale and drawn. 'You'll feel a bit better after a good night's sleep,' I said. 'Call out if you need me in the night. You know where I am. Then tomorrow we'll unpack your bags.' I smiled, adjusted the duvet again and then stood, ready to go.

'Cathy?' he said quietly.

'Yes, love?' I paused and looked at him.

'Why did I have to leave?'

'Rosemary and Edward's?'

He nodded.

I sat on the bed again and chose my words carefully. 'Because Rosemary and Edward hadn't thought enough about adoption and what it would mean. It was nothing to do with you. It was them, they weren't right for you.'

'Was it because of James?' he asked.

'In a way, yes. He wasn't used to having a brother or sister and didn't know how to behave. But that should have all been talked about and sorted out a long time ago, before they ever met you. This should never have happened, Alex, and we're all very sorry and upset that it has.'

'I'm upset,' he said quietly. He looked so sad.

'I'm sure you are, love, and you have every right to be. But it will pass in time, and you know you can talk to me whenever you want. Remember that, all right?' He gave a small nod and rubbed his cheek against Simba's soft fabric. 'Good boy. Now I think you should get off to sleep. You must be exhausted.'

'Cathy?' he asked again in the same small voice.

'Yes, love?'

'Will you give me a hug?'

'Yes, of course,' I smiled, delighted, but it also made me sad. Alex hadn't wanted a hug or kiss from me before, as he'd been saving them for his mummy. Now there was no mummy to hug and kiss him, just a foster carer.

I cradled him in my arms and held him close, his body slight and warm against mine and his breath shallow.

'My mummy hugged me on the first few nights,' he said quietly after a few moments. 'Then she stopped. I think that's when she stopped loving me and didn't want me any more.'

My eyes filled and I held him closer. He was probably right. I remembered Rosemary's comment when I'd visited her, that cuddling Alex had felt unnatural. Now, for me, it felt completely natural. 'I don't think she understood how lucky she was to be given the chance to adopt a lovely little boy like you,' I said. I rested my head on his as he wrapped his arms tightly around my waist.

'Mum!' Adrian called from his bedroom. 'I'm in bed.'

'Good boy,' I returned. 'I'll be in soon to say goodnight.'

'Do you have to go now?' Alex asked.

'In a minute. There's no rush. Adrian will look at a book until we've finished.'

I held Alex close, stroked his head and hoped and prayed he'd find the strength to get over the rejection.

'Why did they stop loving me?' he asked presently.

'They had problems,' I said. 'It was nothing to do with you.'

'I tried to play with James, honestly I did, but he kept getting angry and telling on me.'

'He didn't know how to treat a brother. He'd never had one.'

'Will I have to go back there if they change their minds again?'

My heart ached for him. 'No, love. Never.'

'Good. Because I don't think I would like them so much next time. I'd worry they'd give me back again.'

'That won't happen,' I reassured him. 'Debbie will tell us what the long-term plans are, but for now you are staying here with me.'

I sat on Alex's bed, holding him, until he was nearly asleep and then I gently eased him onto the pillow, drew up the duvet and tucked his cuddlies either side of him.

'Night, love,' I said quietly as I stood.

But there was no reply. His eyes were closed and his face had relaxed in sleep. I crept from his room, switching off the light and leaving his bedroom door slightly ajar. My heart was heavy and full of sorrow. I went into Adrian's room.

He was sitting up in bed waiting for me. 'You were a long time,' he said.

'Sorry, love. Alex needed to talk about why he had to move from Rosemary and Edward's.'

'OK,' he said easily, and snuggled down ready for his good-night hug and chat.

I gave Adrian as much time as he wanted, and with my arm around his shoulders we chatted about the subjects he brought up: school, football club, his father and what we were doing at the weekend. Only once he'd finished and was ready to go to sleep did I say goodnight, tell him I loved him (as I do every night) and then come out of his room. I knew from experience how easy it was to let the needs of your own children slip into second place when fostering, especially with a child like Alex, who would need a lot of support over the coming weeks. Sometimes as a foster carer it feels as though there isn't enough of you to go round, but you can only do your best and hope that all the children will see that and forgive your shortcomings.

CHAPTER THIRTEEN

ANGRY OUTBURSTS

Alex slept through Friday night without waking and was still asleep when I checked on him at seven o'clock the following morning. He must have been exhausted, for he continued to sleep through Paula waking and getting up at 7.30. Refreshed after a good night's sleep, she could be very chirpy in the morning, and I explained to her that Alex was in his room again and asleep, so we needed to be quiet.

'Alex!' she said. 'Oh good. I like Alex.'

He finally woke at 8 a.m. – the same time as Adrian. I heard him get out of bed and I went to his room. 'You slept well,' I said. He gave a small nod. Paula was with me and she smiled at Alex and then went to find Adrian.

I'd brought up one of Alex's bags containing his clothes and now laid out a fresh set on the bed. I then left him (and Adrian) to dress while I took Paula downstairs to make breakfast. 'I like Alex,' she said once more, clearly pleased to see him again.

Alex's bike was still in the kitchen, so once the boys were down and could stay with Paula I took it to the shed. Alex was less pale and drawn this morning but still very quiet. He didn't want a cooked breakfast, but agreed to some cereal and a glass of orange juice. I made light conversation as we sat around the table and ate. Adrian and Paula joined in but Alex remained quiet throughout breakfast, just nodding or shaking his head, or managing a small yes or no to my questions. I wasn't surprised he was withdrawn, given what he was having to deal with.

After breakfast I settled the children with some games in the living room so I could unpack Alex's belongings. I knew Adrian would call me if I was needed, but even so I checked on them each time I came down for another bag. By lunchtime the hall was clear except for Alex's school bag, which I left with Adrian's by the coat stand, as they contained their homework. Although I didn't know how long Alex would be staying with us, unpacking and re-establishing a routine was important in helping Alex to settle and feel at home, just as it had been the first time he'd arrived, and for any child I fostered.

My mother telephoned shortly after lunch to see how Alex was, and I said he was slowly settling in but was quiet and withdrawn, which was only to be expected. She said again we should get together as soon as possible and we tentatively arranged for us to visit them the following Saturday. We'd confirm nearer the day. The grey overcast skies of the morning turned to rain in the afternoon, so I suggested to Alex and Adrian that this was a good opportunity to do their homework, then if it was fine the following day we could go out. The boys fetched their school bags and sat at the table to work. Paula didn't want to be left out, so I settled her at the table with some crayons and a colouring book. I was on hand to help with school work if necessary. Alex did his with the same quiet resignation that he had played with Adrian and Paula earlier on. Complying rather than engaging is how I would have described it. But he did his homework and when they'd both finished I suggested we made pizza for dinner – most children love donning aprons and getting messy with the ingredients: flour and water. Alex met my suggestion with quiet acquiescence, and went along with the activity rather than wholeheartedly enjoying it as Adrian and Paula did. When we'd finished and the pizzas, topped with sliced peppers, cheese and ham, were in the oven cooking and everyone was clean again, I took Alex aside to have a chat with him.

'Alex, love, I want you to try to relax and be yourself, like you were before with us. You seem as though you are on your best behaviour, but you won't upset us. You know Adrian, Paula and me and we know you, so try to be yourself. We like you that way.' I wondered if he might be trying to live up to some high and undisclosed standard and was perhaps fearful of saying and doing the wrong thing.

He nodded, but then remained quiet and compliant for the rest of the day, so I guessed it would take time before he was able to relax and be himself again.

I gave all three children a bath and hair wash that night, so I spent most of the evening upstairs. Once they were ready for bed they came down in their dressing gowns for a drink and to watch some television before going to bed: Paula went up first, then Alex and Adrian. Alex was still quiet but now looked more comfortable in his room, surrounded by his belongings and a choice of soft toys. It was the monkey's turn tonight. Alex didn't want a hug or to talk as he had done the night before, so I tucked him in, kissed his forehead and, reminding him to call me in the night if he needed me, left him to go to sleep.

All three children slept well and so did I, and I woke refreshed to a fine day. I told the children that after breakfast we could take their bikes to the park if they'd like to. There was a resounding 'Yes!' from Adrian and Paula, but Alex looked anxious.

'What's the matter, love?' I asked him.

'I won't be able to keep up,' he said quietly. 'I can't ride very fast.' I knew where that had come from.

'You'll keep up OK,' I reassured him with a smile. 'We can't ride along the roads here as you can in the country. You will have to stay beside me on the pavement as we take the bikes to the park, and then once there you can ride around at your own speed. It's not a race. Paula has stabilizers on her bike, so she's not going anywhere fast, and I'll be on foot.'

He looked relieved, but I wondered how many other worries and fears of failing he now harboured from his time at Rosemary and Edward's.

The trip to the park was a success. The children enjoyed it, although Alex remained comparatively quiet, and we returned home with cheeks glowing from the fresh air and exercise. I prepared dinner and we ate in the afternoon – around two o'clock – as we usually did on a Sunday, after which the children amused themselves while I cleared up. Then we settled in the living room and the children played while I read the newspaper. John telephoned at five o'clock to speak to Adrian and Paula, and before he did we exchanged a polite 'hello' and 'how are you?' He also said he was planning on seeing the children the following Sunday, and I said I'd make a note of it in my diary, and then passed the handset to Adrian. He settled on the sofa to chat with his father, and Paula would have her turn afterwards. Alex, who'd heard me say their father was on the phone, left what he was doing and came over to me. 'Will I have to talk to my father on the phone?' he asked quietly.

For a moment I thought he meant his natural father, who, as far as I knew, he'd never had any contact with, but then I realized. 'Edward?' I asked him. He nodded. 'No, love, you won't. You don't want to talk to him, do you?' He shook his head and returned to the Lego he and Adrian had been playing with. But it was another reminder of just how confusing Alex's experience of parents and families had been.

On Sunday evening I had all three children in bed at a reasonable time, as we had to be up for school and nursery the following morning. Alex didn't want any hugs again that night and when I asked him if he was all right he nodded. I tucked him and his soft toy in, kissed his forehead and then, reminding him again to call out if he needed me in the night, I left him to go to sleep. I hoped that when he returned to school the following day its familiarity would help him recover from the trauma of what had happened and bring him out of himself again. Although he was going to have to tell his friends something, and that could be very awkward. He'd been taken to school and collected by his adoptive mother for the past two weeks and now I'd be there again. Children in care have so much to cope with, not only at home, but at school as well. They are often so worried about what their peers will think and ashamed of being in care that they don't make friends, or invent elaborate stories to explain why they are not with their birth families and who the woman meeting them in the playground is. It would be even more difficult for Alex because many in his class had been aware he was going to be adopted and had shared in his happiness. Doubtless they'd want to know what had gone wrong.

As it turned out Miss Cork, Alex's very perceptive and sensitive teacher, was one step ahead of me and came to the rescue. When we arrived at breakfast club that Monday she was on duty and watching out for us. She came over straight away, said a cheerful good morning to Alex and then as he hung up his coat she said to me, 'The Head is going to see Alex at the start of school while I have a word with the class. We think it's best if we explain to the children a little of what has happened, so Alex isn't faced with a barrage of difficult questions.'

'Thank you so much. That's fantastic,' I said, relieved. I could have hugged her. 'I'm sure that will help enormously.'

'When the Head sees Alex she will tell him that if he has any worries to see her or me. We're obviously all very sorry this has happened, but we'll do our best to help him while he's here in school, and obviously we'll stay in close contact with you. Let us know if there is anything else we can do.'

I thanked her again, said goodbye to her and Alex and then left to take Adrian to school and Paula to nursery. Schools can play an important role in helping looked-after children through difficult times, but they don't always appreciate this and assume that once the child is in care they'll be fine.

When I returned home that morning I set about doing some housework. It was while I was in Alex's room returning his clean clothes to his drawers that I noticed a torn greetings card poking out of his waste paper basket. I could see the words 'Good Luck' printed on the front. Setting down his clothes, I took the two halves of the card out of the bin and opened them. As I'd thought it might be, the card was from Rosemary and family – the leaving card Debbie had mentioned. Beneath the printed message inside, Rosemary, Edward and James had signed their names. No kisses or extra words, just their names. Clearly it was Alex's decision whether he kept the card or not – he'd kept the ones from his previous foster carers – but I could appreciate why he didn't want any reminders of his time with Rosemary, Edward and James. I returned the card to the bin. There was no sign of the twenty-pound note that Debbie had said had been in the card, so I hoped Alex had had the good sense to keep it.

Jill telephoned during the morning to see how Alex's move had gone and I updated her, saying that while Alex wasn't visibly distraught or angry, he remained very quiet. Like me, she thought this was only to be expected and that hopefully it would pass in time, but added that Alex was probably very confused right now and his anger might come out later. Her words proved to be highly prophetic, although not straight away.

That afternoon, when Paula and I collected Alex from school, Miss Cork came over to me in the playground and said that Alex had had a good day but had been very quiet. I thanked her for letting me know and for keeping an eye on him. As we walked to the car I asked Alex (as I always asked Adrian and any other children I fostered at the end of school) if he'd had a good day. Alex said a small, 'OK,' then added, 'Miss talked to my class and told them I was living with you again.'

'Was that all right?'

'I guess so,' he said, with a shrug.

'Don't worry, love, by tomorrow they'll have forgotten you ever left me.' In my experience children have an amazing capacity to accept news like this and move on.

Jill visited us on Tuesday after school as arranged and Alex was still very quiet. He was with us at the start, but then Jill said he could go and play if he wished and he went up to his room. It's good practice for a support social worker to see the child at their monthly visit. Once he'd left the room Jill and I discussed how best I could help him and any foster-carer training that might help (ongoing training is part of fostering now), then she read and signed my log notes. Before she left we arranged her next visit for four weeks' time, although I'd speak to her before then as and when necessary. She called goodbye to the children as I saw her to the door.

The evening continued as most school nights do with dinner, homework, some television, a bedtime story and then a bath and bed. Once in his room Alex took a long while choosing a soft toy and I wondered if he was delaying going to bed. But then he looked at me and asked, 'Am I too old to have a cuddly now?'

'No, love, of course not.'

'James said I was. He laughed at me.'

'You're never too old for a cuddly. Adrian has a favourite teddy bear that sits on his bed. I have a fluffy cat on mine that Adrian and Paula gave to me as a Christmas present.'

I think this helped a little, as Alex didn't hesitate any longer but quickly chose a soft toy and climbed into bed. I didn't blame James, although he could have been a bit more sensitive, but siblings do make unkind comments and laugh at each other sometimes; it's part of having a brother or sister. And in the context of a loving and strong sibling bond unkind words and laughter are soon forgotten. But of course that bond had never been established between James and Alex, and Alex was still struggling with everything that had happened and was dwelling on it and taking it personally. All I could do was reassure him and help him move on.

On Wednesday afternoon when I collected Alex from school I reminded him that Debbie was coming to visit us. 'We're very popular this week with social workers,' I quipped lightly. 'Jill yesterday and Debbie today.' But he wasn't amused. Some children have a negative view of their social worker, holding them responsible for taking them away from their family, but all that had happened to Alex a long while ago, and from what I'd seen so far he had a good relationship with her – up until now.

'Do I have to see her?' he asked me in the car.

'Well, yes, you do really. Why? What's the matter?'

'I don't like her any more.'

'Because of what happened with Rosemary and Edward?'

He gave a small nod.

'It wasn't really her fault,' I said. Although of course to some extent it was. 'I know she's very sorry it all went so wrong. She'll just want to have a chat with you to make sure you're OK and then you'll be able to go off and play, like you did with Jill.' He didn't reply and was silent for the rest of the journey home.

Debbie arrived five minutes after we were home, very smart in a navy suit, having come straight from court. Alex followed her resignedly into the living room and I made us all a drink. I settled Adrian and Paula with their drinks and some activities at the table in the kitchen-cum-diner, and then took Alex's and Debbie's drinks into the living room, where I set them on the coffee table. Alex was sitting beside Debbie on the sofa and she was talking quietly to him in a reassuring voice. I didn't hear what she was saying. I asked her if she wanted time alone now with Alex and she said that would be good and I should join them later – after they'd had a chat. The child's social worker always spends time alone with the child during their visit in case there are any issues the child doesn't feel comfortable mentioning in front of the carer. I left the room and joined Adrian and Paula at the table, but a few minutes later we started as we heard Alex shout at the top of his voice: 'I hate you! I hate you all!' We'd never heard Alex shout before and Adrian and Paula looked at me anxiously. Then a moment later the living room door burst open and Alex ran upstairs and into his bedroom. The door slammed shut. 'Stay here and I'll see what the matter is,' I told them.

I went into the hall where Debbie was coming out of the living room. 'Sorry, he's thrown the drinks everywhere.'

'I'll fetch a cloth,' I said. 'What's the problem?'

'I was talking to him about leaving Rosemary and Edward and what would happen now, and he seemed OK. But then he suddenly jumped up from the sofa and shouted and threw the drinks. I've never seen him like that before.'

'No, neither have I,' I said. 'I'll give him a few minutes and then go up.' It was quiet upstairs now. If a child is screaming, crying, shouting or throwing things I go up immediately to calm them, but otherwise most children benefit from a little cooling-off period.

I fetched a damp cloth from the kitchen and set about mopping up the tea and juice as Debbie sat at the dry end of the sofa writing in her notepad, about Alex's outburst I guessed. Some of the carpet and sofa would need a more thorough sponge later, but as a parent and foster carer you can't be too precious about spillages.

'I'll go and see how he is,' Debbie said, setting down her notepad.

She went upstairs as I returned the cloth to the kitchen, reassuring Adrian and Paula that Alex would be all right. Ten minutes later Debbie came down. 'He won't talk to me,' she said. 'I'll try again later before I go.'

'But he's not distressed?' I asked. I would have gone up straight away if he had been.

'No. Just refusing to talk to me.'

We returned to the living room, where she sat on the sofa and then handed me the placement form I needed to foster Alex.

'I wasn't ever given much background information on Alex before,' I said.

'I'll see what I can send you.' She made a note. 'How has Alex been generally since he came back?'

'Until now, very quiet. Withdrawn. He's been the same at

school.' She wrote as I spoke. 'He obviously feels very rejected. I know by the little he has said. He's got a lot to come to terms with – all that hype of being found a permanent family and now this.'

Debbie paused from writing to look at me. 'Do you think a referral to CAMHS would help?' CAMHS stands for Child and Adolescent Mental Health Services, which offers assessment and treatment for children and young people with emotional, behavioural or mental health difficulties.

'It might,' I said.

'I'll make a referral,' Debbie said, again writing on her notepad. 'There's a long waiting list.' Then, 'Remind me who lives in this house with you?'

'Just my children, Adrian, aged seven, and Paula, three.'

'So Adrian is the same age as Alex?'

'Yes.'

'And the boys got on all right? I know Alex wasn't here for long.'

'Yes.' I could guess at the comparison she was making. 'But Adrian is used to having children in our home. He and Paula have grown up with fostering – sharing their toys and me. James was an only child all his life, then Alex suddenly appeared and changed everything. To be honest I'm not surprised James was upset, but I don't think Rosemary and Edward were prepared for it.'

'They attended the adoption preparation course,' Debbie said defensively. I didn't comment. She knew as well as I did that theory and practice can be very different. 'Given what happened between Alex and James,' she continued, 'when we look for a long-term foster family for Alex the ages of any other children in the family will need to be taken into account. We can't risk another disrupted placement.'

'No,' I agreed. 'Alex has had more than enough moves. Is that the care plan for Alex then – a long-term foster placement?'

'Very likely.' And I knew from her comments about Adrian and Alex being the same age that I'd be ruled out for keeping Alex long term, which would mean another move for him. And how many more after that? Long-term foster placements do break down, although they are supposed to be permanent.

'I'll need to arrange a LAC [looked-after children] review soon,' Debbie said, moving on. 'Can we hold it here?'

'Yes.' This was normal. It's usually held in the foster carer's home. The social worker, teacher, foster carer, the foster carer's support social worker and any other adults closely connected with the child meet to ensure that everything is being done to help the child, and that the care plan (drawn up by the social services) is up to date. 'It's half term next week, I'll see if I can arrange the review for then,' Debbie said. 'Alex should be present. Otherwise one day after school the following week.' This was normal too. Very young children don't usually attend their reviews, while older children are expected to, as it is about them. 'I'll send you an invitation once I've set the date.' I nodded. 'I think that's everything. Do you have any questions?'

'No. I don't think so.'

'Well, thanks for taking Alex back. You can never tell how adoptions of older children will work out.' Which comment grated with me as I thought it rather too easily exonerated anyone of responsibility. Debbie returned her notepad to her bag and placed it beside her. 'I'll go and see if Alex is prepared to talk to me now.'

We both stood. Debbie went upstairs to Alex and I went to Adrian and Paula. Two minutes later Debbie returned downstairs. 'He's under the duvet and won't talk to me, so I'll leave it for now,' she said.

'I'll go up and see him shortly,' I said.

She fetched her bag from the living room and I saw her out, then I went straight up to Alex's room. The door was pulled to but not shut. I gave a small tap and went in. Alex was no longer under the duvet but sitting on the edge of his bed, holding a soft toy. 'Are you all right, love?' I asked, going over.

He nodded.

'Debbie has gone now. She said to say goodbye. Do you want to talk to me about what made you angry?' He shook his head. 'Sure?' He gave a small nod. He'd recovered now, so I didn't pursue it. 'OK. Come downstairs then. I don't want you sitting up here alone.'

He obediently stood, set the soft toy with the others at the end of the bed, and with his face expressionless came over and slipped his hand into mine. I gave it a reassuring squeeze and we went downstairs and into the living room, where Adrian, Paula and he watched some television while I made dinner. Although Alex's anger had subsided as quickly as it had erupted, I had little doubt it would surface again as he struggled to come to terms with everything that had happened to him. The brain is like a pressure cooker and it can only take so much before it blows.

CHAPTER FOURTEEN

NOBODY'S SON

The following afternoon, when Paula and I collected Alex from school, Miss Cork came to see me in the playground. I knew from her expression and the way Alex was walking beside her, head down and subdued, that it might not be good news.

'We've had a couple of incidents today,' she said, glancing at Alex, intending him to hear. He kept his head down. 'This morning in the classroom I asked Alex a question about the lesson and he became very angry and ran out of the classroom. Then at lunchtime in the playground another boy accidentally bumped into him and Alex thumped him.'

'Alex!' I said, shocked. Miss Cork threw me a look that said she, too, was surprised.

'It's all right, we dealt with the incidents,' she said. 'I've talked to Alex about ways he can manage his anger, and he apologized to the boy, but I thought you should know.'

'Yes, thank you,' I said.

'He hasn't done much work today,' Miss Cork added. 'He seems to find it difficult to concentrate.' I could see she didn't think this was surprising either. 'Perhaps he could finish the work at home so he doesn't get behind. It's in his school bag.'

'Yes, of course.'

'It's the half-term holiday next week, which should give him a chance to recover.'

I nodded, although of course I'd been hoping that school with its familiarity and friendships would help Alex recover from his upset, but that clearly wasn't happening.

Miss Cork wished us a pleasant evening and we said goodbye.

'Do you want to talk to me about anything?' I asked Alex as we walked to the car. He shook his head. 'Sure?' He nodded. 'Whenever you do, you know I'm here.' He shrugged.

He was quiet in the car on the way to collect Adrian from school, despite Paula talking to him, and he remained quiet and also compliant for the whole evening, obediently doing his homework and coming straight to the table when I called him for dinner. I looked at him as we ate. I was worried. He'd been with us for nearly a week now and there'd been no improvement in the way he was interacting with any of us. Indeed, he *wasn't* interacting with us – not as he had done before. I knew he was internalizing his pain and that it would come out in tears and more angry outbursts. This wasn't the Alex we'd known before, and I knew I needed to keep a close eye on him. But it wasn't close enough as it turned out.

That evening the children came downstairs in their dressing gowns to play for a while before I began taking them up to bed. I was sitting on the sofa with Paula beside me, reading her a bedtime story. Alex and Adrian were sitting cross-legged on the floor and moving toy cars along the road on the play mat. They were playing independently of each other, not together. Suddenly, Alex jumped up and, throwing down the car he'd been holding, fled the room in tears.

'I only moved one of his cars so mine could get by,' Adrian said, worried. 'He didn't used to mind.'

'It's all right. It's not your fault. Alex is a bit sensitive at present.'

Leaving Adrian with Paula in the living room, I went upstairs to Alex's room. He was lying face down on the bed, his little body shaking as he wept into the pillow.

'Alex, love,' I said gently. I sat on the edge of the bed.

'Leave me alone. I don't like you or Adrian any more,' he sobbed. 'I hate you all.'

I placed my hand lightly on his shoulder. 'Alex, I understand you're upset, but it's not really about Adrian or me, is it, love? It's about other things that have happened.'

'Go away. I don't need you. Or Rosemary or Edward or James. I'm going to run away and live by myself. I don't need any one. You're all horrible.'

I didn't take it personally – he was upset. 'Alex, we all need someone. I understand you're hurting, but I want to help you.'

'No, you don't,' he sobbed. 'No one does. I'm leaving.' Then as quick as a flash he was off the bed and out of the door. I went after him but he was halfway down the stairs. By the time I reached the hall he was at the front door, trying to open it. I flicked the lock down and put my arms around his shoulders and turned him towards me.

'Get off!' he cried through his tears, trying to push me away. 'I'm leaving. I'm running away.'

'No, you're not, love,' I said evenly, holding him close. 'I want you to stay here with me.' I held him as he pushed against me. I wasn't going to let him go for fear he could unlock the door and run off, but also beneath his anger and tears was a frail child in desperate need of comforting and reassuring arms.

'I hate you! I hate everyone!' he cried. He struggled some more and then collapsed against me, crying.

Adrian and Paula appeared at the other end of the hall looking very worried. 'It's OK,' I said to them. 'Alex will be all right soon. Adrian, could you look after Paula while I talk to Alex?'

He nodded and, taking Paula's hand, returned with her to the living room. 'Thank you, good boy,' I called after him.

Alex was still collapsed against me, crying quietly. 'It's going to be all right,' I told him, holding him close. 'Let's go and sit down.'

I kept my arm around him and guided him into the front room, flicking on the light as we went. I sat on the easy chair and took him onto my lap. He didn't resist – his anger had subsided now. I cradled him in my lap and soothed his head. He relaxed against me and presently his tears stopped. I wiped his cheeks with a tissue and then we continued to sit in silence. Sometimes a hug can say far more than words – at any age. In the distance I could hear Adrian's voice drift in from the living room as he read Paula a story.

After a few moments and without raising his head Alex said quietly, 'I'm very sad, Cathy.'

'I know, love. About Rosemary and Edward?'

'And other stuff.'

'Like what?' I asked gently, holding him close. 'Can you tell me?'

'My life,' he said. 'It hasn't been a good life for me.' Tears immediately stung my eyes. To hear a seven-year-old, who should have been full of joy and not have a care in the world, say his life hadn't been good touched me deeply. I drew him even closer.

'I want to help you get over this sad time,' I said quietly, stroking his hair. 'So the rest of your life is good.'

'It's not possible.'

'Why?'

'You can't give me what I want. The kids at school all have proper families with mums and dads and brothers and sisters, but I don't. I never have and I won't now. I thought I was going to have a family with Rosemary, Edward and James, but they didn't want me in the end. No one does. I'm nobody's brother or son.'

My eyes filled again. 'I want you,' I said. 'And while you are here with me you will be my son, and Adrian and Paula's brother.'

'But that won't last,' Alex said. 'Debbie told me she's going to look for another foster family for me. That's why I got angry.'

I obviously couldn't lie to him. 'I know, love, but that might take many months. They'll need to be sure they find you the right family this time. So while they're looking you'll be here and I will think of you as my son. I'll try to make you as happy as I can. So will Adrian and Paula. We all like you lots, Alex. Adrian and Paula have told me how much they like you. And on Saturday you are going to meet my parents. They're looking forward to meeting you.' I was drawing on all the positives I could think of to try to build up his confidence and ease his pain. I couldn't change his past or the plans for his future, but helping him to live in the present and enjoy the little things in life – of which there are many – might comfort him a little.

'Perhaps my real mummy will have me back,' Alex said after a moment. I swallowed hard.

'Your mummy loves you, pet, but she can't look after you. That's why you had to come into care.'

'I know, Debbie said, but can I see her again?'

The answer would be no. Alex's contact with his mother had been terminated in preparation for him being adopted (after a judge had ruled that his mother could never look after him). Although the adoption had failed, it didn't mean he could see her again. Cruel though this sounds, to have reinstated contact would have given Alex (and his mother) mixed and confusing messages. Alex would very likely now be in care until he was eighteen.

'It's not my decision, love,' I said gently. 'What did Debbie tell you?'

He sank against me, only too aware of her response. 'My mummy can send me birthday cards, but that's all. I had to say goodbye to her at the contact centre. She was very upset and we both cried.' It was at times like this that I felt guilty for being part of the social care system that separated families, although I knew that the judge would have made the decision that Alex couldn't live with his mother for very good reasons.

'Can I go to bed now?' he suddenly asked, looking up at me.

'Yes, of course, love. You'll feel a bit better in the morning after a good night's sleep. And the next day you'll feel better still, and then the next, until one morning the old Alex will be back and you'll leap out of bed full of laughter and fun, just as you used to. It will take time, but you will get over this.' I gave him a final hug and he eased himself from my lap.

'I'm just going to take Alex up to bed,' I called to Adrian and Paula from the hall.

'All right, Mum,' Adrian replied. 'I'm looking after Paula.'

'I don't need looking after. I'm a big girl,' I heard Paula say.

'Yes, you do, love,' I returned from the stairs as I took Alex up.

Alex was already in his pyjamas and had had his bath, so I waited on the landing while he used the toilet, then I saw him into bed. He snuggled his face against his soft toy penguin and I tucked them both in. Alex looked sad but also very tired, so I hoped that, as I'd told him, a good night's sleep (and the fact that he was now talking about his worries) would set him on the path to recovery. Reminding him to call me in the night if he needed me, I kissed his forehead and came out. Downstairs, I spent some time sitting with Adrian and Paula, explaining why Alex was likely to be upset for a while yet and that we had to make allowances for his behaviour.

'I will,' Adrian said.

'Good boy.'

While Paula said, 'I'm a big girl. I'm going to bed after Alex tonight.'

'Yes, just for tonight,' I said with a smile.

Alex had a nightmare that night. I heard him call out and I was immediately out of bed and throwing on my dressing gown. I went straight to his room. He was lying on his back, eyes closed, tossing and turning and calling out in his sleep. 'I'm not saying goodbye. No! I'm not leaving. You can't make me.' No prizes for guessing where that had come from: Alex had spent most of his short life saying goodbye to families. I sat on his bed, stroked his forehead and reassured him that he was safe and everything would be all right. He didn't wake fully and once he was in a deep sleep again I returned to my room.

On Friday there was another incident at school. Miss Cork came to find me in the playground at the end of the day and said that during afternoon playtime a boy in another class who lived on the same estate as Alex's mother had asked Alex where his mother was. While keeping a looked-after child at the same school offers continuity, the downside is that this type of question can arise as children in the area know the birth family. Embarrassed, upset and unable to answer the boy's question, Alex had run off to the school gate, which was high and locked. But he spotted an escape route, and before the playground supervisor had a chance to intervene Alex had scaled the lower trunk of one of the nearby trees and was crawling across an overhanging branch that bridged the gap to the gate. It was then he realized that if he climbed over the gate there was a very long drop on the other side. The playground supervisor rushed over and persuaded him to come down – in fact, there was nowhere else he could go. She and Miss Cork talked to Alex about the danger of what he'd done. Miss Cork also told me that the caretaker had been informed and he would be cutting back any overhanging branches during the half-term holiday. I thanked her, apologized for all the worry Alex had caused them and, wishing each other a good half term, we said goodbye.

'That was a dangerous thing to do,' I said to Alex as we walked to the car. 'If you'd fallen you would have been badly hurt.'

He shrugged. 'Don't care.'

'Where were you thinking of going if you had got out?'

'Somewhere by myself,' he said sullenly. I had been expecting him to say home, to my mum, which is what most children in care would have said, so I thought that deep down Alex knew that living with his mother wasn't an option.

The school had dealt with the matter, so I didn't labour the point. I asked him what he'd like to do over the half-term holiday. He shrugged.

'I'd like to go to the park,' Paula said, slipping her hand into Alex's.

'Yes, we can do that if the weather is fine,' I said. 'I was also thinking of going to the cinema and an indoor activity centre.'

'Oh yes,' Paula said, giving a little skip of delight.

'Would you like to go there, Alex?' He managed a small nod. 'Excellent,' I said.

* * *

When I collected Adrian from school he was pleased to be breaking up for the week, as indeed I was. Most foster carers welcome the break from the school routine with its long school runs, so that they can spend more time with the children and go on outings and similar. Alex slept well that night, but the following day didn't get off to a good start and the visit to my parents wasn't the success I'd hoped for. The children I foster usually take to my parents, and very quickly call them Nana and Grandpa. Perhaps it was asking too much of Alex, who'd not long ago met James's grandparents and then had his hope of a family dashed. Before we left the house that morning Alex said he didn't want to go to see Nana and Grandpa, but I chivvied him along and said he'd have a lovely time. There wasn't really an alternative. I couldn't ask someone to babysit him at such short notice on a Saturday, and I wasn't going to cancel our visit, as Adrian, Paula and my parents would be very disappointed. I always take a child's wishes into account where possible, but this was one of those occasions when he would have to go along with what I'd planned. I was sure that once he got there he'd feel differently.

Mum and Dad welcomed Alex warmly, as they did all the children I fostered. While Alex wasn't rude to them, he remained quiet and separate – distant from us, despite our best efforts to include him. He sat with us at the table and ate a little but didn't join in with the conversation or smile. Then after lunch we went for a walk in the country not far away and we took food for the ducks on the river. Alex maintained his distance and didn't want to feed the ducks. I watched him carefully, as the river was deep and there was no railing between us and the water. My father thought that Alex might be nervous of the ducks and encouraged him to feed them by saying, 'Come on, lad, stand by me, they won't hurt you.'

'I know they won't,' Alex said moodily. Then he suddenly darted off – up the path that ran alongside the riverbank and around the corner. Leaving my parents looking after Adrian and Paula, I dashed after him and caught up around the bend. I held his arm.

'Alex! You mustn't run off here,' I said very firmly. 'It's dangerous. That river is deep. You could drown.' It had given me a shock and I think he could see that. 'Now take hold of my hand and we'll go back to Nana and Grandpa. They'll be worried about you.'

'I'm not going back,' he said. 'I don't like your nana and grandpa. They stink.'

Despite my fright I had to stifle a smile. 'I'm sure they don't stink,' I said lightly. 'They shower every day. But we're going back, Alex. You don't have to feed the ducks if you don't want to. Grandpa was only being kind.'

He shook his head.

'Alex, you can't stay here by yourself, so you have two choices. You can either hold my hand like a big boy and we'll walk back together, or I'll carry you like a baby. What's it to be? Either way, you're coming with me.' Just as well he was slightly built, I thought. I could carry him if necessary. I waited. He stood for a moment and then snatched my hand, and we returned to our little group.

The rest of the day passed in much the same manner, with Alex there on the edge of activities and conversation but not really joining in.

'He'll be better the next time he meets us,' Mum said to me as we prepared to leave. 'He won't be so shy.' I nodded, but I doubted that Alex keeping his distance and not wanting to relate to my parents had anything to do with shyness. It was more about Alex protecting himself. If you knew for certain that in a few months' time you were going to have to leave, what would be the point in bonding with a set of grandparents you would never see again? I doubt I would have.

CHAPTER FIFTEEN

AN EERIE NOISE OUTSIDE

On Sunday Adrian and Paula went out with their father for the day, so I was able to give Alex my complete attention, which I hoped would be positive for him. We began by finishing his school work and then I asked him what he would like to do. He shrugged.

'We can stay in or go out somewhere?' I suggested. It was chilly but dry.

He shrugged again.

'We could play a few board games, then after lunch we could take your bike to the park?'

'I guess so,' he said, meeting any suggestion from me with the same lack of enthusiasm he now showed for everything.

Alex played the various games I produced, ate his lunch and then rode his bike in the park without really engaging with me at all, or showing any enjoyment for what he was doing. I was starting to wonder if he was depressed. Children, like adults, can suffer from depression, and I would make a note of my concerns in my log and also tell his social worker. Debbie had said she was going to refer Alex to CAMHS but that there was a long waiting list. Perhaps his appointment could be brought forward? I'd ask.

It was mid-afternoon when we returned home from the park. I was still attempting to make conversation with Alex but receiving little or no response. I carried his bike through the house and out to the patio, then Alex wheeled it to the shed at the bottom of the garden where I put it away. When I came out of the shed Alex was nowhere to be seen, so I assumed he'd gone indoors. The sun had gone and the temperature was dropping quickly now. I entered the house through the back door and called his name, but there was no reply. Clearly he hadn't heard me, so after slipping off my coat and leaving it on the hall stand I went from room to room, looking for him and calling his name. I continued upstairs and looked in all the bedrooms, the bathroom and toilet. If he was hiding, this wasn't funny any more. Then a horrendous thought struck me and I ran downstairs to the coat stand. His coat wasn't there! Opening the front door I ran out onto the pavement, where I frantically scanned up and down the street. It curved out of view but surely he hadn't got that far? My heart pounded as fear gripped me. I stood torn between going up or down the road, for he must have gone in one of these directions. Then out of the corner of my eye I caught a flash of blue in the shrubbery. I turned. The blue material of Alex's anorak? I went closer.

'Alex! Whatever are you doing in there? Come out at once.' He was crouched low and almost completely hidden in the middle of the evergreen shrubs in the front garden. I was annoyed and relieved at the same time. 'You scared me silly. Come out now.'

He stood, unfazed and expressionless, and then made his way out, his shoes caked in mud and dry leaves, and twigs clinging to his trousers.

'That was naughty,' I said. 'Don't you ever do that again! I was worried sick. You've lost half an hour of your television tonight.'

Alex wasn't bothered, and of course he had wanted to worry me. He'd been hurt and now he wanted to hurt others. This act of rebellion had proved effective and had elicited the response he sought.

He didn't say anything as we went in and he took off his shoes and coat. I thought it wouldn't be long before he tried running off again – this was the second episode – and I put the latch down on the front door. Foster carers aren't allowed to lock a child in the house in case there is an emergency, so I couldn't Chubb lock the front door and remove the key. Alex could reach the latch if necessary, but it would buy me extra time if he tried to run off again. The back garden was secure with a fence and padlocked side gate, not that he'd be playing in the garden in winter. I tried talking to him, explaining that he needed to share his worries with me rather than running away, and he gave a desultory nod, which said he agreed to nothing.

Adrian and Paula arrived home at 5.30 eager to tell me all about the fun day out they'd had with their father, so once they'd said goodbye to John we went into the living room to chat. Alex was in the room too to begin with but then quietly stood and left. 'Are you OK?' I called after him.

'I'm going to play in my room,' he said. Which he did sometimes, so I thought nothing more about it. He'd had my attention all day and it was Adrian's and Paula's turn now.

They continued telling me about the fair they'd been to with their father, and while I was pleased for them, it still hurt that I hadn't been part of their enjoyment and able to witness their pleasure first-hand. It's a feeling that I think many single parents will recognize and share. Then suddenly, mid-conversation, we fell silent; a scratching noise was coming from the patio doors. Both children looked at me anxiously. It was dark outside now and I'd closed the curtains.

'Toscha,' I said, but then I immediately saw her curled up by the radiator. I stood, went to the curtains, parted them and peered out. There was nothing to be seen. 'Perhaps it was a neighbour's cat,' I said, closing the curtains again. I returned to my seat. 'And what did you have for lunch?' I asked, picking up the conversation. Before they had a chance to answer the scratching came again. 'I'm scared,' Adrian said, grabbing a cushion to hide behind. 'What is it?'

'I don't know.' I went over, opened the curtains and looked as far as I could into the dark, but there was nothing. Although I didn't show it, I was becoming unsettled and feeling spooked too.

I'd just sat down when we heard the scratching again. Adrian squealed and buried his head in the cushion, which frightened Paula.

'That's not helping,' I said to him. 'It's nothing to be worried about. Stay here with your sister and I'll go and see.'

'No, don't go!' Adrian pleaded. 'I'm frightened.'

'You're safe in here. If it's not a cat it's probably a fox.'

But as I left the living room with my senses on full alert, I wondered at the wisdom of going outside. Supposing there was someone out there? What would I do? Perhaps I should call the police, but if I told them I'd heard a scratching sound outside they'd probably say it was a fox or badger – they'd been spotted around here. Of course it would run off when I opened the curtains, I told myself.

Going into the kitchen, I switched on the light and then raised all the blinds so the light shone out onto the patio. I was tense with apprehension, unsure if I was doing the right thing and not knowing what I might find. But I couldn't think of a reasonable alternative if the children and I weren't to spend the entire evening scared and on edge. I was about to turn the key in the back door when I realized it was already unlocked, and for a moment fear gripped me. I thought an intruder must already be in the house. I always kept the back door locked. Then logic returned and I realized that someone hadn't let themselves into the house, but out. I continued outside.

'Alex! Is that you?' The outline of a boy darted from the patio doors and down the garden, quickly disappearing into the dark. 'Alex! Come here now. I'm not playing games with you. It's cold and dark.'

I began down the garden, lambasting myself for not keep-ing a closer watch on him, but it was impossible to see anything. Our garden is long and narrow and has plenty of dense foliage, even in winter. I could hear him moving around in the bushes but couldn't see him. I needed a torch. I kept one in the cupboard under the stairs. 'Alex!' I called one last time, but there was no reply. I returned to the house and went first to the living room where Adrian and Paula were huddled together on the sofa.

'It's Alex,' I said. 'He's run off down the garden. It's naughty. Stay here while I find him. I'm taking a torch.'

'Do you want some help?' Adrian asked. Reassured by it being Alex, he spied the opportunity for an adventure. 'I can fetch my torch.'

'So can I,' Paula added.

'I'd rather you both stayed here. You can see me through the window if you like.' I didn't think it would help to have them in the garden too.

They crossed to the curtains and I went to the cupboard under the stairs, where I took the torch from its hook. Leaving Adrian and Paula looking through the glass of the patio doors, I returned outside and switched on the torch. Thankfully the batteries were good so the beam was strong. Two little faces were pressed against the glass and I threw them an encouraging smile, then headed down the garden. It was cold and damp but not freezing.

'Alex!' I called, flashing the torch around. 'Alex, I want you inside now.' Nothing. No reply or movement. He must be hiding behind a bush. Then the torch beam picked up what could have been a figure, and as I advanced he ran off and hid in another part of the garden. 'That's another half an hour you've lost from television tonight,' I said into the dark. 'I mean it, Alex.' But the night air was quiet again.

Some children would have thought this a funny game, but Alex wasn't laughing or making any noise. The night was eerily still, the only sounds coming from my voice or the sudden rustle of his feet as he moved from one hiding place to another. 'Alex, I'm not telling you again,' I said, following his movement. 'You need to come in now or you'll lose your television tomorrow night as well.'

A window suddenly opened in my neighbour's house. I looked up to see my good friend and neighbour Sue looking out of her bathroom window. 'Cathy, is that you out there?' she called. 'I can hear voices.'

'Yes, Sue. Sorry I disturbed you.'

'What are you doing out there, love?' she asked in a dead-pan voice. She knew I fostered and she made allowances for the unusual behaviour she sometimes witnessed, but losing a child in the garden was a first.

'Alex is out here somewhere and he needs to come in,' I called back, flashing my torch around as I spoke.

'Do you want some help?' she asked.

'No, it's OK, thanks. But if he doesn't come in soon he won't be going on any of the activities I've planned for next week. I'll have to leave him with another foster carer when we go to the cinema and activity centre,' I added, labouring the point for Alex's benefit. These sanctions might have sounded excessive, but Alex needed to understand that he couldn't just run off when he felt like it.

'I'm sure he won't want to miss out on those fun days,' Sue called back so Alex could hear. 'Not if he's got any sense. I've just got out of the shower, but let me know if you want any help.'

'Thanks, Sue.' She closed her bathroom window and the garden fell silent again.

'Right, Alex,' I said firmly. 'You heard what I said. I'm going indoors now and if you are not inside in five minutes there will be no outings at all for you next week and no television either.'

I turned and began decisively up the garden, the torch beam concentrated a little in front of me. It's essential when issuing an ultimatum to a child who has been behaving badly not to hesitate, otherwise they can spot a flaw in your resolve and call your bluff. I didn't know if I would carry out my threat and I hoped I wouldn't have to be put to the test. Adrian and Paula still had their faces pressed against the window and could see I was coming in without Alex. Inside I took off my shoes and then, leaving the back door slightly open, I went into the living room.

'Isn't Alex coming in?' Adrian asked, worried.

'I hope so, in a minute. But close the curtains now.' I didn't want Alex to feel he had an audience and would lose face by returning.

A few minutes later we heard a movement in the kitchen. I went in. Alex was sitting on the floor taking off his muddy shoes. I didn't say anything but busied myself with drying some dishes until he'd finished. Without speaking he went into the living room to join Adrian and Paula. I quickly locked the back door and put the key out of reach on a nearby shelf, then I went into the living room, where I read Paula a story while the boys played separately on the floor.

I didn't let Alex watch any television that evening and he didn't ask if he could. He also had an early night. As I said goodnight I reminded him that he could talk to me at any time about his worries, but he wasn't to run off again. He turned away from me and, pressing his cheek against his soft toy, closed his eyes.

'Goodnight then, love,' I said. 'Tomorrow is a new day and a new start.' I waited to see if he would say anything or if he wanted a hug, but he remained on his side, facing away from me, so I came out.

Alex must have been exhausted from riding his bike in the park and running around the garden, for he slept until after eight o'clock without waking in the night. Adrian and Paula, tired from a fun day out with their father, slept well too.

I always start each day afresh and encourage children to do the same, so I greeted Alex with a bright, 'Hello, love. You had a good sleep. How are you?' There was no reply. I began setting out his clothes for the day and as I did I talked about the fun things we were going to do during the week, starting with a trip to the cinema that afternoon. Alex met my enthusiasm with expressionless silence, so with a cheerful 'come down for breakfast when you're ready' I left him to get dressed.

The morning was free, so after breakfast I covered the table in the kitchen-cum-diner with a plastic tablecloth, set out paints and paper and gave each child an apron. Most children love painting, but Alex approached this activity as he was now approaching everything – with silent apathy, as if it was a chore, with no real interest or commitment, despite my enthusiasm and encouragement. Debbie telephoned while they were painting, and I took the call in the hall where I could keep an eye on them but remain out of earshot. She began by saying that she had arranged Alex's LAC review for Friday at 10.30 a.m. and she'd put the invitations and questionnaires for the review in the post. She then asked how Alex had been and I gave her an update, including my concerns that Alex might be depressed. I asked her if it was possible to bring forward his appointment for CAMHS and Debbie said she'd see what she could do but didn't hold out much hope. She had children on her books with problems far more urgent than Alex's who were still waiting for a first appointment. I thought it was sad that so many children were now in need of urgent counselling and therapy. When I told Debbie that Alex had been running away at home and school she said, 'But his behaviour is manageable?'

'Yes. At present.' I knew why she was asking. The care plan for Alex was that he should live with a foster carer long term, but if his behaviour was very challenging then the social services would struggle to find him a suitable home. 'Although I don't suppose another move will help him,' I added.

'There were no concerns about his behaviour before. It's bound to take a while for him to settle down again after his disappointment.'

Disappointment! I thought. Devastation might be a better word to describe what he must have felt when he'd heard that his adoptive family didn't want him.

Alex came to the cinema with the same silent lethargy that now seemed to dominate most of his waking hours – he was present in body but not in spirit. He watched the film and ate the popcorn without sharing the enjoyment shown by Adrian, Paula and the other children around us, who laughed, cheered and shouted as children do at kids' movies when they are having fun. When the film finished and the lights went up I asked Adrian, Alex and Paula if they'd had a nice time. Predictably, Adrian and Paula said they had and asked when we could come again, while Alex said nothing.

That evening, while I was making dinner, Alex came to me. 'What did Debbie want?' he asked in a small voice. I was pleased he was taking the initiative and instigating conversation. Although I'd told him this morning why Debbie had phoned, I was happy to tell him again.

'To see how you are getting on and to tell us about the review.' Alex knew what a review was from having attended previous ones before.

His face set. 'I don't want a review,' he said. 'I'm not going. All those people lie.' Turning, he fled from the kitchen and then stomped upstairs to his room. I heard his door slam shut. I set down what I was doing and went after him. I was in the hall when I heard the first crash.

CHAPTER SIXTEEN

SAY SOMETHING POSITIVE

'What's that?' Adrian cried in alarm from the living room. 'It's Alex. I'm going to him now.'

I hurried up the stairs to his bedroom as one crash followed another. After giving a perfunctory knock on his door I went in. A toy car zoomed past my head and crashed into the wall behind me.

'Alex! Put that down,' I said as he picked up another toy ready to throw. 'You'll break it.'

'Don't care!'

He threw it. The floor was already littered with items he'd thrown in the short time it had taken me to leave the kitchen and come upstairs: toys, books, his new trainers: in fact, anything that had come to hand.

'That's enough!' I said as he raised his hand again. A box of crayons flew across the room. I went over and, taking him by the arm, drew him away from the toy box.

'Leave me alone!' he cried, struggling.

'No. You're going to regret breaking your toys. I know you're angry and upset, but this isn't the way to show it.'

'Yes, it is!' He pulled against me, trying to reach a book, possibly to hit me with.

'No, Alex. Come and sit down and calm down.'

'I hate you!' he cried. He was easily held, he was so small and light.

'Alex, if you're angry punch the pillow,' I said, directing him to the pillow on his bed. 'It's better than breaking your toys or hitting me.' I thumped the pillow hard with my fist to demonstrate. 'You can hit the pillow as hard as you like.' I'd encouraged other children I'd fostered to pillow or cushion thump when they needed to let go of their anger. It was one of the techniques I used. 'Go on. Thump it hard, like I am,' I said, pummelling the pillow. He followed my example and thumped the pillow a few times, then turned his anger on his soft toys and thumped them too. He immediately regretted it and burst into tears.

'I'm sorry,' he said, picking up Simba and hugging him. 'I'm sorry, I didn't mean to hurt you.'

I eased him down to sit on the bed and I sat next to him. 'Simba will be OK,' I said gently. 'Lions are very strong.'

Alex buried his face in his soft toy and cried quietly, his anger spent for now. I slipped my arm around his waist. 'It's OK,' I said. 'You'll be all right soon.'

Footsteps sounded on the stairs and then Paula appeared at Alex's bedroom door, looking very worried. I threw her a reassuring smile. 'You go down with Adrian. Alex and I will be down soon.' She gave a small nod, turned and went downstairs.

'We're all worried about you,' I said to Alex. 'Adrian, Paula, me and Debbie.'

'I'm not going to my review,' he said through his tears.

'If you really don't want to, you don't have to. You can tell me what you want to say.' But I knew this wasn't the only reason for his anger.

He sniffed and drew his hand across his eyes. I reached for a tissue. 'You can tell them I don't want to be adopted again,' he said tightly.

'OK. But I think Debbie has already told you that she's looking for a special foster family for you where you will be the youngest or only child.'

'Because of what happened with James?' he asked astutely. I wiped his eyes. 'I tried to get on with him, honest I did.'

'I know, love. It wasn't your fault. You need to believe that.'

'They lie at my reviews,' Alex said bitterly. 'At my last one they promised I'd have a forever family. I'm not going to any more reviews because they lie.'

'I understand it must look that way. But no one knew this would happen. We all thought it would be good for you.' His little face was so sad and pitiful. I dearly wished I could take his pain away. It was difficult to know what else I could say. We were quiet for a moment. 'Alex, I know what happened seems dreadful now, and of course you are feeling upset and angry, but I have found in life that often things happen for a reason. Even things that go wrong and seem very bad at the time can turn out for the best in the end. Does that make any sense?'

He shook his head. 'I wanted a family, but they didn't want me.'

'Perhaps that wasn't the right family for you,' I suggested.

'But you all said it was.'

'I know. We thought so. They seemed right, but perhaps if you'd stayed there you would have been unhappy. We won't ever know. But what I'm saying is that possibly in the future you may think that what happened was for the best.' Unlikely though this seemed at present, I had to give him some hope.

Alex didn't say anything further, and very likely my philosophy was too much for a seven-year-old. We sat together for a while longer, Alex cuddling Simba and me with my arm around him. I was aware that Adrian and Paula were alone downstairs and worried. 'Do you feel you could come down now?' I asked. 'Adrian and Paula will be wondering where you are.'

He nodded, tucked Simba into bed and then we stood, stepping over the thrown toys as we left his room. Downstairs Alex joined Adrian and Paula in the living room and, squatting on the floor, he continued with the puzzle he'd been doing previously. Adrian and Paula glanced at him and then at me. I nodded and they resumed what they were doing. I knew they wouldn't say anything to Alex about his outburst, for they appreciated that all children get angry and upset sometimes, and no one wants a reminder once they're over it. Alex would be helping me clear up his room later though, which should make him less likely to throw things in anger again in the future.

If I'm honest the half-term holiday grew more and more fraught, despite the activities I'd arranged. Alex's behaviour steadily deteriorated. He exploded into anger at the smallest provocation, although he was never cruel or unkind to Adrian and Paula. He was also running away whenever we were out, despite my watching him very carefully. His running off not only caused me a lot of worry but also embarrassment. Losing a child once is forgivable, but losing them regularly isn't. On Tuesday Alex disappeared while we were at the indoor activity centre, and after a frantic search by me and the staff he was found hiding in the men's toilets. I told him off and cut half an hour of his television time. Then on Wednesday morning, while we were shopping for some new school trousers for him, I turned to the hangers to select another size and he was gone. Adrian and Paula didn't see in which direction he'd vanished, and we began calling his name and hunting around the rails of clothes. With no sight of him I became increasingly anxious, and I reported him missing to one of the assistants, who put out a call over the Tannoy system. After another very anxious fifteen minutes he was found – the security guard had stopped him as he was about to leave the store. Reunited, I thanked the guard profusely, told Alex off and warned him of the dangers of running away. I also said that if he didn't stop running off I wouldn't be able to take him out again. The thought of what could have happened to him had he left the store tormented me for the rest of the day. That evening I heard Adrian say to Alex, 'You must stop running away. It makes us all worried and Mum upset.'

'She's not my mum,' Alex replied tellingly.

And of course producing a reaction in us was most likely the reason Alex was running off – if we were worried and upset then it proved we cared. I told him often that we cared, but for a child like Alex who'd been badly let down and was convinced that no one loved him, seeing our concern was far more effective than me telling him: actions speak louder than words. Did he believe I cared? I didn't know, but on Thursday morning I cut short our trip to the swimming pool, as Alex kept leaving the water and running off into the changing rooms, male and female. I couldn't leave Adrian and Paula unsupervised in the water, so I had to keep getting everyone out of the pool to go and find him. It was very stressful, so after about thirty minutes of this I apologized to Adrian and Paula and said it was best if we all left.

'It's OK, Mum,' Adrian said amicably. 'I've had a nice swim.' I knew he would have liked to have stayed longer, so I was touched and grateful that he was being so understanding.

The questionnaires for Alex's review had arrived in the post on Tuesday morning. One for me and one for him. They were only short – ten or so questions, printed on a form for the carer and a child-friendly booklet for the child. The questions for the carer were around how the child was doing in the placement, while the booklet for the child asked how they felt about being in care and what life was like with their carer. I'd completed my form on Tuesday evening – it had taken about fifteen minutes – but I'd put off giving Alex his as I knew that there were at least two questions he would find upsetting: 'What has gone well for you since your last review?' 'What hasn't gone well?'

I usually sat with the child while they completed their booklet to help with any questions they couldn't read or didn't understand. Both forms would be handed to the independent reviewing officer (IRO) at the start of the review. As the foster carer I was expected to encourage the child to complete the booklet, so after dinner on Thursday, with the review the following morning, I knew I couldn't put it off any longer. Once Adrian and Paula were occupied in the living room, I took Alex aside and, handing him the booklet, said we needed to fill it in now and that I'd help him if he wished. He knew what was involved from the reviews he'd attended before.

'I'm not writing in that,' he said firmly. 'I'm not going to my review.' He passed the booklet back.

'I think we should try to answer a few questions,' I said, opening the booklet to show him. The first one is easy: 'Do you know why you're in care?'

'I'm not answering any,' he said, and turned away.

'What about if I do the writing and you tell me what to write?' Which is what I'd done previously with some of the children I'd fostered, especially those with learning difficulties who couldn't read or write.

'No. I'm not telling you what to write,' he said, and his face set. 'They lie. They don't care.'

'They do care and they'd like to know what you think. But if you really don't want to fill it in, OK.' I wasn't going to make an issue of it and I closed the booklet.

'Can I go now?' he asked.

'Yes.'

He looked slightly surprised, perhaps thinking I was going to lecture him or stop his television, but managing a child's behaviour is as much about what you can reasonably let go as what they have to do. So while it was crucial that Alex stopped running away, for his own safety, completing the booklet was desirable but not essential.

* * *

That night Alex didn't have a nightmare as such but did a lot of sleep talking, clearly grappling with the issues he was having to deal with. One time when I went into his room to settle him I had to smile, as he was talking about his social worker being eaten by a lion. Simba? I reassured him there wasn't a real lion and he went back to sleep. Dreams are nature's way of cleansing the subconscious.

The following morning, by 10.15, I had the children settled at the table in the kitchen-cum-diner with lots of activities to keep them occupied while the review was taking place in the living room. LAC reviews tend to be formal wherever they are held, and Adrian and Paula knew that once everyone had arrived and the meeting was taking place we weren't to be disturbed unless there was an emergency. Alex was still refusing to attend his review or speak to anyone who came to it.

Jill arrived first and as I took her coat she asked me how Alex's behaviour had been since the last time we'd spoken. I said mixed. I'd go into more detail at the review. She looked in on the children to say hello. Adrian and Paula managed a small, shy hello, but Alex kept his head firmly down and, true to his word, said nothing. Debbie arrived next and as I took her coat I told her that Alex was refusing to attend his review and we hadn't completed his questionnaire. 'Perhaps he'll join us later,' she said. I showed her where the children were and she said, 'Hi, how are you?'

Alex said nothing, while Adrian and Paula managed another small hello. Debbie joined Jill in the living room and I made them coffee. A few minutes later the independent reviewing officer (IRO), Lorraine, arrived. I hadn't met her before, although I knew from the paperwork that she had been the reviewing officer at Alex's previous, more recent reviews.

'I certainly didn't expect to be seeing Alex again so soon,' Lorraine said regretfully.

'No,' I agreed. Once a child is adopted they are no longer in care, so no longer have reviews.

I took Lorraine through to Alex and she said hello and received the same response. We both joined Debbie and Jill in the living room. Lorraine didn't want a coffee. The number of people attending a LAC review varies. There can be a room full, but today there would just be the four of us – five if Alex attended. His teacher would have normally been present, but because it was the half-term holiday she was away. Lin, who'd been present at Alex's previous review – the last before the introductions to Rosemary and Edward had begun – wouldn't be coming, as her involvement had finished with the end of the adoption.

I handed Lorraine the questionnaires, explaining that Alex hadn't wanted to complete his, and sat down. Lorraine opened the meeting by asking us to introduce ourselves, which was usual at the start of all LAC reviews. She made a note of the date and time of the review and the names of those present, then recorded apologies for absence from Miss Cork and also from Shanice, who apparently was a member of the permanency team and had been invited but couldn't attend. Debbie said she'd include Shanice's progress in finding Alex a long-term foster family in her report. I felt there was a strange atmosphere as we sat there completing the formalities before the meeting began in earnest, which could best be described as reserved trepidation, perhaps defensiveness, as though we were on guard and bracing ourselves, for this was the first review since the adoption had failed and it wasn't going to be easy.

'I understand from Cathy that Alex doesn't want to join us,' Lorraine said, addressing us all. 'I saw him before this meeting and I'll see him again at the end.' It was good practice for the IRO to at least see the child as part of the review. She drew a breath. 'I was very sorry to learn that Alex's adoption had failed, and so quickly.' IROs are usually updated prior to a review. 'I understand a disruption meeting will be held. Has a date been set for that yet?' she asked Debbie.

'Not yet, no,' Debbie said.

'I think the sooner the better, don't you?'

'I'll speak to Lin and arrange it,' Debbie said, making a note.

Lorraine now looked at me. 'Thankfully, Alex was able to return here, or it would have been another new set of foster carers. How is he doing? Is he coping?'

'Just,' I said. I stopped, as a worrying thought occurred to me. 'Sorry,' I said, standing. 'I won't be a minute. I just need to check on something.' Leaving them looking slightly bemused I went quickly down the hall to the front door where I checked that the latch was on, and then hurried through to the back door to make sure the key was out of reach, which it was. As I passed the children I threw them a smile and then hurried back into the living room.

'Sorry,' I said again as I took my seat. 'I needed to check the doors. Alex has been running away and I now keep the latch down on the front door and the key out of the back door. We can get out in an emergency, but it gives me extra time to stop him if he tries to run away.'

'Has he been trying to run away much?' Lorraine asked, concerned.

'Yes, and it's on the increase.' I then related the instances.

'And he didn't try to run away when he was here before?' Lorraine asked.

'No.'

She made a note and then looked at me again. 'Please tell us more about Alex.'

When asked about a child I'm fostering I like to start with the positives – their strengths and what is going well for them, although at present for Alex that was going to be difficult. 'Alex is eating well,' I said, 'and he sleeps reasonably well, although he has started having nightmares. He has good self-care skills – he washes and dresses himself, and his play is age-appropriate. He does his homework when asked, although his teacher said he had difficulty concentrating last week. There were also a few incidents at school – Alex became angry and tried to run away.'

'As I remember he was doing well at school,' Lorraine said, glancing up from writing to look at Debbie.

'Yes, he was,' Debbie said. 'I have spoken to his teacher and the school is doing all they can to help him settle again.'

'So this behaviour is a result of what happened with the Andrews?' Andrews was the family name of Rosemary, Edward and James.

'Yes,' Debbie said. 'It should pass once Alex recovers from his disappointment.'

Lorraine looked at me to continue.

'I also have concerns that Alex may be depressed,' I said. 'Debbie is referring him to CAMHS.'

'What makes you think he is depressed?' Lorraine asked.

'Alex has outbursts of anger, but most of the time he is very quiet and withdrawn. I include him in all activities, but nothing seems to interest him now.'

'Does he talk to you about how he is feeling?'

'Only a little. I think he is keeping a lot to himself. He's obviously devastated by what happened. He was so looking forward to having a family of his own, and of course we told him it would be his last move.'

Lorraine nodded thoughtfully as she wrote and then asked Debbie, 'Do we have an appointment yet for CAMHS?'

'No. I've made the referral, but it could take two months. There is a waiting list and Alex's case isn't classified as urgent.'

Lorraine wrote. 'This is all so sad,' she said, voicing her thoughts. 'It should never have happened.' Then, looking at me: 'You have two children. How does Alex get along with them?'

'When he was here before they all played together nicely, but now he doesn't want much to do with them. He sits with Adrian and Paula – as they are doing now – but he won't be playing *with* them. He doesn't talk to them much either. He is often in the same room as them but alone, if you know what I mean.'

Lorraine, Jill and Debbie nodded. Jill and Debbie were taking notes too.

'Have there been any issues between Alex and Adrian?' Lorraine asked.

'No. Alex is very good at getting on with other children, or rather he used to be. I think he's had to fit in with so many foster families that he knows about sharing and taking turns. He's not a child who squabbles or is always demanding attention. I'm aware that the permanency team is looking for a long-term foster family where there are no siblings of a similar age to Alex, but I really don't see that as an issue.'

Lorraine nodded as she wrote, and then said, 'Thank you, Cathy. Is there anything else you would like to tell us about Alex?'

'He does get angry sometimes, but that's only to be expected.' I then outlined the instances of his anger at home and the ones I knew about at school. 'But that's not the real Alex,' I said. 'He's upset at present. I'm doing all I can to help him, but it breaks my heart to see him so unhappy.' Embarrassingly, I teared up.

Lorraine smiled at me kindly. 'Hopefully the referral to CAMHS will come through before too long.' I nodded. 'When I saw Alex at his last review it was clear then that he had all his hopes pinned on his new family,' Lorraine said. 'Do you think that finding a suitable long-term foster family will help him? He's never had a family of his own and he obviously knows he's only here temporarily.'

'I don't know,' I said. 'I suppose it might. I would offer to keep him, but I'm aware of the concern that Adrian is the same age.'

'Thank you, Cathy,' Lorraine said noncommittally. 'And thank you for looking after Alex so well.'

It was Debbie's turn to speak now. She began by giving an update on what had happened since the last review, including

Alex's first move to me, the introductions to Rosemary, Edward and James (which she said had gone well), Alex's move to them and then the swift breakdown of the place-ment, and Alex's return to me.

'And their reasons were that Alex and James didn't get along and that James was happier as an only child?' Lorraine clarified.

Debbie nodded. 'Rosemary said they'd made a big mistake in wanting to adopt at all.'

'Some mistake,' Lorraine said dryly, making a note. Then she looked up. 'But sadly this is not the only case I've come across recently. Last month I was the reviewing officer for two brothers – aged six and seven – who were placed for adoption and then returned to care after only a week.'

CHAPTER SEVENTEEN

NOT TO BLAME

Debbie continued her report to the LAC review by confirming the changes in the care plan for Alex – that the permanency team were looking for a long-term foster family for him. She said that as they couldn't find a suitable family locally they were widening their search (through independent fostering agencies) to other parts of the country. This is not unusual and some children in care end up living hundreds of miles from their place of origin because there isn't a suitable carer nearer. None of us commented. The priority was to find Alex the right family, but I'm sure we all thought that a move out of the area would mean more disruption for him – leaving all that was familiar, including his school. And supposing that placement didn't work out? It happens.

Lorraine nodded sombrely, noted what Debbie had said and then referred to her checklist to see what else she needed to include in the review.

'Has Alex had any serious illnesses or accidents since his last review?' she asked. Debbie confirmed he hadn't and that his health checks were up to date.

'Friends and family?' Lorraine now asked. 'Contact with his mother was stopped in preparation for the adoption. Does Alex have friends at school?'

'Yes,' Debbie said. 'But I'm not sure he sees them out of school.'

'I've asked Alex if he would like to invite a friend here,' I said. 'But he doesn't want to at present. I'll ask him again.'

'Thank you,' Lorraine said, and made a note. All the points raised would be revisited at the next review to see what progress had been made.

'Any complaints from anyone?' Lorraine now asked. It was a question the IRO was obliged to ask at the review.

'No,' Debbie confirmed.

'No,' Jill and I said.

Satisfied that she'd covered everything on her checklist, Lorraine now asked Jill if she would like to add anything to the review.

'As Cathy's support social worker I visit her at least every month and we speak on the phone in between when necessary. I didn't see Alex when he was here before on the bridging placement, but I have seen him since. I think Cathy has given an accurate account of how he is at present. He's upset and obviously has a lot to come to terms with. Cathy provides a high level of care for Alex and I know she will ask for help if she needs it.'

'Thank you,' Lorraine said. She then set a date and time for the next review – in three months. Although Alex might not be with me by then, possibly having moved to his long-term carer, I noted the date in my diary just in case.

'I'll go and see Alex now,' Lorraine said. She tucked her notepad and pen into her bag and stood.

'Would you like us all to come?' Debbie asked, putting away her pad and pen.

'No. I think it could be a bit overwhelming for Alex, as he's feeling wobbly.' This was sensitive of her. Most children in care take part in reviews far bigger than this one, with all the attention focused on them. They do incredibly well to cope with it.

'That's a lovely picture, Alex,' we heard Lorraine say as she went in. 'Can you tell me about it?' There was no reply. 'Do you like art at school?' she asked. 'Is that one of your favourite subjects?' If Alex replied, it was too quiet for us to hear. 'Do you remember who I am?' Lorraine then tried, 'We've met a few times before at your previous reviews.' Nothing.

There was silence and then Paula ran into the living room, looking concerned, and jumped onto my lap. 'There's a strange lady in there talking to Alex,' she said. Jill and Debbie laughed.

'I know, love,' I said. 'It's OK. Alex knows her.'

We heard Lorraine compliment both boys on their artwork and then she returned to the living room. 'Alex doesn't want to talk to me today,' she said easily. She picked up her bag and Debbie and Jill stood.

The three of them went into the kitchen to say goodbye to Alex and Adrian, and then Paula and I saw them to the front door, where I helped them into their coats. Once they'd gone, we returned to Adrian and Alex. 'You've all done well,' I said. They'd been amusing themselves for over an hour.

'Thank you for your cooperation. I was thinking we might go out for lunch and then to the cinema this afternoon. There's the new Walt Disney film showing.'

'Yes!' Adrian cried. 'Chicken nuggets and chips for me!' Going to a fast-food restaurant was a treat for my children, as we didn't go that often.

'Chicken nuggets and chips for me,' Paula agreed.

While Alex managed a small, indifferent nod.

I'd suggested this outing as being seated in a restaurant and then the cinema offered less opportunity for Alex to run away. It was a pity I had to think this way, but I needed to be practical.

It was the end of the half-term holiday, so families were making the most of the last day and the restaurant and cinema were busy. Alex was quiet as usual, looking around and taking it in but not saying much, while Adrian and Paula chatted excitedly as they ate, and also after the film. I think Alex liked the film as much as he liked anything at present, but as soon as we were home he went straight up to his room and began throwing things in anger.

'Not again,' Adrian sighed, and he took Paula through to the living room to look after her.

Once I'd calmed Alex down and he'd had a little cry, I asked him why he'd suddenly become angry after a nice day out. I was puzzled as well as concerned.

'All the other kids in McDonald's and the cinema were with their families,' he said gloomily. 'But I was with a foster carer. I should have been with my family.'

'And that's why you're upset?'

He nodded and I wiped his eyes.

I knew that Rosemary and Edward had promised Alex lots of outings over the half-term holiday, but his upset wasn't about missing those activities as missing the family he'd been promised. I comforted him as best I could and said that when we missed something we often noticed it more in others and it seemed that their lives were better than ours. I couldn't offer any reassurance about being with a foster carer because when Alex left it would be to go to another foster carer, albeit a long-term one. Having foster parents rather than a mum and dad is something many children in permanent care have to come to terms with, and often after a while they think of their foster family as their own family and call their carers Mum and Dad. Thankfully, as before, once Alex's anger was spent he let me give him a hug.

The following week was shaky at school and at home for Alex. Miss Cork saw me with a brief update either before or after school on most days. She was very kind and caring, but acknowledged that the half-term break had done little to improve Alex's behaviour, and he remained quiet and withdrawn with outbursts of anger at school – just as he was at home. She apologized for not being able to attend Alex's review and said she'd sent Debbie a copy of Alex's latest personal education plan. I appreciated that she and the other staff were making allowances for Alex's behaviour (as we were at home), but if he didn't do his work in class then he finished it at home.

Halfway through the week Alex started bedwetting – a sure sign of stress. I reassured him that it didn't matter, quietly changed his sheets and tried again to talk to him about his worries, but all I got in return was a resigned shrug. Aware that on top of all his feelings of rejection and being unloved and unwanted he was probably also feeling very insecure, I told him that he wouldn't have to move from me until Debbie was sure she'd found him the right family. But to be honest my words sounded feeble even to me, for how many times had something similar been said to him before? He shrugged, unconvinced.

On Thursday morning Jill telephoned to see how Alex was and also to advise me that Debbie had arranged the adoption disruption meeting for the following Tuesday at 11 a.m. I had been invited and Jill would be going too. 'You'll need to prepare yourself for meeting Rosemary again,' she said. 'And possibly Edward, if he can get the time off work.'

'They're going?' I asked, slightly surprised.

'Yes. Rosemary was reluctant to begin with, but Debbie explained that it wasn't going to be a witch hunt. That the social services wanted to learn lessons from what had happened to avoid something similar happening again.'

'All right. I'll have to arrange childcare for Paula. She's not at nursery on a Tuesday.'

'Thank you. The meeting is at the council offices. Shall I see you in reception?'

'Yes, please.'

I noted the time of the meeting in my diary and then straight away telephoned my parents, who were free that day and happy to come over and look after Paula. They would stay until Adrian and Alex came out of school so they could see them, although Mum understood that Alex might not want much to do with them.

The remainder of the week and then the weekend continued in much the same vein. Alex was very quiet or angry; there was nothing in between. I asked him again if he would like to have a friend home, but he said despondently that he didn't have any friends. This wasn't true, he had friends at school, but I knew from Miss Cork that he wasn't having much to do with them at present. Alex's unhappiness and low self-esteem was blighting all aspects of his life, and despite my efforts he didn't seem to be improving. I kept a note of my concerns and incidents of his anger in my log so that I could update Debbie (and Jill), and I hoped it might help bring Alex's referral to CAMHS forward. At what point did his case become urgent?

On Sunday evening as Alex climbed into bed he suddenly asked me, 'Was it because I wanted to learn the guitar?'

I hadn't a clue what he was talking about.

'Sorry, love, what do you mean? Are you going to learn the guitar at school?'

He shook his head vehemently. 'When my dad – I mean Edward – said I should learn a musical instrument I said I wanted to learn the guitar so I could be in a boy band. He laughed and said that I needed to learn a classical instrument that would teach me the scales like James. Is that why he didn't want me?'

'Alex, of course not!' I said, shocked. 'It had nothing to do with that, and he shouldn't have laughed.' Despite all my assurances, Alex was still clearly going through the conversations he'd had with Rosemary and Edward, dissecting them to see if he could find out what he had done wrong. 'It was nothing you said or did,' I said firmly, sitting beside him on the bed.

'Are you sure?'

'Yes. Positive. If you'd wanted to learn every musical instrument in the whole wide world it wouldn't have made any difference. The reason you left was because Rosemary and Edward hadn't thought enough about adoption and what it would mean to them and James. They should have done. It was a big mistake that they didn't. But it was not your fault. You must understand that. Sometimes adults get it wrong, just as children do. We all make mistakes.' I could feel the heat rising to my cheeks. I was passionate in what I said – he had to believe me. I looked at him carefully. 'But Alex, do you know what the biggest mistake of all would be?' He shook his head. 'If you continue to let this make you so unhappy. You need to try to let it go and look to the future. I think you could if you tried really hard. I will help you.' Without replying, he picked up his soft-toy polar bear, climbed into bed and turned away, rejecting me.

'Please think about what I've said.' I tucked the duvet around his shoulders. 'You need to get over this. It can't stay with you forever.' Although I knew that to what degree he did get over this would depend largely on what happened in his future. If the long-term carers he went to provided him with a stable, loving home and he became a permanent member of their family then there was a good chance he'd be able to leave behind the upset of his unsettled early life. But if the move to the next family didn't work out and there was another move and possibly another one after that, then his experience with Rosemary and Edward would be compounded: another brick in a wall of unhappiness and rejection. I knew too many cases where a series of placement breakdowns (as they are called) had damaged a young person so much that they turned to drink and drugs and promiscuity in an attempt to block out the pain and convince themselves they were lovable. Hopefully that wouldn't be Alex's fate, but at present it was impossible to be sure, and if – heaven forbid – it was his future, then not only Alex's mother and Rosemary and Edward, but every foster carer and social worker who had been part of Alex's life would hold some responsibility.

The adoption disruption meeting had been playing on my mind since Jill's telephone call, and by Monday morning it was completely dominating my thoughts – or, more specifically, seeing Rosemary and Edward was. Debbie had said that the meeting wouldn't be a witch hunt – they weren't looking to blame someone – but that the department wanted to learn lessons. I thought this was very magnanimous of Debbie, as I was struggling not to blame Rosemary and Edward for all the grief they had caused – and were still causing – Alex. Each time he said something about them it hit me afresh. But I knew I needed to be professional when I met them. I had to concede that it was decent of them to attend the meeting at all, and that they hadn't set out to reject and upset Alex, but must have been convinced they were doing the right thing in applying to adopt. Furthermore, I doubted that they had any idea just how devastated he was.

I didn't tell the children what the meeting was about, only that I had to go to a meeting and Nana and Grandpa would be looking after Paula, and they would see Adrian and Alex at the end of school. Paula and Adrian were pleased to be seeing their nana and grandpa again, while Alex just accepted the arrangement with the same resignation he accepted anything that involved him now.

Although it was March, Tuesday morning was bitterly cold with a cruel northeasterly wind, so the children and I wrapped up warm to leave the house. I drove Alex to school first and then took Adrian to school before returning home with Paula. My parents arrived in plenty of time and I made us a coffee before I changed into my black trousers, smart jersey and best coat, ready for the meeting. Saying goodbye, I left and began the drive to the council offices, my feelings of trepidation increasing. I wasn't altogether clear what my role would be at the adoption disruption meeting, but from what Jill had said my input was likely to be minimal: to answer some questions about Alex from the present foster carer's point of view. I hadn't brought any notes with me and intended to play it by ear. As I drove and my apprehension increased, I reminded myself that Rosemary and Edward must be feeling significantly worse, having to face all of us again.

I parked the car in a side road close to the council offices and walked round to the front, where I met Jill on the way in.

'Good timing,' she quipped. 'All ready?'

'As ready as I'll ever be.'

We crossed to the reception desk and signed the visitor's book. Jill asked which room we were in and we hung our one-day security passes around our necks. The room was on the second floor, next door to the one I'd been in previously for the adoption planning meeting. As we arrived outside, Jill took a deep breath. 'Well, here goes,' she said before knocking, which did nothing to allay my nerves. She opened the door and I followed her in. A sea of faces greeted us.

I find you can gauge the atmosphere of a meeting as soon as you enter the room. In complete contrast to the adoption planning meeting, where Jill and I had been greeted by lively conversation and four smiling faces, now there was silence and sombre expressions. A dozen or more people around a large oblong wooden table sat upright and formal. Most had paperwork in front of them. I felt my anxiety level rise. I recognized Rosemary, Edward, Lin and Debbie, but no one else. The person in front of us moved along a seat so Jill and I could sit together.

'Thank you,' Jill said quietly as we sat down. I slipped off my coat, hung it over the back of my chair and tried to relax.

After a moment the chairperson asked, 'Are we expecting anyone else?'

No one appeared to know.

'If we could introduce ourselves, I'll tick everyone off my list,' she said. The chairperson would be an IRO not connected with the case. She was a mature woman, confident in her role, and with a calming, conciliatory manner designed to put everyone at ease. She squared a sheet of printed paper in front of her and looked to the person on her left to start the introductions.

'Elaine C—, team manager, fostering and adoption,' she said.

The chairperson ticked off her name on the sheet and then looked at the next person, who was Debbie. 'Debbie G—, social worker for Alex.'

And so it continued: 'Lin B—, adoption social worker for Alex.'

'Lara M—, team manager.'

'Shanice K—, social worker from the permanence team.'

As the introductions continued the door opened and to my surprise Miss Cork walked in. 'Sorry if I'm late,' she said, a little flustered. 'I was only told about the meeting this morning.' She took one of the two remaining chairs and I threw her a reassuring smile.

'Adele W—, social worker, looked-after children's team,' the next person at the table said.

I glanced at Rosemary and Edward across the vast expanse of oak table, but there was nothing to be read in their expressions and they kept their gazes down. When it was their turn to introduce themselves they said only 'Rosemary Andrews' and 'Edward Andrews' without any reference to their role as Alex's adoptive parents. Edward and a trainee social worker who was also taking minutes were the only males present.

Next was the nurse for looked-after children, then another social worker and me. 'Cathy Glass, Alex's foster carer,' I said, addressing the chairperson.

'You were his carer before the move as well?' she asked.

'Yes, just for a few weeks.'

She nodded.

There were fifteen of us in all, including three team managers, the size of the meeting reflecting the importance that was being attached to what had happened to Alex.

Introductions over, the chairperson noted an apology for absence and then looked at us as she spoke. She began by thanking us for coming – she knew how busy we all were –

then made a special point of thanking Rosemary and Edward. She appreciated that coming to this meeting would have been difficult for them. Edward gave a perfunctory nod, but he and Rosemary remained expressionless.

'The purpose of this meeting', the chairperson continued, 'is not to apportion blame, but to see if we can identify any significant factors that led to the disruption of the placement. This information will help the department assess if its preparation, matching and support of families is adequate and also plan for Alex's future. We shall hear from all those who had a role in Alex's case and participants will have a chance to share information and their feelings.' She then asked Debbie, as Alex's social worker, to speak first. Judging from the thickness of the papers she had in front of her, I guessed she was well prepared.

'Alex is seven now,' she began, then stated his date and place of birth, his ethnicity and that he was the subject of a Full Care Order. 'I took over Alex's case nine months ago after his previous social worker left.'

'Do we know how many social workers Alex has had?' the chairperson asked.

'I'm not completely sure,' Debbie said, 'but more than five.'

The chairperson nodded and Debbie continued by giving some background information on Alex's mother and the reason she and Alex had come to the attention of the social services. She then summarized Alex's time in care, some of which I already knew from the placement information. However, hearing it said out loud highlighted just how unsettled Alex's life had been, even since coming into care. His return to me was his seventh move since he first came into care. The original care plan had been for Alex to return to his mother, which I didn't know. But despite her enrolling on a drug rehabilitation programme, she hadn't made the necessary changes to her lifestyle to enable Alex to be returned to her. Face-to-face contact had been stopped in preparation for the adoption and it was intended that she would have 'letterbox contact' only, which meant that she could send Alex a card and letter on his birthday and at Christmas, but that was all. Debbie said that generally Alex had coped well during his time in care, although he had become unsettled since returning to me, after all the recent changes. I saw Edward look up as though he might be about to say something, but he didn't comment.

Debbie continued by saying that Alex was generally in good health, was developing normally and didn't require specialist support, although she had made a referral to CAMHS. She explained the reasons for this – that some of Alex's behaviour suggested he could be depressed; that he had angry outbursts, and generally wasn't coping well with the adoption breakdown. She added that Alex had been doing well at school until now.

I saw Edward straighten in his chair and, clearly unable to contain his thoughts any longer, he said very brusquely, 'You can't blame us for all of this! The child clearly had issues before we ever met him.'

CHAPTER EIGHTEEN

LABELLED

I drew a breath, about to speak and leap to Alex's defence, but Jill touched my arm, advising me not to say anything at present.

'No one is blaming you,' the chairperson said calmly to Edward. His and Rosemary's defences were up and they were both staring confrontationally at her.

'It certainly sounds like it,' Edward said. 'My wife and I have sat here for over twenty minutes listening to how well Alex coped until he came to us.'

'I'm sorry if that was the impression, it wasn't the intention,' the chairperson said evenly. Debbie nodded. 'If we could let Alex's social worker finish her report. You and Mrs Andrews will both have a chance to speak later. I find it's useful if we hear the background information from the social workers involved in the case first, before the rest of us speak.' Said in such a calm, non-confrontational manner, it would have been unreasonable for Edward to object further. He clearly didn't like it and gave a small *humph*, but then, folding his arms across his chest, he sat back in his chair. 'Thank you,' the chairperson said, and looked to Debbie to continue.

'I've nearly finished,' Debbie said. 'In respect of Alex at school, I'm in regular contact with his teacher, Miss Cork, and the school are being very supportive of Alex. It's the same school he attended before the move. Lin was the social worker involved in placing Alex and she'll be able to say more about that process. The care plan now is to find a suitable long-term foster family for Alex.' She briefly consulted her notes and then said, 'I think that's all for now.'

'Thank you,' the chairperson said. Then, looking at Edward and Rosemary, 'I'd like to hear from Lin next and then it will be your turn.'

Edward gave a curt nod and the chairperson now asked Lin to speak. She began by explaining her role in the adoption and said she had been involved from the start. She gave a brief résumé of the selection process for would-be adopters, then more specifically in respect of Edward and Rosemary. She said they were a strong family unit who presented as being in a good position to give Alex an adoptive home and to meet his needs. She said that Edward's parents lived nearby and that she had met them and they had backed the adoption. Rosemary and Edward had attended the preparation course for would-be adopters and then, during the assessment, she had met with them eight times. She had also met James – with them and separately. During the assessment they had discussed their lifestyle and how different it was to that of any child who was likely to be placed with them. Rosemary and Edward appreciated this and the lasting impact that early-years experiences could have on a child. Lin said that they were keen to adopt a boy of a similar age to James. This was discussed at length and James was asked how he would feel, having been an only child. He had no cousins, although he did have friends who were invited home from school. All James's responses were very positive and he said he was looking forward to having a brother, as it was lonely being an only child. I could see Edward shifting in his seat, clearly uncomfortable at having his family discussed in front of him, which was understandable, although Lin was being as tactful as possible.

Lin then gave the date when she had taken Rosemary and Edward to the adoption panel, where they had been approved as adopters – there were no concerns from the panel members. By now Alex had been matched to Rosemary and Edward, although he was still living with his previous foster carers. Lin then covered Alex's move to me as an emergency bridging placement in some detail, as this could be relevant: the upheaval might have had a knock-on effect on Alex's behaviour after the move to Edward and Rosemary. She then mentioned the adoption planning meeting, which I'd attended, and described the introductions, which had gone very well. She said there was nothing in Alex's behaviour to suggest he'd been distressed from the last move.

'And Alex didn't display any behavioural problems during the bridging placement with Cathy, despite the sudden move?' the chairperson asked as the minute-taker wrote furiously.

'No,' Lin said. Debbie confirmed this to be so.

I glanced at Rosemary and Edward, who continued to stare at Lin with grim, fixed expressions. Although everyone was being very tactful, I knew this wasn't what they wanted to hear. Lin poured herself a glass of water from one of the jugs in the centre of the table and took a sip before continuing. A couple of others poured themselves water too.

'There were no real issues during the introductions beyond a bit of sibling rivalry,' Lin said, 'which was dealt with by Rosemary – the main care giver. Alex's move continued as planned and he went to live with Rosemary and Edward on –' She gave the date. 'Difficulties began almost immediately – mainly as a result of James and Alex. I received a phone call from Rosemary on the Thursday morning. She was very distressed and said that the boys weren't getting on at all – not as they had done during the introductions – and she didn't know how to deal with it. I spent some time talking to her on the phone and then visited the family that evening. I had hoped they would all be present, but there was only Rosemary and Alex. James had gone to his grandparents and Edward was going to collect him on his way back home from work later that evening. Rosemary said she felt it was better that the boys spent time apart.

'During my visit', Lin continued, 'I talked to Rosemary and Alex together and also separately. Alex was quieter than usual but appeared to be unaware of any problems between him and James. He said he loved his brother and missed him when he wasn't there. I asked Rosemary if she thought it would help if she talked to Cathy Glass, who is an experienced foster carer and also knew Alex from having fostered him. She thought it might, so I arranged for Cathy to visit Rosemary the following Tuesday. She spent two hours with her and was able to suggest some strategies to help with the boys. She also told Rosemary that she'd found in fostering it took time to bond with a child when they first arrived, and to gel as a family. Cathy told me afterwards that she felt her visit had been useful, and that Rosemary had mentioned the long school runs she was doing. We were considering changing Alex's school when the placement was terminated.'

'It is unusual for a placement to disrupt so quickly,' Lin's manager, who was seated beside Lin, now added.

This was the green flag Edward needed. 'That's because Alex wasn't the child you said he would be!' he snapped. 'You've just admitted that all those moves to different foster carers could have unsettled him, yet you are still trying to blame us! The boy couldn't relate to James or us, and I doubt he ever would have.'

There was a brief silence before Lin's manager spoke again, addressing Edward. 'Going to live with a new family is a huge life-changing experience for any child. It takes time for them to understand the new routines, expectations and customs of the family, before they start to relax and feel at home.'

'We had two weeks of introductions so he could get to know our "customs", as you put it,' Edward said, agitated. 'Unless you were expecting us to come down to his level?'

'His level?' Lin's manager queried.

'Yes. You know what I mean,' Edward retaliated. 'The boy has clearly been through a lot. I know he can't help that, but don't make us the scapegoats. We should have been made more aware of the significance of his early-years experience and the effect it was likely to have on him later.'

'What early-years experience exactly?' Debbie's manager now asked.

'His mother going to prison, for one,' Edward said.

Rosemary nodded vehemently. 'You can't leave all that behind. It's not his fault – it's in his genes.'

I leaned slightly forward to speak. I couldn't let this assassination of Alex's character continue. Jill didn't stop me this time. 'I'm sorry,' I said. 'I really don't understand what is being said here.'

'You may not be aware of all Alex's history as we are,' Rosemary said tersely, which was true. Adopters usually have access to all the child's history, whereas foster carers are given information on a 'need-to-know' basis. 'Alex's mother had been to prison a number of times for drug offences. She was a heavy drug user. That's bound to have affected him deep down.'

The chairperson looked to Debbie. 'Do we know if Alex was born with neonatal abstinence syndrome?' she asked. This is the term used to describe babies born with a drug dependency as a result of the mother being a drug user during pregnancy. The baby can suffer dreadful withdrawal in the first few weeks of life and, depending on the severity of the drug abuse, can go on to suffer development and behavioural problems later in life.

'He wasn't,' Debbie said. 'His mother managed to stay clean while she was pregnant.' I didn't know this and I thought it was very sad that his mother had managed to stay off drugs long enough to deliver a healthy baby, but not long enough to parent him.

Rosemary and Edward were now on the offensive. 'You said yourself that the damage can come out much later,' Edward said to Lin.

'Our early-years' experiences – good and bad – shape us all,' she said evenly. 'But as far as I'm aware Alex wasn't displaying signs of disturbed or challenging behaviour.'

'No, he wasn't, not with us,' I said.

'You didn't have him that long,' Rosemary said. I wanted to reply, 'Neither did you,' but stopped myself. The meeting was becoming very heated.

'What about his previous carers?' the chairperson asked, looking at Debbie and her manager. 'Did Alex show signs of disturbed or challenging behaviour there?'

'No,' Debbie said. 'There were no concerns.'

'The carers might not have told you,' Rosemary said.

I shook my head in dismay. I was sure this wasn't about Alex's behaviour but more about Rosemary's and Edward's unrealistic expectations of him, and they were now trying to justify their actions.

'No one is blaming you,' the chairperson said again to Rosemary and Edward. 'But it would be helpful if we could establish the reasons for the placement breakdown, as it could affect where Alex goes next.' It certainly would have an effect if Alex was labelled as having difficult or disturbed behaviour, which he didn't – even now, with his angry outbursts.

Edward and Rosemary fell silent.

'Perhaps we could let Lin finish her report,' the chairperson said, 'and then return to you.' Edward shrugged acquiescence.

Lin continued by saying that before the decision was made to move Alex, Rosemary and Edward were offered support, but they didn't think it would make any difference. Two days later they asked for Alex to be removed and Debbie took him back into care. As I was free he came to me.

'How did Alex react when he was told he was leaving?' the chairperson asked.

'He was very upset and confused,' Debbie said. 'Since then he's been quiet and withdrawn at home and at school, with occasional angry outbursts. He's also been trying to run away.'

'There!' Rosemary said, and Edward nodded, as though this proved their point.

The chairperson finished writing, asked Lin if there was anything else she wanted to say – there wasn't – and she then looked at Rosemary and Edward. 'Would you like to speak now?'

Rosemary glanced at Edward, who took the lead. 'It was clear to us from early on – even before Alex moved in – that he wasn't the child we were expecting. He appears and acts much younger than his age, and is not at all like James or his friends, so it was difficult for James to relate to him.'

'Did you tell Lin or Debbie this during the introductions?' the chairperson asked.

'My wife and I didn't think it was appropriate with all the hype going on of meeting him, and then the move. And it was possible the lad was just shy and would be different once he'd moved in.'

The chairperson gave a small nod, although I doubted it was in agreement but rather for Edward to continue.

'He wasn't any different after the move,' Edward said. 'In fact, he was worse, despite my wife's best efforts. I work long hours, so much of the childcare is left to Rosemary. You may not agree with this, but it's how we run things in my house. When the boys started fighting it all became too much for

Rosemary and I came home from work one evening to find her in tears.'

'When you say fighting, were the boys physically fighting – intending to do each other harm?' the chairperson asked.

'No. More squabbling,' Rosemary put in. 'James didn't like it that Alex was always following him around – "in his face", as he put it.'

'Couldn't James have gone to his room if he wanted to be alone?' the chairperson asked.

'He could,' Edward said. 'But why should he? It was his home.'

There was a poignant silence before Lin said what I was thinking: 'When Alex moved in it became his home too.'

'And Rosemary did all she could to make him feel at home,' Edward snapped, clearly annoyed. 'But it was obvious after a week that it wasn't going to work. We felt it was better if we said so rather than let it drag on indefinitely, so Alex could be found a new home where he would be happy.'

'What made you think he wasn't happy with you?' the chairperson asked.

'Well, he couldn't have been, could he?' Rosemary said. 'With James rejecting him.'

The chairperson made a note and then waited for them to continue.

'The rest you know,' Edward said. 'Rosemary telephoned Debbie. She and Lin both visited, so did the foster carer, but the situation didn't improve and Alex went back to his carer.'

'And how is James now?' the chairperson asked.

'Fine. Normal. Although he said he missed Alex.'

Beside me I heard Jill sigh in exasperation.

'You don't think that if you'd given it longer the problems between the boys might have been resolved?' the chairperson asked. 'Not that that is an option now.'

'No,' Edward said. 'To be honest I had doubts about the whole adoption thing from the start. I probably should have said sooner.'

'Yes,' the chairperson said dryly. I saw Debbie and Lin exchange a pointed look. 'Do either of you wish to add anything?' the chairperson asked.

Edward shook his head, while Rosemary said, 'I hope Alex is happy in his new family.'

'Thank you,' the chairperson said, and managed a weak smile. She consulted her list of those present and then looked at me. 'I think it will be useful if we hear from you now, Cathy. You provided the bridging placement prior to Alex's move to Mr and Mrs Andrews and are Alex's present foster carer.'

I straightened and sat upright in my chair, but embarrassingly, given the opportunity to speak, with all those faces looking at me my mind went completely blank for a moment before I found my voice. 'I have been fostering for over eight years and I have two children: a boy of Alex's age and a girl of three. I know the situation is different between a temporary foster placement and a permanent home – Alex might have been on his best behaviour with me – but I can only tell you what I saw. Alex didn't show any signs of disturbed or difficult behaviour while he was with me on the bridging placement, despite the abruptness of his move to me. He fitted in well and was looking forward to having a permanent family of his own. That's all he talked about.'

'Can you tell us a little about what it is like to look after Alex?' the chairperson asked.

'Yes. He is a sweet, kind, gentle and likeable child who is usually happy. He has no malice in him. He has age-appropriate self-care skills and washes and dresses himself competently. He was sleeping and eating well before the move and making good progress at school. He played nicely with both my children and joined in with family activities and adapted well to our routine. I took over from the previous carers just before the adoption planning meeting, and the introductions went well. Alex was a bit quiet and nervous to begin with, but that was only to be expected. One time he mentioned that he usually had to play what James wanted, and that James thought his soft toy – which he took to bed at night – was babyish, but he wasn't upset by it. I didn't think any more about it – no siblings get on all the time – and the move went as planned.'

'Did you have any contact with Alex after the move?' the chairperson asked.

'No, we were going to wait to visit until he'd settled in – that was decided at the planning meeting.'

'Did your children miss Alex?' the chairperson asked.

'Yes, especially Adrian – they are the same age.'

'And you say they got on well? I appreciate Alex wasn't with you for very long on the bridging placement, but there weren't any problems?'

'No. Adrian is used to having other children in the house and Alex fitted in easily. When my support social worker telephoned and said there were problems I was very surprised. I went to see Rosemary and I thought my visit had helped. The problems she described appeared quite minor and similar to many experienced by new carers. I was shocked to hear that Alex was returning to foster care. I've fostered children before with behavioural difficulties and in my opinion Alex didn't have any behaviour that was likely to cause a problem between him and James. Although Alex *is* finding life difficult now.'

'In what respect?' the chairperson asked.

'He is very quiet and withdrawn and doesn't want much to do with any of us, although we try to involve him. As Debbie mentioned, he has angry outbursts and he's also started running away. I've tried talking to him, but he doesn't say much. What he has said suggests he is blaming himself for what happened, although I've told him it wasn't his fault.' I was about to continue when a chair scraped back and Edward rose to his feet.

'Come on,' he said to Rosemary. 'We're not staying here to listen to any more of this.' She also stood.

'Mr Andrews, if you could –' the chairperson began.

But Edward turned his back and, touching his wife's arm, led the way out of the room. The door swung shut behind them with a bang.

'I'm sorry,' I said. 'I didn't mean to …'

'It wasn't your fault,' Jill said.

The room was quiet as the chairperson wrote and the others concentrated on their papers on the table in front of them. I felt awful. I'd tried to be tactful and sensitive, but it had been difficult not to implicate Edward and Rosemary while giving an honest account of Alex as he had been before and now after the move. The chairperson looked up at us all.

'It's a pity that Mr and Mrs Andrews didn't feel they could stay.' Then addressing Debbie: 'Would you pass on my thanks to them for attending?' Debbie nodded and made a note, and then the chairperson asked me to continue.

In some ways it was easier without Edward and Rosemary present. I felt less inhibited in choosing my words as I continued to describe Alex's behaviour since he had returned to live with me: his tears, nightmares, anger and deep feelings of rejection and that nobody loved or wanted him. When I'd finished the chairperson asked, 'Have you received an appointment from CAMHS yet?'

'No,' I said.

She thanked me and then asked Alex's teacher, Miss Cork, to speak. As she and I were in almost daily contact, I knew most of what she told the meeting – the change in Alex's personality and his performance at school, that he wasn't joining in class activities as he used to and was struggling to concentrate. She mentioned his angry outbursts and that he'd tried to run away, but the saddest part of all was when she described him alone in the playground, not wanting to play with his friends. She finished by saying that she hoped he would turn a corner soon, but felt that his last move had proved one too many for a child with such an unsettled past. Having given her report, she then asked if she could leave so she could return to her class, and the chairperson agreed and thanked her for coming.

The chairperson now went round the room so that everyone had a chance to contribute. There wasn't really anything new; it had all been said. When it was the turn of Shanice and her manager from the permanency team they confirmed that they were family-finding for Alex and were looking for an experienced foster carer with no similar-aged children, but they hadn't identified a suitable family yet. When they'd finished the chairperson returned to Debbie and asked if Alex's mother had been informed of the adoption disruption. Debbie said that she hadn't been and there were no plans to do so. As a matter of procedure the chairperson then said that Alex's case would need to be presented back to the panel, and Debbie's manager nodded. She then thanked us all for attending and closed the meeting. It was now 1.15 p.m. – we'd been there for over two hours, and I don't think I was the only one who felt emotionally exhausted. The room quickly emptied. I left with Jill, and on the way out she reminded me to telephone the agency if I needed any advice or support, otherwise she'd be in touch again later in the week. She was going straight to another meeting and hoped to pick up a sandwich for lunch on the way.

I drove home in a gloomy mood, going over what had been said at the meeting. I hadn't meant to upset Rosemary and Edward, and I thought they might have been feeling guilty, which was why they'd gone on the offensive. However, I was concerned that if I hadn't spoken up Alex could have been labelled with behavioural problems. He might still be, for the main reason given for the adoption failing was the friction between James and Alex. I hadn't been to an adoption disruption meeting before and I wondered how useful it had been, both in respect of planning for Alex's future and changing the social services' procedure in future adoption cases.

However, my gloom lifted the moment I arrived home and Paula, pleased to see me, ran into my arms and gave me a big hug and a kiss. Mum had lunch ready and as we sat around the table, talking as we ate, I was again reminded of how lucky I was to have a stable, loving family of my own.

CHAPTER NINETEEN

CONFLICTING EMOTIONS

We had another rocky week with Alex and then his behaviour started to improve. There was no obvious reason for the change, so I put it down to the healing effect of time and that he was starting to feel settled again. He began playing with Adrian, Paula and Toscha – whom he'd also been ignoring – and talking to us all more. Miss Cork said she'd seen an improvement at school, and while we were both very pleased we knew that at some point in the not-too-distant future Alex would have to move again. How would he cope with that? Not very well, I thought, and Miss Cork, only half-jokingly, asked, 'I don't suppose you could keep him?'

'I wish!' I said with a smile.

But to be honest, it had been on my mind since the adoption breakdown. The next time Jill visited I brought up the matter, and asked her if she thought there was any chance of Alex being allowed to stay with me as a long-term foster placement. She didn't hold out much hope.

'The social services are going to need to be ultra-careful after what happened with James,' she said. 'I'll speak to

233

Debbie and find out where they are on this. If they can't find the perfect match then they might consider you.'

'Thank you,' I said. 'I don't mind being second best. And what happened with James wasn't Alex's fault.'

'I know.'

Jill telephoned three days later, having spoken to Debbie, and the news was worse than I'd anticipated. Not only would I not be considered for keeping Alex, but a long-term foster family had now been found and Debbie and Shanice were going to visit them the following week. Jill gave me a moment to digest this and then said, 'The match looks very good on paper.'

'So did the last one,' I replied caustically.

'This family are different,' Jill said. 'They've been fostering for twenty years and have three teenagers, one of whom has Down's syndrome. Alex would be the youngest by seven years. They live in H——.' She named the neighbouring town, which was about a thirty-minute drive away.

I couldn't argue; it wasn't my decision.

'If it goes ahead, you'll meet the couple once the match has been approved by the permanency panel.' Which I knew could take weeks, if not months.

We visited my parents at the weekend and Alex related well to them. They were pleased. 'He's such a poppet,' Mum said, seeing the real Alex for the first time.

Debbie visited us the following week for one of her statutory visits, and she asked me to stay while she talked to Alex. She told him she was pleased to see him looking so well and happy again, and that what happened at Rosemary and

Edward's was now past and it was important that they concentrated on the future. She gradually led the way into telling him they were looking very hard for a wonderful family for him where he would be the youngest, so he would have older brothers and sisters. While she spoke in general terms, I knew she was referring to the family that had already been identified and would go to panel soon – this was the first step in preparing him. Similar would have happened before with Edward and Rosemary. 'Won't that be nice?' she finished.

Alex looked as unimpressed as I felt, but I set my face to a positive smile and, wearing my professional foster-carer hat, said brightly, 'That sounds fantastic, doesn't it? I always wanted older brothers and sisters.' Debbie threw me an appreciative look.

Debbie didn't say anything more specific to Alex about the family; she'd wait until the match had been approved by the panel. After she'd gone Alex stopped playing with his toys, didn't want much dinner and then that night he had a nightmare – the first for some weeks. Of course the talk of a new family and having to move again had unsettled him – it was only natural. He was very quiet for a few days, wouldn't talk to me about his worries or Debbie's visit, and then slowly recovered. Children are able to bounce back many times, but there is a cut-off point.

It was April now. Spring had arrived with the promise of summer not far behind. Birds were busy nest-building in the hedgerows, spring flowers bloomed and the trees were bursting into new life, budding fresh green leaves. Alex was his old self again, although he never spoke of Edward, Rosemary and James or what the future held, which probably wasn't altogether healthy. Our lives continued reasonably smoothly and then at the beginning of June I heard that the match had been approved by the panel. Also the appointment for CAMHS finally arrived. Because we would be starting the introductions soon and Alex would have that to cope with, followed by another move, it was decided it would be better for him to wait until after he'd moved and settled in before commencing therapy with CAMHS. This is normal practice in England.

The planning meeting to work out the timetable of the introductions was in my diary and Jill telephoned the day before with more details of the couple I would soon meet: Gareth and Gwen. They were in their fifties and had two boys – Mark, fourteen; Taylor, sixteen – and a girl, Kaylee, nineteen, who had Down's syndrome.

'Sounds like they've got their hands full already,' I said a little sourly.

'You're not the only one to think that,' Jill said. 'A panel member asked how they'd cope and why they wanted to adopt again.'

'Sorry? Did you say adopt?'

'Yes. They want to adopt Alex.'

'I thought they were foster carers and this was a long-term foster placement.'

'They have been fostering, but they found that all the social worker visits unsettled the boys. The boys had severe behavioural issues when they first arrived, having been in and out of care all their lives. Gareth and Gwen worked wonders with them; they settled down and they went on to adopt them.'

'And that's what they're planning for Alex? Not that he has behavioural issues.'

'Yes,' Jill said.

'There is no way I can sell another adoptive family to Alex, not after what happened the last time,' I said bluntly. 'And Debbie has already told Alex she's looking for a long-term foster family for him.'

'I know. Gareth and Gwen are aware of Alex's history and what happened with the Andrews. They've agreed to take him as a foster placement to begin with, with a view to adopting him when the time is right. It's what happened with Kaylee.'

'Kaylee – with Down's syndrome. Is she adopted too?'

'Yes.'

I was starting to feel a grudging admiration for Gareth and Gwen, although I still had big doubts.

'Supposing the time is never right for Alex to be adopted,' I said. 'What then? If they don't want to foster, would he have another move?'

'Hopefully not. Although of course nothing can be guaranteed.' Didn't I know it!

'And you say their two boys, Mark and Taylor, had behavioural issues and were very unsettled when they first arrived?'

'Yes, and for some time after. The couple are highly experienced and competent. If Alex does become unsettled again they'll be able to deal with it, just as you have. Debbie said they are a very kind and caring couple but can be firm when necessary. They have no illusions and are down to earth, so let's give them a chance tomorrow, shall we? And then take it

237

from there. I'll meet you just before ten o'clock in reception at the council offices.'

It was like a flash of déjà vu the following morning as I parked my car outside the council offices and met Jill on the way in. With our security passes around our necks we made our way up to the second floor. The meeting was in the same room as the first adoption planning meeting, which seemed a bad omen to me. Did I hope for a last-minute reprieve whereby, for some as-yet-undisclosed reason, I would be allowed to keep Alex and we'd all live happily ever after? Yes, of course I did. It's most foster carers' dream come true to be able to keep all the children they foster, but realistically that wasn't going to happen.

What did happen was that as Jill and I stepped into the room we were greeted with light convivial chatter and smiling faces. My gaze immediately went to the couple sitting at the far side of the table, whom I deduced must be Alex's new carers. They met my critical gaze with a smile and then came round to greet me. And sometimes when you meet someone for the first time, before they've even spoken a word you know they are going to be OK.

'Hello, love, so pleased to meet you. I'm Gareth,' he said, warmly shaking my hand. 'We've just been hearing what a great job you've been doing with young Alex.' Not patronizing but genuine. Taller than average, with broad shoulders and a rugged jawline, Gareth was dressed casually in corduroy trousers and a knitted jersey. He had the confidence of a man at ease with himself and others.

'Nice to meet you too,' I said.

Then Gwen took my hand between hers – not really a handshake, more an affectionate embrace – and, looking me straight in the eyes, said, 'You're going to miss Alex, but we'll be keeping in touch, won't we?'

'Yes, please,' I said.

She was wearing a cosy woollen dress and cardigan and carried a few extra pounds, which gave her a cuddly, mumsy appearance. Good-natured, with a kind, open face that suggested she was used to smiling.

Jill and I took our seats at the table and the meeting began with the introductions. There were nine of us: Gareth and Gwen and their support social worker, Debbie and her team manager, Shanice and her team manager, and Jill and me, all with our diaries ready in front of us. Debbie led the meeting and we began with a general discussion about how Alex was now, during which I gave Gwen and Gareth some recent photographs I'd brought with me for this purpose. They'd already seen an older photo of Alex, so they knew what he looked like, but these were up to date. They would show them to their children this evening when they told them more about Alex, for they, too, had to be thoroughly prepared. Having Alex come to live with them would be life-changing for the whole family. In return, Gwen produced a small photograph album that would be given to Alex later, just as I'd done with Rosemary and Edward. However, this time Debbie said she would come to my house this afternoon after school to tell Alex about Gwen and Gareth and show him the album then. This would be the start of the introductions.

Jill said it would be useful if Gwen and Gareth could tell me a little about themselves and their family and what they liked to do in their spare time so that I could answer any questions Alex might have later. Gwen began by saying that they hadn't been able to have children of their own, so they'd started fostering over twenty years ago. To begin with she was the main caregiver while Gareth went out to work. 'But when we started caring for very challenging children,' she said, 'Gareth cut his hours at the factory, and for the last eight years he's been working part time so he can help with the children.'

Gareth joined in, describing their home life, and when they talked about how naughty Mark and Taylor had been when they'd first arrived they spoke with an indulgent smile, as if boys will be boys. I saw a confidence in their partnership, which suggested that whatever was thrown at them they would deal with it and come through as a family. 'The boys had had so many moves and upsets before coming to us,' Gareth said. 'I told them from day one that this would be their last move. They didn't believe me to begin with. Taylor had lost count of the number of homes he'd lived in, but he reckoned it was over fifty, which was confirmed by the social services records.'

When Gwen spoke of Kaylee, their adopted nineteen-year-old daughter with Down's syndrome, a tear came to her eye. 'Her mum died when she was twelve. She came to us the same day, sobbing her heart out and not able to understand why she couldn't stay at home and live with her mummy. It was heart-breaking. She'd been with her mum when she'd died and had sat beside her, trying to wake her up, and had then gone to a neighbour. She came as a short-term placement initially, and our first attempt to adopt her was blocked by an aunt who said she was making plans to look after her, but nothing came of it. Two years later we applied again and were successful.' Gwen smiled at the recollection. 'We threw a little party for family and friends. We had Mark and Taylor with us by then. Kaylee is such a kind, gentle soul, although she doesn't stand any nonsense. She puts the boys in their place, I can tell you, sometimes better than I do.'

They talked about their family holidays and activities and days out. As they spoke I warmed to them more and more, and gradually put many of my concerns aside. We then went on to plan the timetable of introduction as we had with Rosemary and Edward. It was similar – spread over two weeks – although there were a few extra visits, as everyone agreed we needed to take it slowly to give Alex a chance to adjust. It could be longer than two weeks if necessary. Debbie would start the ball rolling with her visit after school today, and then tomorrow Gwen and Gareth would telephone and speak to Alex, just to say hello and have a little chat for a few minutes. The following evening they would visit for an hour and then come to dinner the next day. Alex wouldn't meet Kaylee, Mark and Taylor until the end of the week so that he had a chance to get to know Gwen and Gareth first and wasn't overwhelmed. At each stage Debbie and Shanice would phone us for updates and then adjust the timetable if necessary. However, I should say here that although we could prolong the introductions if necessary, at some point Alex would definitely be moving to his new home, as it had been decided by the social services and approved by the permanency panel as being in his best interests. It doesn't happen often, but there are times when a child has to be physically carried into the car if they don't want to move – whether it is to another carer or home to a relative. It's different with older children who would 'vote with their feet' if moved against their wishes, but younger children in care have the decisions on where they will live made for them.

By the end of the meeting I only had two main concerns left and they weren't small: one, that Alex might reject the whole idea of going to a new family, and his behaviour and well-being would therefore suffer a huge setback. The other was that he might feel overwhelmed and swamped by having three teenagers in the house, all with their own needs. I had no doubt that Gwen and Gareth and their family were wonderful, but how would Alex fit in? I couldn't imagine Mark and Taylor having much time for a seven-year-old who may be acting up, and how would Alex and Kaylee relate to each other? I couldn't picture it at all. But the meeting ended as convivially as it had begun, with warm handshakes all round and calls of 'see you soon' as we said goodbye.

That afternoon, when I collected Alex from school I told him Debbie was coming to see him at 4.30. 'Not again,' he sighed. 'The other kids at school don't have all these social worker visits.'

'I know. It's a real bummer,' I said lightly. This was a term Alex had brought home from school and I didn't normally use. He managed a small smile. And of course if all went to plan and Alex was adopted by Gwen and Gareth, he wouldn't have the disruption or stigma of social worker visits, LAC reviews or any of the other intrusions that are part of a child in care's life, although I couldn't tell him that now.

Once home I told Adrian and Paula that Debbie was coming ('Yes – again') and I would be spending time with her and Alex in the living room while they played nicely at the table. Alex sat with them, playing with the activities until the doorbell rang.

'That'll be Debbie,' I said. 'You'll be able to play again later, after she's gone.'

I let Debbie in and showed her through to where the children were. She said hello and then Alex took quite a bit of persuading before he stopped playing and came with Debbie and me into the living room, where she sat on the sofa beside him.

'I've had a very special meeting today,' she began with a big smile. 'I met two wonderful foster carers called Gwen and Gareth who want to look after you.' Alex glanced at me and I felt guilty. He knew I'd been to a meeting today, but I hadn't told him what it was for, and now he'd made the connection. It felt as if I'd been part of a conspiracy against him.

'Gwen and Gareth live in H—, which isn't far away,' Debbie continued enthusiastically. 'They have three teenage children: two boys and a girl. They also have a dog, a cat and a rabbit. Isn't that fantastic? They've sent some photographs just for you.' She took the album from her bag. Alex sat impassively, his hands in his lap and his face expressionless. Debbie set the album between them and opened it to the first page. 'Here they are,' she said brightly. 'There's Gwen and Gareth. That's Mark, Taylor and Kaylee, and that's their dog, Rupert.' The first picture showed them standing at the front of their house with the door open behind them, smiling and ready to welcome Alex in. It was a similar shot to the one at the beginning of Rosemary and Edward's album – not coincidence; standard guidelines are given when preparing these albums as part of a child's move to permanency. It crossed my mind that I hadn't seen Rosemary and Edward's album since Alex had returned to me. I supposed, not wanting it, he'd left it with them.

'Here is the living room,' Debbie continued enthusiastically, turning the pages. 'The house looks very cosy, doesn't it? And there's Mark again. He's playing on his PlayStation and giving you the thumbs-up sign.'

And so Debbie continued the picture tour of the house. I watched Alex's expression, just as I had done when I'd shown him Rosemary and Edward's album. Then he'd been very excited, but now he maintained a passive indifference to the photographs and Debbie's commentary. His gaze was on the pictures, but he could have been looking at a pile of bricks for all the interest or emotion he showed.

The tour went into their back garden with a photograph of their rabbit, Flopsy, sitting in her hutch. Then back into the house and upstairs, into the bathroom, other bedrooms, and finishing with what should have been the grand finale – Alex's room.

'Well, what do you think?' Debbie asked brightly, the album open at the page showing his bedroom. It wasn't as large or as lavishly furnished as his room had been at Rosemary and Edward's, but it was comfortable and decorated appropriately for a boy of seven. 'It's a nice house, isn't it? And they're a lovely family,' Debbie said. She paused and looked at him, waiting for feedback.

'Can I go now?' he asked sullenly.

'Alex, Debbie is talking to you,' I lightly chastised.

'I know this is difficult,' Debbie said to him. 'But they are really lovely people who are so looking forward to meeting you. This is the long-term family I told you we were looking for. I am sure you will be happy with them.' I half expected him to say, 'You said that last time,' but he remained silent, head down and now looking at the carpet.

'Is there anything you want to ask me?' Debbie said. Alex shook his head. 'I know there's a lot to think about, so when you're ready and have some questions you can ask Cathy or me. The album is yours. They made it especially for you.' She placed it squarely on his lap.

'No, thank you,' he said, and placed it firmly back on her lap. 'Can I go now?'

She looked a little disappointed, although I'd have been more surprised if he'd welcomed all of this with the same unbridled enthusiasm he'd shown the last time.

'Yes, you can go now,' Debbie said. 'We'll talk again soon, and remember to ask Cathy if you have any questions.'

Alex stood and left the room in silence. I heard him go upstairs to his room.

'He'll need time to adjust,' Debbie said.

'Yes,' I agreed. 'I'll do what I can.'

'Well, I don't think there's anything else. I'll phone you the day after tomorrow to see how the telephone call tomorrow evening has gone.'

I saw her to the front door, and then after she'd left I checked on Adrian and Paula and then went up to Alex's room. His door was ajar so I gave a small knock and went in.

He was sitting on the edge of his bed cuddling Simba. He wasn't crying or angry, just sitting there, holding his soft toy and gently rocking. I went over and sat next to him. We were silent for a few moments.

'Can you tell me what you're thinking?' I asked gently. He shrugged. 'I expect you're thinking lots of different things and some of them are very confusing. I know I did when I first heard Debbie had found you a new family. One of the thoughts I had was that you'd have to move again, which didn't seem fair after all the other moves you've had already. But then part of me thought the family sounded nice, and different from Edward and Rosemary in many ways. I liked that Gwen and Gareth have been fostering for a long time and the children have stayed with them.' I hoped that by acknowledging my conflict of feelings and emotions it might help Alex to deal with his, although I purposely didn't mention that Mark, Taylor and Kaylee had been adopted, and Debbie hadn't mentioned it either. Adoption was still a very raw subject for Alex. He'd stopped rocking now and had slightly loosened his grip on Simba.

'I tried to keep an open mind for when I met them,' I continued. 'But part of me said I wouldn't like them. I didn't want to like them. Yet as soon as I walked into the meeting this morning I knew straight away they were good, kind people. Sometimes you can just tell. Then, when they started talking about their children and that they wanted you to be part of their family, I felt really good about them. I know this is a lot for you to take in and you need time. But when you're ready we can have a look at the photographs together and I'll tell you more about them. Is there anything you want to ask now?' He shook his head. 'OK, let me know when you think of something, but for now I want you to come downstairs. I don't want you sitting up here alone, and I need to start making dinner. You can carry on playing with Adrian and Paula.'

We both stood. Alex set Simba on his pillow and then came with me downstairs. He quietly joined Adrian and Paula at the table and continued with the puzzle he'd been doing before Debbie's visit. About ten minutes later Adrian asked if they could watch some television, and I went with them into the living room where I switched on the television and checked that what was showing was suitable for all three of them. The photograph album was where Debbie had left it on the coffee table. 'Is that Alex's?' Paula asked.

'Yes,' I said.

'Can I look at it?'

'Not until Alex is ready to show you,' I said, glancing at Alex. He kept his gaze on the television screen.

'Can I look at the other one?' she asked, meaning the one from Edward and Rosemary.

'I haven't got it,' Alex said, without turning. 'Rosemary kept it. She said I wouldn't want reminders of them.' Which was probably true, although something would have to be included in Alex's Life Story Book; those two weeks couldn't just be ignored.

The children watched television, then we ate, and after dinner we went into the living room where I heard Adrian and Alex read. The photograph album remained untouched on the coffee table and did so for the rest of the evening. It seemed to loom at me like a beacon, warning of all that lay ahead. I wasn't going to mention the album again to Alex – only when he was ready. But neither was I going to put it away. The album was his, and it was the first step in acknowledging his new family and preparing himself for meeting them and eventually moving in.

CHAPTER TWENTY

NOT MUM AND DAD

The following day, after dinner, I reminded Alex that Gwen and Gareth would be phoning at around 6.30. I hadn't told him the whole timetable of introduction as I had before, as it would have been too much for him to cope with all at once. I was taking it a stage at a time and had said only that Gwen and Gareth would be telephoning this evening and visiting the following evening. He was still ignoring the photograph album.

'I'm not talking to them,' he said with scowl.

'That's a pity,' I said. 'They're phoning especially to speak to you.'

'Don't care,' he said with an even bigger scowl. After a restless night, Alex had been 'a little grumpy', as his teacher had put it, but she appreciated that he had a lot on his mind and had excused his behaviour.

We were all in the living room at 6.30 when the call came. I was reading Paula a story and the boys, having done their homework, were on the floor assembling a construction kit.

'I expect that's Gwen and Gareth,' I said brightly, and picked up the handset from the corner table. 'Hello?'

'Cathy, Gwen here. How are you?'

'Very well, thanks, and you?'

'We've had a good day. Lovely to see the sun. It's got real warmth in it.'

'Yes, it's been a beautiful day,' I said. 'I managed to do a bit of gardening this afternoon.'

We continued chatting generally for a few minutes. As an experienced foster carer Gwen appreciated that it was important for Alex to see us getting along, as it gave her the stamp of approval.

'How was Alex after Debbie's visit?' Gwen asked. 'Not rushing to meet us, I bet.'

I laughed. 'Not yet. Alex is just in front of me making a fantastic bridge out of the construction kit.' Both boys looked over.

'Great. Does he feel up to talking to me?'

'I hope so.' I lowered the handset slightly and said, 'Alex, Gwen would like to speak to you.'

He shook his head and kept his gaze down. 'She's telephoned especially to say hello to you,' I said.

'I'm not talking to her,' he replied grumpily.

'It would be nice if you could just say hi,' I said. Gwen could hear what we were saying. 'Oh well, if you're not going to talk to her, I will.'

'Can I talk to Gwen?' Paula asked. I heard Gwen chuckle.

Strictly, this call was specifically for Alex, but I thought a bit of child psychology wouldn't go amiss. Children often want what is coveted by other children.

'Gwen,' I said, raising the handset to my ear again. 'Would you like a quick chat with Paula until Alex is ready to talk?'

'Yes, of course. Put her on.' I could hear the smile in her voice.

I passed the handset to Paula, who held it a little away from her ear so she could share the call with me. 'Hello,' she said in a small, shy voice.

'Hello, pet. How are you?'

'I'm fine, thanks,' Paula said quietly.

'What have you been doing today?'

'I've been to nursery.'

'Fantastic. What did you do there?'

'I painted a picture of Mummy, and we had a drink and sang some songs.' I saw Alex look over, his interest piqued.

'That sounds good,' Gwen said enthusiastically. 'Can you sing a song for me?'

Shyness got the better of Paula and, after saying a quick goodbye, she returned the phone to me.

Gwen chuckled. 'She sounds a darling.'

'She has her moments,' I said. 'I wonder who is going to speak to you next … Adrian or Alex?'

I knew Adrian wouldn't have much desire to make small talk with a grown-up he hadn't even met, but the suggestion that he might was all that was needed.

'I will,' Alex said, standing. 'It's my turn.'

'Well done,' Gwen said to me down the phone.

Alex came over and sat beside me. I passed him the phone and then I continued quietly looking at a book with Paula. I didn't want him to feel he was on show.

'Hello,' he said in a subdued voice.

I couldn't hear Gwen, but I knew that with all her fostering experience whatever she said would be right and designed to put Alex at ease. Alex said a few yeses and nos in reply to Gwen's questions, then she must have asked him about the construction set, as he explained that the bolts needed to be tightened with the spanner in the kit. Then there was a pause and Alex said hello again, so I guessed Gwen had passed the phone to Gareth. Alex answered a few questions about the bridge he was making and then said goodbye.

'Well done,' I said as he handed back the phone. He returned to sit on the floor beside Adrian and resumed playing.

'He did just fine,' Gwen said as I took up the call. 'He managed to speak to Gareth as well.'

'Excellent.' I could see from Alex's expression and body language that he was more relaxed now, probably relieved at having overcome the first hurdle. 'So we'll see you tomorrow then,' I said to Gwen.

'Cathy, before you go would you mind saying hello to Kaylee? She's beside me now and really wants to talk to you. She's like a big kid, really,' Gwen added affectionately.

'Yes, I'd be happy to.'

There was a pause as Gwen passed the phone to Kaylee and I heard Gwen say, 'Now, not too long, Cathy has things to do too.'

After a moment a small, measured voice said carefully, 'Hello, my name Kaylee.'

'Hello, Kaylee, I'm Cathy. How are you?'

There was another pause before she answered – characteristic of many young people with learning disabilities as she thought of her reply. 'Well. How are you?'

'Very well, thank you. What have you been doing?'

'Playing Flopsy.'

'You've been playing with your rabbit?'

'Yes. You friend Mummy?' she asked.

'Yes, I am.'

People with Down's syndrome often talk in short 'telegraphic' sentences, leaving out conjunctions and prepositions, and relying on nouns and verbs, which can make understanding them difficult. However, I had no problem in understanding what Kaylee told me next and it brought tears to my eyes.

'I have two mummies,' she said. 'Both love me. I live with Mummy Gwen. My other mummy in heaven.'

I swallowed hard. 'You must have been sad when your first mummy left you, but Mummy Gwen is a wonderful mummy.'

'Yes. Love her much.' Stated so simply, but with such warmth and depth that my eyes filled again.

'I am sure you do, and she loves you very much too. I know she is very proud of you.' I saw Alex steal a glance at me.

Then I heard Gwen prompt Kaylee – 'Say goodbye now, love.'

'Goodbye,' Kaylee said obediently.

'Goodbye. It's been nice talking to you.'

'Nice talking to you,' she repeated. Then Gwen came back on the phone.

'Thanks, Cathy. She'd talk all night given the chance.'

'She sounds delightful.'

'Yes, she's a good kid. She brings us so much happiness. They all do. The boys are very protective of her.' Which sealed in my mind just what a loving and caring family they were.

We confirmed arrangements for their visit the following evening and said goodbye. As I replaced the handset Alex asked, 'Who were you talking to?'

'Kaylee, one of Gwen and Gareth's children. There's a photograph of her in the album. Shall I show you?' Alex shook his head.

I finished reading Paula her story and then left the boys playing while I took her up to bed. When I came down again to my surprise and delight Alex and Adrian were sitting side by side on the sofa with the photograph album open on Alex's lap. He was turning the pages as Adrian read out the captions beneath. I didn't comment but sat down and picked up a form I'd been meaning to complete all day. When they got to the end Alex closed the album and returned it to the table.

The boys continued playing until it was their bedtime. I took Alex up first as usual, and as he said goodnight to Adrian he picked up the album and tucked it under his arm. He took it up to his room, where he placed it under the bed. A very positive sign, I thought. Once he was in bed and I was tucking him in, I said lightly, 'If you have any questions about Gwen and Gareth and their family then do ask me.' That was all I said. I wasn't going to start telling Alex what a wonderful family they were – he'd heard all that before in respect of Rosemary and Edward, and it would have sounded hollow now. I hoped that in time, once he met them, he would gradually warm to them.

Alex slept well and the following morning I anticipated building on the positive end to the day before. However, when I went into his bedroom to wake him he was already wide awake, sitting up in bed with the photograph album open on his lap. But I knew straight away he wasn't happy; his face was pinched and white.

'They're lying!' he said, glaring at me. 'They're lying like the others did.'

'What ever do you mean?' I went over. 'Who's lying? About what?' I perched on the edge of his bed.

'They are,' he said, agitatedly flipping over the pages in the album. He was going forwards and backwards as though looking for something. 'Debbie said they had a cat, but there isn't a cat here. They're liars like the others.'

'You mean because their cat isn't in the photographs you think they haven't got one?' He nodded and brusquely turned another page.

'Alex, because they haven't included a picture of their cat doesn't mean they don't have one. We can ask Gwen and Gareth this evening, but I expect the cat was out when they took the photographs. Cats often roam.' But this wasn't really about an absent cat. Alex was trying to catch Gwen and Gareth out and prove them liars, as he now deemed Rosemary and Edward to be. And who could blame him?

'Let's just wait and see what Gwen and Gareth say,' I said. 'We'll put away the album now as it's time for you to get washed and dressed ready for school.' I gently eased the album from him, closed it and placed it on the bed. I didn't want him going to school agitated and in a bad mood.

'I bet they are liars,' he mumbled under his breath as he climbed out of bed.

'We'll see,' I said, and left him to get ready. However, I knew that regardless of what lovely people I now believed Gwen and Gareth to be, there was going to be an uphill struggle before Alex began to trust and accept them.

I made notes in my fostering log of Alex's reactions and comments to the introduction so that I could update Debbie and Jill. It would also allow me to monitor Alex's acceptance (or not) of Gwen and Gareth. If I thought there was a case for prolonging the introductions then I would have written evidence in these notes – incidents and comments – which I might otherwise have forgotten. It's so important for carers to keep good log notes.

That afternoon, when I collected Alex from school, Miss Cork made a point of telling me that Alex had worked very well in Science. We both praised him and then as he stood to one side with Paula I quietly asked Miss Cork if Alex had mentioned Gwen and Gareth at all. She was aware that we'd started the introductions.

'Not a word,' she said. 'But I guess that's probably to be expected after the disappointment of last time. I won't mention it to him unless he does, and I'll keep you posted.'

'Thank you.'

Gwen and Gareth were due to arrive at our house at six o'clock and to stay for an hour, so I made an early dinner, which we'd finished well before six. Adrian and Paula knew they were coming and why, but appreciated that Alex didn't want to talk about it. When the doorbell rang we were all in the living room. I was helping Alex learn his spellings while Adrian, having done his homework, was helping Paula fit together a large-pieced puzzle of a zoo. Alex closed his spelling book and looked at me.

'Do you want to come with me to answer the door?' I asked him.

'No,' he said bluntly and, folding his arms across his chest, put his head down. His body language said it all.

The days were growing longer now and it was still light at 6 p.m. so when I opened the front door it was to a still pleasantly warm evening and the cheerful smiles of Gwen and Gareth. 'Welcome,' I said. 'Good to see you again. Come in.' We greeted each other with cheek kisses and hugs as one would old friends, which they were very quickly becoming. 'We're in the living room. This way.'

I led the way down the hall and into the living room, where Alex was still sitting on the sofa with his arms tightly folded and his face like thunder.

'Hello,' Gwen said lightly. She sat on the sofa a little way from him, setting the shopping bag she was carrying at her feet.

'Alex, this is Gwen and Gareth,' I said.

'Hi, Alex,' they both said.

'And this is Adrian and Paula.'

'Good to meet you,' Gareth said. 'You look busy.' He sat in one of the easy chairs close to them. 'Fine jigsaw, that,' he said, smiling at Paula.

'It is indeed,' Gwen said.

Unfazed by Alex's hostility, Gwen and Gareth continued chatting, including Alex in the conversation but not saying anything directly to him that required an answer, which could have made him feel uncomfortable. He kept his head firmly down as we talked, but after a while I saw his arms start to relax. That he had even stayed in the room I viewed as positive; I'd half expected him to flee to his room when the doorbell rang.

'So you've got a cat too!' Gwen exclaimed as Toscha sauntered in. Sensing new friends, she went to Gwen and began rubbing around her legs, purring as Gwen stroked her.

'Alex was wondering about your cat,' I said, seizing the opportunity. 'We couldn't see him in the photographs.'

'No. He's a bit of a wanderer. He likes a nice warm fire in winter, but come the spring and summer he's off hunting. Sometimes he brings things home that he's caught. I don't like it, but that's cats for you.'

Intrigued, Alex glanced up at Gwen and then down again.

'In your bag, love,' Gareth now reminded Gwen.

'Oh yes,' she said. 'We've brought one of our family albums with us. I'm sure there's a picture of our cat, Tom, in there.' She dipped her hand into her shopping bag and brought out the album, then flipped through until she came to a photograph that included their cat. 'There he is,' she said, tapping the page and tilting the album towards Alex. He still had his head down, but the album was in his line of vision. She set it on the sofa between them.

'I've also brought you a few cupcakes,' Gwen said, delving into her shopping basket again. 'Kaylee and Mark made them. Do you like cake?'

'Does a duck like water?' I said, laughing.

Gwen unclipped the lid of the airtight container and showed us its contents. A dozen mouth-watering cupcakes iced in blue, yellow, pink and green, and decorated with different-coloured sugar strands, sprinkles and mini marsh-mallows, were arranged in neat rows.

'Yummy,' Adrian said, his eyes rounding.

'Yes, very yummy,' I said.

'You can have one now if your mum says it's OK,' Gwen said to Adrian. 'We made them for you all.'

'Thank you,' I said. 'I'll fetch some plates and some drinks. Would you like a tea or coffee?'

They both said they'd like tea, so I went into the kitchen where I set a tray with plates, juice for the children and then the tea I made for us. Returning to the living room, I placed the tray on the coffee table and handed out the plates and drinks. Alex still had his head down, so I slipped a plate onto his lap and put a glass of juice within his reach. Gwen offered around the box of cakes. When she came to Alex he raised his head enough to quietly take a cake with blue icing.

'Good choice,' Gwen said. 'Those are Gareth's favourites too.'

The next few minutes was given over to eating and sighs of delight as we enjoyed the delicious, light cakes. I asked Gwen to pass on my thanks to Kaylee and Mark who'd made them. We continued chatting and Gwen told us more about their family, as Adrian and Paula played and Alex sat on the sofa. I asked Alex a couple of times if he would like to play a game or join Adrian and Paula, but he shook his head. The hour passed quickly, and although Alex hadn't contributed anything he had been listening, and simply being in the same room as Gwen and Gareth meant that they were becoming familiar to him and were no longer complete strangers. With ten minutes to go and their family album still open on the sofa, Gwen said quietly to Alex, 'Would you like to see the photo of our cat now before we have to leave?'

Alex gave a small, almost imperceptible nod. 'Good,' Gwen said. She picked up the album and, moving a little closer to him, pointed to the photograph of Tom. She said he was five years old and got on well with their dog, Rupert, most of the time. Then she returned to the front of the album and began going through it, saying a few words about each picture, while Adrian and Paula continued playing and I talked quietly with Gareth. Alex was looking at the photographs, although he didn't say anything or nod. Once Gwen came to the end of the album she said, 'You can look at that again another day, but it's time for us to go now.' She returned the album to her bag and she and Gareth stood. They admired the puzzles Adrian and Paula had completed and then began saying goodbye. Without actually looking at them, Alex managed a small 'bye'. It was the first word he'd said to them all evening and I saw Gwen and Gareth exchange a smile.

As I saw them to the front door I said, 'I hope you weren't disappointed. It is difficult for him.'

'Of course not,' Gwen said, and Gareth nodded. 'He did very well. You should have seen our Mark when he first arrived. The only words he ever said to us for a month were, "I hate you," and, "I wish you were dead," and worse. We'll see you tomorrow then, around the same time.'

'Yes.'

We hugged goodbye, and I thanked them again for the cakes and then opened the front door. The sun was beginning its descent now, casting a mystical pink glow across the skyline and over the rooftops of the houses opposite. It was quite magical and seemed to augur well for what was to come. Once they were in the car I returned to the living room, where Alex had left the sofa and was playing with Adrian and Paula. 'They're nice,' Adrian said.

'Yes, very nice,' I agreed. I began collecting together the cups, saucers and plates.

'Are they coming again tomorrow?' Alex asked.

'Yes, just for an hour again.'

'I'm not going to call them Mum and Dad,' he said emphatically.

'No, they don't expect you to. Their names are Gwen and Gareth.'

And that was all Alex said about them for the rest of the evening.

CHAPTER TWENTY-ONE

THE FAMILY

G wen and Gareth visited us again the following evening as arranged and Alex began talking to them a little. Not with the unconditional enthusiasm and affection he'd shown Rosemary and Edward at the start of their introductions, but with a reserved distance. His defences were up. He was protecting himself from being hurt again, which all the adults understood. However, when Debbie telephoned for an update I was able to say that the evening had gone well and Alex was coping. The next evening when Gareth and Gwen visited, it had been agreed that they would take Alex out for a short walk. As they left the house I heard Gareth telling Alex that one of their family usually took their dog for a walk around this time. When they returned Alex seemed more relaxed and Gwen said he'd been asking questions about their dog, Rupert, and also what they did in their spare time. Although going out alone with Gwen and Gareth and talking to them was obviously a big step forward, none of the adults harboured any doubts that before long there could be a backlash – probably quite a few.

It was my turn first, and that evening, after they'd gone, Alex came to find me in the kitchen. 'How come they want me and you don't?' he asked, his face set.

I stopped what I was doing to talk to him. 'I do want you,' I said. 'But Debbie and the other social workers think you would be happier long term with Gwen and Gareth and their family. I'm hoping we will still be able to see you after you move.'

'She's fat,' Alex said, trying to think of something horrible to say about Gwen, which to be honest was difficult.

'No, she's not,' I said. 'She's cuddly, like my mother.'

'I'm not going on bike rides with them or learning the violin or having a tutor,' Alex said, becoming increasingly angry.

'Did they say you would do those things?' I asked, surprised.

'No. I'm just telling you, because Rosemary and Edward wanted me to do those things.'

I lifted Alex onto the breakfast stool, so that I was at eye level, and looked at him carefully. 'Alex, Gwen and Gareth and their family are completely different to Rosemary and Edward. They're different people, their routines will be different, and they'll do different things. We don't know that much about them yet, but what I do know is that they won't put you under pressure to do activities you don't want to do. We will learn more when we see them tomorrow. Once we've been to their house and you've met Mark, Taylor and Kaylee I'm sure you will feel much better.'

'Have you met them?' he asked.

'No, not yet, but Debbie has.'

'She met Rosemary, Edward and James lots of times,' he said pointedly.

'I know, and it didn't work out. I understand your worries, but we must give Gwen and Gareth a chance. I like what I've seen so far. Let's try to be positive. Can you tell me something you like about them?'

He thought for a moment and then said, 'They have a dog.'

'Good. Anything else?'

'They didn't lie about having a cat.'

'That's true. Good. What else?'

He thought again. 'Their kids have been with them a long time and can stay forever.'

'Fantastic,' I said. So he had been listening. 'One last thing?'

'They make great cupcakes!' he said, finally smiling.

'Yes, they do,' I agreed, pleased.

'Can I have another one?'

'Go on then.'

I asked my parents to babysit again the following evening while I took Alex to Gwen and Gareth's house for the first time. I invited them to dinner and we ate early so that Alex and I could set off at 5.30. Because Adrian and Paula loved being looked after (and spoiled) by their nana and grandpa, they didn't feel they were being left out or left behind. But it was important I could give Alex my full attention when he saw his new home for the first time and met his new siblings. He was nervous, understandably, and asked me twice before we left the house if I would stay with him for the whole hour. Then in the car he was silent, apart from clicking his fingers while staring agitatedly out of the side window. I reassured him that there was nothing to worry about.

I found the house easily from the directions Gareth and Gwen had given me and from my knowledge of the area. It was a Victorian semi-detached house in a row of similar houses, with a compact front garden and street parking only; very different from Rosemary and Edward's house, which didn't escape Alex's notice.

'At least it's not in the country,' he said, with a small sigh of relief, as I cut the engine.

'No. It's on the edge of the town, like my house is.'

'So they don't go for bike rides?' he asked. The episode at Rosemary and Edward's when Alex had failed to keep up on their first bike ride together had really left its mark.

'As far as I know they don't,' I said. 'Although I'm sure you'll be able to ride your bike if you want to. We'll ask them.'

'You can ask them,' he said, and we got out.

He slipped his hand into mine and we walked up their front path. I rang the bell. 'That's nice,' I remarked, pointing to the hanging basket of flowers in the porch as we waited for the bell to be answered.

Alex squeezed my hand tightly as the door opened. 'Hi, I'm Mark,' the teenage lad said. Gwen appeared just behind him, taking off her apron as she came to the front door.

'This is Alex,' I said to Mark as Gwen welcomed us in. Although I knew Mark to be fourteen, he looked a couple of years younger.

'Lovely to see you both again,' Gwen said. 'Come through.'

The house smelt deliciously of cake baking. We followed Gwen through a door to our right where two rooms had been knocked into one, creating a large open-plan room running from the bay window at the front of the house to the patio doors at the rear.

'This is a lovely room,' I said. All the wood had been stripped, revealing the original pine doors, surrounds and floorboards. The end of the room we were now in was the lounge area, which had two sofas, an armchair, beanbag and television arranged around a large stone fireplace. At the other end was the dining area with a pine table and six chairs. Although it was a townhouse, it had a rustic country feel about it, but no one was in the room except us and Gwen, and Mark had disappeared.

'Make yourselves comfortable,' Gwen said. 'I'll go and find out where everyone is. Trust them to vanish when they're needed.'

'Don't worry, we'll be fine,' I said. Indeed, not having to meet everyone at once had made it a bit easier for Alex.

Alex and I sat on one of the sofas and gazed around the room. There was a lot to see. On our right was a long wooden bookcase overflowing with books, DVDs, small photos in frames, ornaments and anything else that had needed a place. There were more framed photographs on the walls (mainly of the family), some African wall art and some older, possibly Victorian framed pictures of the countryside. A coffee table stood beside each of the sofas and held a haphazard arrange-ment of magazines and newspapers, a bunch of keys, a packet of sweets and a fruit bowl. A lad's jersey was draped over the back of the armchair and a pair of moccasin slippers was on the floor close by. There was other paraphernalia dotted around the room, which created the ambience of a well-lived-in, comfortable family home.

The door opened and Gareth came in, closely followed by their dog Rupert, a medium-size crossbreed who, at twelve years old, found walking a bit of a struggle. 'Sorry, I've just been trying to fix one of the showers. There's always something to mend around here,' Gareth said genially.

'I know the feeling,' I agreed. Rupert flopped down by the armchair.

'Is someone making you a drink?' Gareth asked.

'No, I'm OK for now, thank you.' I looked at Alex, who shook his head.

Gareth removed the jersey from the armchair with a small good-humoured tut and, laying it to one side, sat down. 'Gwen is rounding up the rest of the clan,' he said, absently patting the dog. 'You met Mark – he'll be back in soon.'

The door opened and Gwen returned, now with Kaylee carrying a large picture book. She had distinctive Down's features, with a round face, small mouth and nose, and almond-shaped eyes, which gave her a vulnerable, child-like appearance even though she was nineteen.

'This is Cathy and Alex,' Gwen said, introducing us.

'Hello, love,' I said. 'Nice to meet you. We spoke on the telephone.'

She looked at her mother uncertainly. 'You talked to Cathy on the phone,' Gwen confirmed.

Kaylee smiled, her whole face crinkling with delight. I guessed she smiled often and easily, like her parents. 'Talked on the phone,' she said to me.

'Yes, that's right. We had a good chat. I enjoyed talking to you.'

She looked so pleased, I could have hugged her, then she sat heavily on the beanbag and the air escaped with a loud whoosh. She laughed and I saw Alex smile. He was watching her closely and I'd answer any questions he had about her condition later.

'Read story,' she said, holding up the picture book she'd brought in.

'I think Kaylee would like to read you a story,' Gwen said to Alex.

Alex shook his head shyly.

'Perhaps a little later,' I said to Kaylee.

'Later, love,' Gwen told her.

She put the book on the floor beside her and reached over to pat the dog. 'Story later,' she said. I hoped she wasn't disappointed.

The door opened and Mark stuck his head round. 'Dad, Taylor says the shower still isn't working properly.'

'Tell him I'll look at it again later, not now. He had a shower this morning, and by the time he's emptied a can of deodorant over himself no one's going to notice.' I smiled.

'We couldn't get him in the shower when he first came,' Gwen said fondly. 'And now we can't get him out of it. He's taking his girlfriend out later.'

'Tell him to make do for now,' Gareth said to Mark.

Mark turned and, with one hand still on the door, yelled the message up the stairs behind him.

'That wasn't quite what I meant by "tell him",' Gareth remarked dryly. I smiled again. The warmth and affection this family felt for each other was palpable.

'Are you going to join us?' Gwen now asked Mark.

'Yeah, I just need a glass of water.'

'Would anyone else like a drink?' Gwen asked before Mark left the room.

'I'm fine, thanks,' I said. Alex shook his head.

'You could bring me a glass of water,' Gwen said. Mark nodded and disappeared.

'Read now?' Kaylee asked her mother.

'Not yet, love, a bit later.'

'Later,' she said, and smiled at Alex.

Alex was looking a bit bemused by all the comings and goings, but we were here so that he could start to get to know his new family, and this was giving him a good feel for what life would be like with them. Did I have any reservations despite their warmth and hospitality? Yes. How would Alex fit in – with what was already a well-established and success-ful family unit? I hoped that would become clear in time as the introductions proceeded.

Mark reappeared with Gwen's glass of water and handed it to her.

'Alex might like a game on your PlayStation,' she suggested to him. 'But a suitable game, mind you.' There was then a discussion on what Mark considered suitable for a seven-year-old – which didn't match Gwen's idea – until they finally agreed on a suggestion of Gwen's. The name of the game didn't mean anything to me, as we didn't own a PlayStation.

'Come on then,' Mark said to Alex. He went halfway down the room where a small table containing a screen with a consul beneath stood against the wall. Mark pulled up a second chair from the dining table.

Alex hesitated. 'It's just there,' I encouraged him.

'Come on,' Mark said, switching on the PlayStation.

Alex stood and went over to join him. Mark gave him a handset and then showed him how to work it. Gwen, Gareth and I began chatting, while Kaylee was content to mainly watch and listen, and occasionally stroke the dog. A few minutes passed and then the door opened again and a taller, more solidly built lad came in, dressed in freshly laundered jeans and a white T-shirt. 'Dad, the shower's still not working, the water just trickles out. I was in there for ages.'

'I'll see to it later,' Gareth replied. 'Taylor, this is Cathy and over there is Alex.'

'Hello, nice to meet you,' I said.

Taylor threw me a friendly nod and then looked down the room to where Mark and Alex were playing. 'Hi!' he called.

Alex turned and smiled shyly. Taylor was standing just behind Kaylee and ruffled her hair.

'Don't do that,' she said, pulling a face and smoothing her hair. She tried to smack his leg, but he jumped out of the way with a laugh. Rupert looked up.

'Taylor, don't tease her, I've told you before,' Gwen said lightly.

'Don't tease me,' Kaylee said, but it was all in good humour.

So the normal interactions of a happy family continued, unscripted and slightly chaotic, but relaxed, easy and non-judgemental. There was no pressure. It felt as if everyone could be themselves. Taylor joined Mark and Alex at the PlayStation while the adults continued chatting. When Alex began letting out little yelps of delight and sighs of exasperation as he won or lost points I knew he was relaxing too.

Rupert didn't stir. Then suddenly Gwen looked at her watch and exclaimed, 'It's six-forty already. I need to show you around the house, then I expect you'll be ready for a cup of tea and a slice of cake.'

'Yes, please,' I said.

I had to persuade Alex to leave the PlayStation. Mark said they could play again later if there was time. 'Or on your next visit,' I added.

We left Mark and Taylor finishing the game and Rupert still spread out on the floor by the armchair. Kaylee went with Gareth into the kitchen while Gwen, Alex and I remained standing in the centre of the room.

'So this is our living and dining room,' Gwen said, waving her arm to encompass the room. 'Every so often we have a big tidy up, but then it fills up again.'

'It's cosy,' I said.

'You could say that,' she said with a laugh, and then opened a door to our left. 'Through here is what we call the study or quiet room.'

We stepped into a small room that was as comfortable and cluttered as the living room. It was at the rear of the house and looked out to the garden. It contained a small desk with a computer, a couple of folding chairs, a beanbag, half a dozen plastic toy boxes stacked against one wall and more overflowing bookshelves on the other wall. The wood in here had been stripped too, exposing the Victorian pine, and a brightly coloured circular rug lay in the centre of the floor. Gwen then led the way into the kitchen, where Gareth was filling a kettle and Kaylee was arranging two large sponge cakes on plates.

'I thought I could smell baking when we first came in,' I said. 'They look delicious.'

'Thank you,' Gwen said. 'Kaylee and I made them earlier. Do you like cooking?' She asked Alex. He nodded.

Alex had now fallen quiet again and as Gwen led the way into the garden he slipped his hand into mine. Immediately outside was a paved patio area with potted plants, a large wooden picnic table and a rabbit hutch, in which sat Flopsy, nose twitching in the evening air. The rest of the garden was mainly lawn; there was a swing at the far end and also a rabbit run – empty at present. A shed stood partway down to the left and resting against it was an adult bike. I saw Alex look at it, but he didn't say anything. Then a ginger cat that I recognized as Tom appeared from behind the shed and leisurely strolled towards us.

'Here comes Tom,' Gwen said. 'I wonder what mischief he's been up to.'

Tom came right up to us, rubbed around our legs once and then went indoors. We returned inside too, passing through the kitchen, where under the watchful eye of Gareth Kaylee was carefully slicing the cakes. Tom was now at his food bowl, eating. As we followed Gwen upstairs she explained that Mark and Taylor shared one of the double bedrooms and she and Gareth the other. Kaylee had one of the two single rooms and Alex would have the other single. Alex slipped his hand into mine again as we went into what, in about two weeks, would be his room. It was decorated in neutral beige and contained a single bed, wardrobe and chest of drawers.

'It looks a bit plain now,' Gwen said to Alex. 'But once you have all your belongings in here and posters on the walls, you'll make it your own.'

'You allow posters on the walls?' I clarified, as I knew Rosemary and Edward hadn't.

'Yes, of course. Wait until you see the boys' room!'

Alex and I had a quick look out of the window, which overlooked the garden, and then we followed Gwen into the room next door – Taylor and Mark's room. My question about posters was answered! All the walls, from floor to ceiling, were covered with large colourful posters, some in 3D. They ran behind the shelves and disappeared round the back of the wardrobe and chest of drawers. Posters of vintage cars, capital skylines, football teams and individual players, Marilyn Monroe, London's Tower Bridge, boybands, movies and TV shows – *Star Wars* and *Doctor Who* featured heavily – and in one corner a collection of scantily clad ladies with large breasts.

'Not for your eyes yet,' Gwen said, lightly placing her hand over Alex's eyes. He chuckled.

We had a quick look in Kaylee's room, which was decorated in her favourite colour – pale yellow – and was very neat and tidy. Then Gwen briefly showed Alex her and Gareth's room while I waited on the landing. We returned downstairs to the living room, where the table was now laid for tea; the two sponge cakes, evenly sliced, sat majestically in the centre. Rupert had finally moved and was beneath the table – waiting, I suspected, for crumbs to fall or any titbits.

We sat down, took a plate and a slice of cake each and began eating. There was a choice of tea or lemonade to drink. Alex was sitting between Gwen and me, and presently she said to him, 'Have you thought of any questions you'd like to ask me?'

He shifted, slightly uncomfortable, and then looked to me.

'Do you go for bike rides?' I asked.

'I don't, although I probably should after eating all this cake,' Gwen laughed. 'Mark has a bike he uses for school. You probably saw it propped by the shed – he never gets around to putting it away. Gareth has a bike too, don't you, love?' She threw him a teasing smile. 'He bought it a couple of years ago as part of a get-fit campaign, but I've told him he needs to ride it to get fit. It won't happen while the bike is in the shed.' Everyone laughed, including Gareth.

'Unfair,' he said good-humouredly. 'I used it last Saturday.'

'Yes, Dad!' Taylor cried. 'To fetch a takeaway!' We all laughed again.

'Alex was given a bike last Christmas. He likes to ride in the garden or the park sometimes,' I said.

'That's good,' Gwen said. 'We have a park just up the road. I can take you.'

'What about hobbies?' I now asked, trying to remember all the issues Alex had raised. 'Do you do things together?'

'Oh yes, sometimes,' Gwen said. 'We may go to the cinema if there's a film we all want to see, or on a day trip, and we have meals out. But at their age Mark and Taylor often want to do their own thing. Kaylee always comes with us though, and we still go on family holidays together.'

'Do any of you play a musical instrument?' I asked. Gwen glanced at me oddly; it was starting to sound like an interview. I met her gaze. 'Just a few questions that have come up after the last time,' I said. I think she understood what I meant.

'I'm afraid we don't have any musicians in the family,' Gwen said. 'Although we like to listen to music – sometimes very loudly,' she added, glancing at the boys. 'Kaylee can play the recorder a little, and Taylor is teaching himself the guitar.'

Alex sat upright and looked at Taylor with admiration.

'Alex would like to learn to play the guitar,' I said.

'That's cool,' Taylor said. 'We can form a boyband.'

Which comment, I could see from Alex's expression, meant everything to him.

CHAPTER TWENTY-TWO

THE LINE WENT DEAD

The introduction of Alex to his new forever family continued as planned. The following evening I took him to his new home and left him for a short while. Adrian and Paula came with me and were able to meet Kaylee, Mark, Taylor and Rupert for the first time – *Mum, why can't we have a dog?* Flopsy was in her hutch and Tom, as usual, was off roaming. When we collected Alex, Gwen and Gareth said he'd done very well and had spent some time with everyone. He and Mark had played on the PlayStation, Taylor had shown him a few chords on the guitar and Kaylee had finally had the chance to read him a story.

'It was a bit babyish,' Alex confided in the car as I drove us home. 'And she wanted me to play with her doll's house.' He pulled a face.

'What did Gwen say?' I asked. I'd already explained a little about Down's syndrome to Alex.

'Gwen said Kaylee often liked to do things that younger children did, and if I didn't want to play with her I should tell her, and she wouldn't be offended.'

'So that was OK then? It was sorted?' I asked, glancing at him in the rear-view mirror.

He nodded. 'I didn't mind her reading me a story, but I didn't want to play with her dolls.' I assumed that Gwen and Gareth would know what to say and do if situations like this arose.

When we took Alex on Saturday for his first overnight we were in the house for longer, and Adrian and Paula had the chance to see Alex's bedroom and play with Flopsy, who was in her run on the lawn. We were also treated to a short musical recital where Taylor helped Alex strum a few chords on the guitar and Kaylee joined in with her recorder. I wouldn't call it music, but it was entertaining!

'We know what we're going to buy Alex for his birthday,' Gwen said quietly to me, referring to the guitar. Alex's birthday was in a little over a month.

'He's a lucky boy,' I said. 'In more ways than one.'

'We're the lucky ones,' she said, 'being able to have Alex. Our family is complete now.'

When we returned to collect Alex on Sunday afternoon we were invited to stay for a cup of tea and a slice of cake and were there for over an hour again. During this time I was better able to see how Alex was fitting into the family and relating to his siblings, and, just as importantly, how they related to him. As he was the youngest by seven years, they treated him simply as a younger brother. There was no sign of jealousy or sibling rivalry, although I could see that Alex could be spoiled, but then he deserved spoiling after all he'd been through.

Debbie visited Gareth and Gwen twice during the introductory period, once with Shanice. She also telephoned Gwen, Gareth and me regularly for updates. Jill phoned me too. Happy that everything was going well and to plan, we confirmed the arrangements for Alex to move the following Saturday, two and a half weeks after he'd first met his family. The Friday before the move he finally told his teacher and one of his friends that he was going to live with a new family and he'd never have to move again. That Alex was able to say this showed how much he now trusted Gwen and Gareth. It was a testament not only to Alex's forgiving and generous nature, but the wonderful work Gwen, Gareth and their family had put into rebuilding Alex's trust. Many children from failed adoptions are not so lucky and bounce around the care system as they struggle with deep feelings of rejection, resentment and anger.

On Friday after school – Alex's last day with us – we gave him a little moving party; it wouldn't be goodbye, as we would be keeping in touch. I had asked him if he'd like to invite some of his friends from school, but he hadn't wanted to. I could understand why – to come to our house for the first time when he was leaving might seem uncomfortable and confusing. Doubtless there would be plenty of opportunities for his friends to go to his permanent home. He was staying at the same school and Gwen was already planning a birthday party for him. I invited my parents and Jill to the tea party. Once Alex had left me, Jill and the fostering agency would no longer be involved, so this was goodbye for her, and it was unlikely that my parents would see him again either. I made Alex's favourite food, including jelly and ice cream, and after tea we played some games and then presented him with his leaving presents: a skateboard from us (he'd admired Adrian's), a compendium of board games from my parents and Jill gave him a card signed by all the staff at the agency and a gift voucher.

That night Alex was very excited – overexcited – and couldn't sleep. I kept going into his room and settling him, and then, overtired, he grew maudlin and started saying things like, 'What if Gareth and Gwen change their minds and don't want me?' Which he hadn't said since before the start of the introductions.

'They won't,' I said firmly.

'But how can you be sure?' he persisted. 'They might.'

'I can be sure because of Kaylee, Taylor and Mark. They didn't change their minds with them and they won't with you.' Which seemed to help.

The following morning Alex had recovered and was looking forward to life with his new family. His excitement was contagious, and over breakfast the noise level rose until Toscha shot upstairs and hid under my bed. I had all of Alex's bags packed and ready in the hall for when Gwen and Gareth arrived at 10.30 a.m. We all helped load the car – even little Paula. Fortunately, they owned a large four-by-four, so all Alex's belongings fitted in, including his bike. We kept our goodbyes short as was advised and said we'd telephone in two weeks. It was sad standing on the pavement and waving him off, seeing his little face at the car window, but I knew he couldn't wish for a better family and I was sure he'd be happy there.

* * *

Life continued as normal for us, and the following week I looked after a child on respite for ten days. Two weeks after Alex left I telephoned him as arranged and we all spoke to him. He sounded the happiest I'd ever heard him and was excitedly looking forward to his birthday the following week. I'd sent a card with some money, which Gwen had put away. Alex knew that Gwen and Gareth had bought a very special present for him, but he didn't know what it was. He said that Mark and Taylor had been teasing him about what it could be. But it was all in good fun and he didn't mind at all – it added to his excitement. When we visited after his birthday he was proudly strumming his new guitar.

Gwen and I said we'd keep in touch, not only so that we could see Alex, but because during the introductions Gwen and I had become friends. However, realistically, with both of us leading busy family lives and me fostering, we wouldn't be meeting up that often. Adrian, Paula and I visited again a month later, met up with them in the summer holidays and from then on we got together as and when the opportunity arose. I saw Alex flourish and grow in height and confidence. He'd fitted perfectly into the family and was obviously very happy. Gwen said they'd felt as if they'd always had him.

When Alex had first gone to live with Gwen and Gareth he'd called them by their first names, but as time went on, hearing Kaylee, Taylor and Mark calling them Mum and Dad, Alex began to do the same – naturally and without any encouragement. Then, when he had been living with them for about eight months, Gwen and Gareth had a chat with him, one to one, and explained that Mark, Taylor and Kaylee had come to them as foster children but they'd then adopted them. They explained what adoption really meant, and that the child became theirs forever, with the same rights and status as if they had been born to them. They suggested that Alex could think about whether he'd like them to adopt him, as they wanted to. Alex thought about it for two seconds and then gave them a resounding yes, smothering them in hugs and kisses.

A year later I was invited to the court when the adoption certificate was presented, and it was one of the happiest days of my life. The number of guests was limited and it was a school day so I couldn't take Adrian and Paula, but Alex's family was there, everyone dressed very smartly, with the men and boys wearing suits. Debbie and Shanice were there too, as were six of Gareth and Gwen's oldest friends – three couples. It was formal to begin with. The judge sat on the podium and spoke about adoption, then he congratulated the family, wished them well for the future and stood ready to present Alex with his certificate. Alex looked so proud (and a little self-conscious) as he walked up to the podium in his suit to collect the certificate. The judge shook his hand and congratulated him personally. Then he and the judge came down into the body of the court and we all posed for photographs. After the ceremony family and friends were invited for lunch. Gareth had booked a table at an Italian restaurant just round the corner. Once there I gave them the presents I'd brought: a crystal vase inscribed with 'Congratulations' and today's date for Gwen and Gareth and a watch for Alex. I'd checked beforehand with Gwen that he would like one.

As we ate the delicious food I chatted with Gwen and Gareth's friends – lovely, warm people who'd known them since their twenties. One of the couples fostered, so we had plenty to talk about. They all said what a wonderful family Gwen and Gareth had created and how pleased they were that Alex was part of it, and that he wouldn't give them the trouble Mark and Taylor had. Little did we realize then, but later I thought how those words must have come back to haunt them ...

We left the restaurant at around 2.30, as most of us had children to collect from school, and once home I showed Adrian and Paula the photographs I'd taken of the day and told them all about the ceremony.

Time passed, months turned into years, and our families got together when we could. We always exchanged Christmas cards and I always sent Alex a birthday card containing money or a voucher. Alex stayed at his primary school until the age of eleven, when he transferred to a secondary school closer to his home. All went well until he was nearly thirteen and hit puberty, then trouble began.

I wasn't aware of just how bad things were to begin with, as Gwen just said that Alex was starting to test the boundaries, but then so do lots of young people at that age. It's part of growing up, as children discover adulthood and seek greater autonomy and freedom. Adrian was the same age as Alex and I'd noticed that he, too, had started questioning my authority sometimes and pushing the boundaries. Given that Mark and Taylor had arrived at Gwen and Gareth's with very challenging behaviour and police records, I didn't think too much about it. Then, by sheer coincidence, I was in the high street one weekday morning when I passed a group of youths behaving rowdily. Of school age, they were shouting, swearing, play-fighting and generally making a nuisance of themselves, and a couple of them were smoking. Passers-by had to step off the pavement and into the road to get by them, but I held my ground. As I drew level, to my horror I saw that one of the lads was Alex. He saw me too and quickly passed his cigarette to the girl next to him. I stopped dead in my tracks.

'Alex! What are you doing here?' I asked, surprised and shocked.

'Is that your mum?' the girl asked with a smirk, referring to me.

'No,' Alex said, and had the decency to look embarrassed. It had been about six months since I'd last seen him at Gwen and Gareth's, but it hadn't been for long as he'd been going out.

'How are you?' I asked. 'No school today?'

'I've been suspended, Miss,' one of the other lads bragged with a laugh.

Alex didn't reply and couldn't look me in the eyes. 'Come on, let's go,' he said to the others.

'Bye, Miss,' the girl said. Dragging on the last of the cigarette, she threw it in the gutter.

The group turned and walked away and I watched them go. Alex didn't look back. An elderly couple coming in the opposite direction had to move out of their way as they passed. I heard the man remark disgustedly, 'The youth of today!'

Shocked and upset by what I'd seen, I continued to my car. I'd finished my shopping and had been on my way home. Whatever was Alex doing here? This town was a forty-minute bus ride from his home, and why wasn't he in school? Surely he hadn't been suspended like the other lad? And smoking. Gwen would be so upset. It was clear he wasn't keeping the best company. My thoughts churned away as I drove home and then for the rest of the afternoon. I kept going over what I'd seen and then returning to the question: should I telephone Gwen and Gareth and tell them? Would I want to know if I was in their position? I didn't want to be the bearer of bad news, but then again I felt I would want to know if it was one of my children. Alex was so unlike the child of a year ago, it had shocked and worried me.

By 9 p.m. when my children were in bed asleep I'd decided I'd make the call to Gwen and Gareth, and with increasing anxiety I dialled their number. Their phone rang for a while and then Kaylee (now twenty-four) answered as she often did with a very polite and well-practised, 'Hello. Who would you like to speak to?'

'Hello, Kaylee, it's Cathy. Is Mummy there?' I knew that if I asked her how she was or engaged her in conversation we would be chatting for some time, and tonight I just wanted to say what I had to and see if I could help at all. There was silence on the other end of the phone, so I said again, 'Kaylee, it's Cathy. Can you tell Mummy I'd like to talk to her, please?'

Then I heard Gwen in the background ask, 'Who is it, love?'

'Cathy,' Kaylee replied.

Gwen came to the phone. 'Hi, how are you?' She sounded upbeat. 'Sorry I haven't been in touch, the time has just vanished.'

'We're fine,' I said.

I knew I needed to come straight to the point, but it still wasn't easy. 'Gwen, I've agonized all afternoon if I should phone and tell you, and I decided that if it was one of my children I'd want to know. I saw Alex this morning in our high street and ...' I didn't get any further.

'Wait a minute while I close the door,' she said. 'So we can't be overheard. Alex has just got back. Gareth is with him now.'

The phone was set down, I heard a door close and then Gwen came back on the line, her voice now sombre and subdued. 'Sorry, Cathy, we're going through hell at present with Alex. The police returned him about twenty minutes ago. Gareth is giving him a good talking to now.'

'Gwen, this is obviously a bad time for me to phone. Shall I call back another time?'

'No, stay. I could do with someone to talk to, and it's safer if Gareth speaks to him.'

'Safer?' I asked, dismayed.

'Alex is very angry with me. He's raised his fist to me in the past and has threatened me.' Her voice faltered. 'Oh, Cathy, you won't believe what we've been going through with him.'

'I'm so sorry,' I said. 'He was doing so well.'

'I know. It's taken us all unawares. We expected this sort of behaviour with Mark and Taylor when they first arrived. They were completely out of control and tested us to the limit. But once they realized we'd always be there for them, and would love them no matter what, they began to settle down and became like different boys. But Alex has been settled and one of the family for the last six years, and then he hits puberty. It's as though all the hurt, anger and resentment from his early years has been unleashed.'

'Oh, Gwen. How are you all coping?'

'I'm not sure we are,' she said. 'You name it and Alex is doing it – smoking illegal substances, drinking, stealing, lying, truanting, getting into fights and trouble with the police. He's due in court next week. And the drugs and alcohol are turning his brain and making him paranoid. He says the most ludicrous things.'

'Is he having counselling?' I asked, horrified and overwhelmed by what I was hearing.

'It's been offered, but he won't attend. Gareth and I have been seeing a counsellor for advice on how to deal with Alex's behaviour, and also to offload. He's pushed us to the limit. I'm not sure how much more of this we can stand. Some of the things he's been saying are really nasty and designed to hurt us. He's so angry.'

'Like what?' I asked, appalled.

'He says he never loved us and it was just an act. We know it's not true, but it still hurts. He accuses us of loving Mark, Taylor and Kaylee more than him, and says we are unfair and show them favouritism, which just isn't true. If anything Alex has had more than his share of love and attention because he's the youngest.'

'I know, Gwen. He doesn't mean it. He's angry.'

'That's what the counsellor said. But he tells Kaylee she's stupid, which is really nasty.' Gwen's voice faltered again. 'When Gareth or I tell him how unkind that is he tells us to go and fuck ourselves and to put him into care. He often says he'd rather be in care. I know it's designed to hurt us, and it works, but the social worker from the post-adoption team said it might be the only option in the end.'

I went cold. 'Oh no, don't say that. Please.'

'Trust me, Cathy, it would be the very last resort, but I honestly don't know how much more we can take. Alex's behaviour isn't just affecting Gareth and me; it's impacting on the others. Mark and Taylor have become very protective of us. They've tried talking to Alex, but they've lost patience. They threatened to give him a good hiding if he didn't sort himself out, and Kaylee just bursts into tears when there is any nastiness. She hates shouting or unpleasantness of any kind. She's such a gentle soul and can't understand why Alex is behaving like this. It breaks my heart. It's a nightmare.'

'It is,' I said. I didn't know what to say. 'And the counsellor says this has all come about because Alex has hit puberty?'

'She explained that children with backgrounds like Alex's often struggle more in adolescence – a combination of all those hormones and the trauma of their early life experiences. She said she'd supported other adopters in similar situations. But it's always more difficult if the younger person won't engage or is using drugs and alcohol to numb the pain. I blame that crowd Alex has got in with for that. I expect he was with them today.'

'He was with a group,' I said. 'Four lads and a girl.'

'That'll be them. I had a phone call this morning from his school to say he hadn't arrived. I knew he wouldn't stay around here, as I've found him before in our town and taken him back to school. Two of the boys are brothers. It's the older one that supplies them with the drink and drugs. This evening when Alex hadn't arrived home by six o'clock – the time he's supposed to be home – we waited an hour and then reported him missing to the police. That's what we're supposed to do as part of the behavioural contract the post-adoption social worker suggested.' A behavioural contract is a signed agreement between the young person and the adult(s) responsible for them, which sets out the rules and expectations to modify their unsafe or unacceptable behaviour. There are rewards for improving their behaviour and consequences for not doing so.

'I'd no idea it was that bad,' I said. 'Is there anything I can do to help?'

'I doubt it. But let me know if you think of anything.' She gave a small, humourless laugh.

Then suddenly there was an almighty crash, as if a large object had been thrown and smashed, together with Alex's voice, almost unrecognizable: 'There's fuck all you can do about it, so don't piss me off!' Then another crash.

'Got to go, Cathy. I'll phone you when I have the chance.'

And the line went dead.

CHAPTER TWENTY-THREE

BEFORE IT'S TOO LATE

S hocked, saddened and extremely worried, I tried to think if there was anything I could do to help Gwen, Gareth and their family through the terrible time they were having with Alex. They were highly experienced in handling challenging behaviour and had successfully survived a very testing time with Mark and Taylor. I hoped and prayed they'd find the strength to be able to do the same with Alex. Although of course this was different, as Mark and Taylor had arrived out of control, and with love, commitment and firm boundaries had finally settled down. Alex, on the other hand, had been much younger, had settled quickly and had been a fully integrated member of their family for six years. I knew that despite what he was now saying about not loving Gwen and Gareth, he had loved them and underneath his anger still did, as they loved him. But how long the family could survive the type of behaviour they were now having to deal with I didn't know. Everyone has a breaking point. Gwen had said they were accessing post-adoption support and seeing a counsellor, but unless Alex engaged and saw the counsellor too, the service could only be of limited help. My heart went out to them as I pictured Mark and Taylor protecting their parents from Alex's anger, and Kaylee, just wanting everyone to be happy, in tears. The worst-case scenario was that Alex would end up in care again or, if he got into further trouble with the police, a young offenders' institution. In the UK a shocking quarter of those in young offenders' institutions are from care.

I desperately wanted to do something to try to help, and after much thought I decided that probably the best offer I could make was to give them some time. I'd suggest that Alex came to stay with me for a few days. It would give them all a break and hopefully Alex the space he needed to take stock of his life and realize what he was doing wrong. I'd also try to talk some sense into him. But there were a number of considerations I had to take into account before I made this offer. One, I was now fostering Lucy (whom I went on to adopt and whose story I tell in *Will You Love Me?*). I'd need to consider the impact Alex staying would have on her, and her social worker would have to approve it, even if it was only for a few days, as would Jill and the agency I fostered for. It's a requirement of fostering that both the foster child's social worker and the fostering agency are informed straight away of any changes in a carer's household. And of course as well as asking Lucy I would need to ask Adrian and Paula for their views, for who knew what damage Alex might do?

I didn't go into all the details when I spoke to the children. I just said that Alex and his family were going through a difficult time and I was thinking of suggesting that Alex came to stay with us for a few days. They said they didn't mind and Adrian made the offer of sharing his bedroom with Alex, which I thanked him for but declined. I would be keeping a close eye on Alex and would minimize any opportunity for him to influence Adrian. Young people at this age can be very impressionable and some of what he might tell Adrian could sound daring and risqué. I'd either give up my bedroom for Alex or he could sleep downstairs on the sofa bed.

I telephoned Jill first. She knew I was still in touch with Alex and his family. I was honest in my account of the problems they were experiencing. I had to be, and possibly she was already aware from a colleague that there were problems. She said she'd need to speak to her manager but she thought he'd agree to Alex staying, and I would obviously supervise him very well. She also said she'd speak to Lucy's social worker. Three days later Jill phoned back and gave me the go-ahead, with the stipulation that I mustn't leave Alex unattended in the house or with Lucy, which I didn't intend to.

When I told Gwen her voice broke with emotion as she thanked me. 'That is kind of you. Let me have a chat with Gareth and I'll get back to you. We'll have to think how to put it to Alex so he doesn't see it as another rejection.' I then suggested that as it was half-term holiday the following week, Alex could come and stay with me then.

Gwen telephoned back two days later, thanked me for my offer but said Alex didn't want to come. In fact, he'd taken it badly and had accused me of plotting with Gwen and Gareth against him.

'Oh dear, I am sorry,' I said. 'That was never my intention.'

'I know, but in his present state of mind he interprets any situation involving him as a conspiracy.'

There wasn't much else I could suggest, so I told Gwen that if Alex changed his mind – the offer stood – or if there was anything else I could do to help, to let me know.

'I'm not sure there is,' she said despondently. 'But thanks anyway. We're just going to have to try to work through this. Although I'm not sure how.'

Gwen had said that Alex had taken my offer badly, and now he was about to show me just how badly. The following night he and his mates threw a brick through the window of my downstairs front room. I don't want to put anyone off applying to foster, so it's important to say that nothing like this has ever happened before or since. But it was one of the scariest moments of my life. It was a little after 11 p.m. Adrian, Lucy and Paula were in their bedrooms, asleep, and I'd just gone up. Thankfully, the front room was empty or one of us could have been badly hurt. I was in my bedroom, still dressed, when the noise of breaking glass startled me, although I didn't know at that point it was the window of the room below. I quickly crossed to my bedroom window and parted the curtains in time to see a group of lads running off up the street. I recognized Alex with what looked like the same group I'd seen him with in the high street, minus the girl. Shocked and trembling, I went downstairs, flicking on the lights as I went. In the hall I saw that the front door wasn't broken, but as I entered the front room my heart stopped. I stared at the scene before me. 'Oh no!' I cried. There was a large hole in the centre of the window with tentacles of fractured glass spiralling out. Shards of glass covered the chair in front of the window and the surrounding floor. I stared in horror at the builder's brick on the floor directly in front of the window. 'Oh, Alex,' I said under my breath. To be honest, I could have cried from the shock of it all and that he had done this to us.

Adrian, Lucy and Paula, woken by the noise, had come out of their bedrooms. 'What was that?' Adrian asked anxiously and began downstairs.

'I heard a crash,' Lucy said.

'The front-room window has been smashed,' I said, my voice shaking.

In their nightwear and barefooted they came into the front room as far as was safe – to the edge of the carpet, where it was glass-free. They looked as shaken as I felt.

'Who did that?' Paula asked, aghast.

'Yobs messing around in the street,' I said as evenly as I could.

'Shall I phone the police?' Adrian asked helpfully.

'No, I'll do it tomorrow,' I said. I needed time to think if I would report it to the police, and if so what I would say.

'You should do it now,' Lucy said. 'They might catch them.' But that was the point. Did I want Alex caught? Was that what he needed right now? I didn't know.

'I think I'll clear up first,' I said. 'And we need to put something over that hole for tonight, then I'll call the insurance company in the morning.'

'Shouldn't you leave everything as it is for evidence?' Adrian asked.

But I wasn't sure I wanted evidence of what Alex had done. I was too shocked to think straight. Then the doorbell rang, making us all jump. For a moment I thought it was

Alex and his mates, returning to do us more harm, in which case I would phone the police straight away. Adrian, Paula and Lucy stared at me anxiously as I began towards the front door. Adrian got there first and, peering through the security spyhole, said, 'Mum, it's OK. It's our neighbour, Sue.'

I opened the door. 'We heard the noise,' she said, concerned. 'Your window is broken. Are you all right?'

'Yes, we were upstairs thankfully, but the front room is a mess.'

Sue came in and gasped when she saw the state it was in. 'Did you see who did it?' she asked, dismayed.

'Teenage lads. I'll report it in the morning. I'm more concerned about boarding up that hole for tonight.'

'Shall I send Steve round? He's still up and he'll know what to do. I'm sure he's got something in his shed to cover that. He has most things in there.' Steve was Sue's husband, who could often be heard hammering and sawing in his shed at weekends. It was a bone of contention between them as to how much time he spent in his shed, but now I was very grateful for the offer.

'Yes, please, if he wouldn't mind. If I phone the insurance company it will be hours before they send a repairer.'

Sue returned next door to fetch her husband.

'I'll get dressed and help Steve,' Adrian said, and went upstairs. Since my husband had left Adrian had in some ways taken over the role of the man in the house, although I didn't allow him more responsibility than was reasonable for a thirteen-year-old.

Lucy and Paula went upstairs too for their dressing gowns and slippers, while I fetched the dustpan and brush, making sure Toscha was shut out so she couldn't come into the front room and risk getting shards of glass in her paws. The girls and I then began the task of clearing up. Paula held open a plastic bag as I swept up the larger pieces of glass and tipped them into it, while Lucy fetched the vacuum cleaner and plugged it in. Steve suddenly appeared outside the window, making us start. 'Just measuring up,' he said through the hole, and opened up the ladder he'd brought with him.

'Thank you so much. I am grateful,' I said.

'Whoever did this wants a good hiding,' he said.

I nodded and continued clearing up.

Once I'd swept up the larger pieces of glass, I began vacuuming the carpet and chairs as the girls moved the furniture. Tiny splinters of glass were everywhere. Just as we thought we had one area clear another sliver glinted in the light. Adrian had returned downstairs in joggers and jersey, and when Steve appeared outside the window again, now carrying a large sheet of plywood, Adrian went out to help him.

Sue returned and joined me and the girls in the front room, and we all watched as Steve and Adrian held the sheet of plywood up to the window to check it fitted. Then they lowered it again and set it to one side. 'That'll do fine,' Steve said. 'I'll use as few nails as possible so it doesn't damage the wood. But this is just temporary, Cathy, to see you through the night.'

'Yes. Thank you so much,' I said again.

We continued watching as Steve gave instructions to Adrian on what he could do to help – hold the bottom edge of the plywood to steady it as Steve went up the ladder, then pass the nails up to him. Already emotional from what had happened, seeing this moved me, as it would have been Adrian helping his father with this job, had he not left us.

Fifteen minutes later the wood was in place and I thanked Steve and Sue profusely. Sue and I were friends as well as neighbours and she and I had helped each other out in the past, but this was not a favour I would easily be able to repay. Not that they expected repayment, but I would buy them wine and chocolates as a thank you. I was so grateful, and it was such a relief to have the house reasonably secure again. It was well past midnight by the time we'd finished and had said goodnight to Sue and Steve. The children and I went straight up to bed, but I slept fitfully. I was agonizing, not only because Alex and his mates – out of control and on the streets – could return and do more damage, but also because I was trying to decide whether I should report them to the police. While I was annoyed and upset by what they'd done, I knew Alex was in a really bad place right now. Would reporting him help him to work through his anger? Or help Gwen and Gareth manage his behaviour? I doubted it. Alex was already in trouble with the police. Adding to his crime list wasn't likely to help him turn a corner, was it? Indeed, I thought it would probably compound his feelings of persecution and make him even more difficult to reach. But on the other hand I didn't want him and his mates thinking they could vandalize my house and upset my family when they felt like it. During that long night, every time I heard the slightest noise outside I was out of bed and peering between the curtains. By the morning I had no clearer idea of what I should do.

As Adrian, Paula and Lucy came down for breakfast they all made a detour via the front room, as I had done when I'd first got up, to check on the boarding. It was still in place and doing its job, thanks to Steve, but the room was dismally dark with the main window blocked up. It occurred to me that if I'd had double glazing, a brick was unlikely to have penetrated, but now John had gone I was having to be careful with money, so double glazing wasn't a priority.

I saw Adrian, Paula and Lucy off to school, and then as soon as the offices at the insurance company opened I telephoned their claims department. I said that a brick had been thrown through my front-room window last night and asked how I should go about having it repaired under the insurance. By the time he'd finished telling me what was involved and I'd checked the details of my policy, it was clear I wouldn't be making a claim. All claims had to be reported to the police, which would involve a trip to the police station to make a statement. Evidence of the damage had to be kept until the loss adjuster had visited and my claim had been approved, resulting in a boarded-up window for however many weeks it took – he didn't know exactly. Then, if my claim was approved, which seemed a big 'if', I had to submit three estimates for the work, and that was before we came to the matter of the excess on my policy, which I was now reminded I'd set at the maximum of £500 to keep the premium low. The decision was therefore made. I thanked him for his trouble, said goodbye and then telephoned a local glazier who said he'd come round in an hour to give an estimate for the work. For £250 he replaced the window that afternoon, so when Adrian, Paula and Lucy arrived home from school we were back to normal.

That evening I telephoned Gwen and Gareth.

Gareth answered and we swapped the usual friendly hellos and how are yous? Then I asked if Alex was there.

'Yes, why?' Gareth asked.

'I'd like to talk to him if I may. I'll tell you afterwards exactly what we've said. Would that be all right?'

'Yes, Cathy, but can I ask you what this is in connection with?'

'The brick that was thrown through my window last night,' I said.

'Oh no. Not Alex?'

'Yes, with some other lads. Would it be all right if I spoke to him now and then explained to you?'

'Yes, of course. I'm so sorry, Cathy. I'll fetch him now. He's in his room.'

'Thank you.'

The handset was put down and then a lengthy silence followed – unusual in their house, as normally there was always something going on and voices in the background. I guessed Alex didn't want to speak to me, for it was over five minutes before Gareth's voice came on the line again. 'He's coming now.'

'Thank you. How is everyone?'

'Not too bad, considering. Gwen's told you the trouble we've been having.'

'Yes. I am sorry.'

'There's only Alex and me in this evening,' Gareth said. 'Mark and Taylor are at their girlfriends'. They spend quite a bit of time there now. Gwen has taken Kaylee to the cinema. I would have gone, but we daren't leave Alex in the house alone.' He stopped abruptly. 'Here he is,' he said. 'I'll put him on.'

Gareth passed the handset to Alex. 'What do you want?' he demanded rudely.

'To talk to you about last night,' I said evenly.

'It wasn't me. I didn't throw it.'

'It doesn't matter who threw it. I'm holding you responsible. Those other lads wouldn't have had the idea without you – they didn't even know where I lived. You brought them to my house and even if you didn't actually throw the brick you incited one of them to do so. You are the only one with a motive, Alex, and I saw you all running away, so please don't treat me like a fool.' I was firm but calm.

'Have you finished now?' he asked insolently.

'Not yet. I've no idea what you thought you would achieve by doing that. I doubt you even thought it through. I made the offer for you to come and stay with me for a few days and you respond by getting angry with your parents and then throwing a brick through my window. The offer was well meant, but you completely misinterpreted it and decided we were plotting against you. Nothing could be further from the truth. We are all trying to help you.' I heard him give a scornful *humph*. 'I haven't reported it to the police yet, Alex, because your parents don't need any more worry. And I'm not convinced that reporting it would help you either. But if there is any repetition of that type of behaviour or if I see you or your mates near my house again – unless I invite you to visit – I will call the police straight away. Do I make myself clear, Alex?'

There was silence.

'Alex, I'm asking you a question. Do you understand what I've said?'

Another silence and then a begrudging, 'Yes. I heard you.'

'Good. I've had the window replaced. It cost me two hundred and fifty pounds and I'm expecting you to pay for it.' He swore under his breath. 'Not all at once – you can put aside a few pounds each week out of your allowance. Your mum and I get together every so often, so she can give me however much you've saved, or, if you prefer, you can give me the money in person. Phone and we'll arrange to meet.'

He muttered another expletive, which I ignored.

'And, Alex, a word of advice before I speak to your dad: please take the help that is being offered and get yourself sorted out. I know you had a rough start to life, but so do lots of children. Don't let it ruin the rest of your life. You've got much to be grateful for. I'm sure that deep down you know you've got the best family ever and how much they love you, and I know you love them. Smoking drugs and drinking alcohol is ruining your brain. This isn't the real you, Alex. I know the real you and so do your parents, brothers and sister. You're a fantastic person – intelligent, funny, loving, kind and generous. Find that person again, Alex. Please take all the help and support that is on offer and find him for your own sake and your family's. Before it's too late.'

There was no reply. I didn't really expect one.

'Please think about what I've said, Alex. Take care. I'll speak to your father now.'

The phone was set down and presently Gareth's voice came on the line. I explained about the brick being thrown through my window and then what I'd said to Alex just now and his limited responses. As his father Gareth had a right to know. He gave a deep, exasperated sigh, apologized and offered to pay for the broken window, but we both knew that Alex should be responsible for repaying me, so Gareth said he would remind Alex each week to put some money aside from his allowance. He thanked me for not reporting the matter to the police, as it would certainly have sent Alex to a young offenders' institution. Perhaps that's what Alex needed – a short, sharp shock – but I didn't want to be the one to put him there. I still remembered the old Alex – the small, rejected child, and then the young lad who had thrived in the heart of his adoptive family for all those years. I hoped and prayed that Alex would return before it really was too late.

CHAPTER TWENTY-FOUR

THE HUG

The next time I met Gwen, about three months later, she looked utterly exhausted. She admitted that she didn't know how much more she and Gareth could take. Alex's behaviour, far from improving, had deteriorated. She and Gareth were now arguing between themselves over the best way to deal with Alex, while Taylor, Mark and Kaylee had little to do with him. 'Whatever happened to my loving, happy family?' Gwen said, with tears in her eyes.

We'd met at a coffee shop in town, and as we talked Gwen told me that although Alex hadn't come to the attention of the police again, this was because he'd evaded being caught, rather than any improvement in his behaviour. She said he was still stealing to buy alcohol and the drugs he smoked, and had stolen from all of them, including Kaylee, who kept cash in a money box in her bedroom. He'd gone in when she wasn't there, emptied the money box and then said she must have forgotten where she'd put it, blaming her learning difficulties for not remembering. Gwen said that Alex was no longer showering or changing his clothes regularly and seemed to take a perverse pleasure in being unwashed and unkempt, then caused a huge scene if they mentioned it at all. He often stayed out all night, and when she or Gareth reported him missing to the police they now treated their concerns less seriously and took longer to respond, as it had happened so many times before. She said Alex hardly spoke to any of them and when he did it was usually to say something spiteful. The previous month he'd been permanently excluded from school so he was now at home all day. She or Gareth had to be in the house to make sure he didn't get into more trouble. She didn't mention the money Alex was supposed to be giving me for the broken window and I certainly didn't bring it up. It was impossible to know what to say, and my well-meant and now overused 'I'm sure he'll turn a corner before too long' sounded feeble and unconvincing even to me.

Ten months passed, during which time I was supposed to meet Gwen twice but she cancelled at the last minute saying she was unwell. On the second occasion she said she was going to the hospital for blood tests. 'I've been feeling low for a while now, so I thought I'd better get checked out, although I'm sure it's stress.'

'Let me know if I can do anything,' I said, and then asked how Alex was.

'The same,' she said, but didn't offer any more.

The next time we met, a few months later, Gwen had been given the all-clear from the hospital – there was nothing physically wrong with her, but her doctor had talked to her about trying to reduce the stress she was under, which of course was impossible with Alex behaving as he was. I began to wonder if – despite all their love and support – he would be able to get his life back on track, and how much stress they could take. But Gwen said more than once to me that he was their son and they'd stand by him, no matter what.

We continued to meet every few months and Alex's name was mentioned less and less. If I asked Gwen how he was she'd say, 'The same. Let's talk about something else.'

There was never any money from him for the broken window and I wrote it off. I hadn't seen Alex or his mates near my house again, so they had heeded my warning. By the age of fifteen Alex had been excluded from four secondary schools. 'I think he must be trying for a record,' Gwen said with the weakest of smiles.

'Not a record you'd want him to set,' I said sadly.

But on a positive note, Taylor was getting married to his long-time girlfriend, Krissy, and Gwen was organizing their wedding. Krissy's mother had died when she was a child and her father was happy to leave the arrangements to Gwen. 'Taylor and Krissy just want a small wedding,' she told me. 'Immediate family with a sit-down meal to follow. But it's so nice to be thinking about something else other than Alex's problems. He's saying he's not coming to the wedding, but hopefully he'll change his mind.'

I hoped so too, for if Alex didn't go to his brother's wedding it could cement the wedge between them permanently.

It was six months before we met again and Gwen seemed much brighter and full of how lovely the wedding had been. Alex had attended and when she showed me the photographs it was lovely to see him clean and smart in a suit. While he wasn't smiling, at least he'd lost the scowl that had been part of him in recent years. Gwen was upbeat and chatty and I thought the wedding had done her a power of good, but there was another reason too.

'We've managed to get Alex into school,' she said. 'It's much smaller. A specialist unit for young people who have been out of mainstream school for a long time. Their classes are small and there's plenty of one-to-one available, and counselling. The children can stay for a year and the expectation is that they then go back into mainstream school.'

'Fantastic,' I said. 'And Alex is attending?'

'Yes. So far, so good. He's been every day for six weeks. I get regular feedback from the Head and he seems to be doing well. Apparently, he's been spending quite a bit of time with one of the girls who attends. He's started showering and changing his clothes again.'

We both smiled. 'A good influence then.'

'Yes, indeed.'

'And the alcohol and smoking?'

'There are very strict rules at the unit,' Gwen said. 'Any hint that they are using illegal substances and they're out. Alex knows this is his last chance, so hopefully he'll use it wisely.'

Like Gwen, I was cautiously optimistic.

I received a Christmas card from them as usual, and Gwen had written a note inside saying that she was sorry she hadn't been in touch and she'd give me a ring in the New Year to arrange to meet.

I was still in bed at 9.30 a.m. on 1 January when the landline rang. My family and I had seen in the New Year with a few friends and I was now having a lie-in. I reached out for the handset on my bedside cabinet, expecting it to be a friend or relative wishing me a Happy New Year. I answered with a bleary, 'Hello?'

'Cathy?' I didn't immediately recognize the voice.

'Yes? Who is it?'

'Alex.'

'Alex?' I sat bolt upright.

'I've got the money for your broken window. Mum says I should come in person to give it to you.'

'Oh. I see.' I couldn't believe my ears. 'OK. Yes, thank you.'

'Today?'

'Yes, I suppose so. What time?'

'Eleven.'

'All right. Are your parents coming too?'

'No. They said I needed to do this alone, and to tell you they'd see you another time.'

'OK. See you at eleven then.'

'Yes. Goodbye.'

I replaced the handset.

Astounded. Astonished. Flabbergasted. I couldn't think of a word to describe my thoughts that morning as I quickly got out of bed, showered and dressed. I then went into Adrian's, Lucy's and Paula's bedrooms and told them that Alex was visiting. Unaware of the problems Alex had been causing, and used to children we'd fostered visiting, they took the news in their stride. Downstairs, I cleared the living room of the debris of last night, taking the glasses, plates, cups and so on into the kitchen, where I filled the dishwasher. Still dumbfounded that Alex was on his way to pay for the damage he'd done over two years previously, I went round the rest of the downstairs tidying up as Adrian, Paula and Lucy slowly got up. What an incredibly wonderful way to start the New Year, I thought.

Alex was ten minutes early, and when the bell rang it was with a mixture of incredulity, relief and joy that I answered it. Now nearly sixteen, he was much taller than me, a good-looking lad, dressed in clean jeans and what looked like a new leather jacket over a grey jersey. He stood nervously on the doorstep wearing a very serious expression.

'Come in, love,' I said, smiling. 'It's good to see you.' Perhaps he'd expected me to tell him off, for as he came in he looked relieved. 'How are you?'

'Good. Thanks.'

He automatically slipped off his shoes as he had done when entering my house as a child, and then hung his jacket on the hall stand.

'Nice jacket,' I remarked.

'Thanks. My Christmas present from Mum and Dad.'

'Very nice. Adrian, Paula and Lucy are just getting up. Come through.' I led the way into the living room, where his gaze swept around.

'It looks different from when I was here,' he said.

'That was eight years ago! We've redecorated since then and changed the sofas.'

'But you still have Toscha,' he said, looking at her asleep on her favourite chair.

'Yes, but she's very old. She just eats and sleeps. Do sit down.'

'Rupert died a while back,' he said, sitting on the sofa.

'I'm sorry.' I knew already, as Gwen had told me. 'I expect you all miss him.'

Alex nodded. 'Dad said we may think about having another dog this year.'

'Great.' I also knew from Gwen that their rabbit and cat had passed from old age. 'Would you like a drink?'

'No, thanks. I'm seeing my girlfriend later. I just came to give you this.' He took an envelope from the pocket of his jeans and handed it to me. 'Two hundred and fifty pounds.'

'Thank you very much. You did well to save up all that,' I said, impressed.

'Dad reminded me. Each time he gave me my allowance he told me to put a bit aside.'

'You did well though,' I said. Indeed, I was astounded, for despite all that had been going on, Alex had kept saving, even when he'd been stealing from others.

'I'm paying them all back now,' he said, as though reading my thoughts. 'I've been a right dickhead. I took money from my family and I'm paying them back. Every last penny.'

I was touched by his honestly and humility. 'That's good. I expect they have forgiven you.'

He nodded. 'They've forgiven me for everything. I don't know why. I don't deserve it. I was horrid, even to Kaylee, who can't help how she is.' His eyes filled with tears and he grabbed a tissue from the box on the coffee table and wiped them. 'Sorry,' he said, embarrassed.

'It's OK. You've been through a lot.'

'I can't believe they still love me after all I've said and done,' he said, his voice breaking.

A lump rose to my throat and felt my own eyes fill. To see him so vulnerable and remorseful moved me deeply. 'They love you more than ever,' I said. 'You've all come through a difficult time and I know they love you as much as you love them.'

His eyes filled again and he took another tissue. Big as he was, I couldn't just sit there from afar and dispassionately watch him, so I went over and sat next to him.

'Don't cry, love,' I said, slipping my arm around his waist.

But his tears fell. 'I don't know what I can do to put it right,' he said. 'I can give back the money, but I can't take back my words and all the horrible things I've done. I'm seeing a counsellor and she said she'd help me.'

'I am sure she will,' I said. 'But, Alex, the fact that you are turning your life around and are recovering will be enough for your family. I know them and I know just how much they all love you. They'll be overjoyed they're getting the old Alex back, and at some point this will all be history. Try to concentrate on the positives and see how much you have achieved, and look to the future. Keep doing what you are doing and I know you will be fine.'

'That's sort of what Mum said,' he said, wiping his eyes again.

'Well, she's as wise as I am then,' I said with a smile. I waited while he blew his nose. 'How is everyone? I haven't seen them for a while.'

'Good. They send their love, and Mum said to make sure I told you that Taylor and Krissy are expecting a baby.'

'Wonderful. Give them my congratulations. So you're going to be an uncle,' I said happily.

He nodded and managed a smile. 'I'm looking forward to it. Mum says a new baby in the family is just what we all need. She and Dad are so excited. I'm going to be the best uncle ever.'

'I'm sure you will be,' I said.

'Anyway, I'd better be going. I just wanted to give you the money and say I'm sorry.'

'Thank you, love. That is kind of you. You're doing very well.' His eyes misted again and I knew he was emotionally fragile and only at the start of his journey of recovery. It would take time.

'I'm meeting Lexi in town,' he said, blowing his nose and throwing the tissue in the waste paper basket. 'I'm taking her out for the day. I'd better go. She tells me off if I'm late.'

I smiled. 'I won't keep you then, but let me just see if Adrian, Lucy and Paula are up so they can say hello.'

Alex waited in the living room while I went to the foot of the stairs and called up that Alex was going and if they were dressed would they like to come down and say hi. They called back that they would. I returned to the living room and within a minute or so the three of them had appeared. They said hello and exchanged a few words with Alex, a bit awkwardly, but then teenagers are often awkward in conversation and they hadn't seen him for a while. Adrian, Paula and Lucy then went into the kitchen to make themselves some breakfast.

'They've all grown,' Alex said.

'So have you!' I laughed.

I picked up the envelope he'd given to me and took out fifty pounds. 'I'd like to treat you and Lexi to your day out,' I said, offering him the money.

'No. It's yours,' he said, and refused to take it to begin with, but I insisted, saying it would make me happy.

I went with him to the front door, and as he knelt to tie his shoelaces my thoughts went back to when he'd lived with us and he had done that as a child. 'I remember you doing that when you were little,' I said.

'So do I,' he said, straightening. He slipped on his jacket. 'I remember my time here very well, and how good you were to me. I also remember how you offered me a hug on my first night, but I didn't want one. I was so pleased you didn't insist.'

'You remember that?' I asked, surprised.

'Yes. And lots more.'

He met my gaze and for a moment I saw again that vulnerable seven-year-old, hurt and confused from previous rejections, and resisting affection yet crying out for love and a family of his own.

'Come here,' I said, opening my arms. 'I'll have that hug now.'

He stepped forward and gave me the biggest hug ever, then thanked me for all I'd done.

'Good luck with everything,' I said. 'Give my love to your family. Enjoy your day out.'

'Thanks, I will.'

With that warm glow from knowing that everything will work out, I watched him go.

If you were to ask Gwen and Gareth what made Alex turn a corner and begin his journey of recovery, they would say it was because he met Lexi. While she may have played a part – Alex dated her for over a year – it was Gwen and Gareth who saved Alex. Their unfailing love, commitment and support, combined with their previous experience of handling very challenging behaviour, provided the safe haven Alex needed to set him on the path to recovery. Without them he would have continued on a downward spiral of self-loathing, anger, resentment and substance abuse, perhaps never coming to terms with his early life experience, even into adulthood.

Early childhood experience shapes us all, and not all adopted children are as lucky as Alex in finding a stable, loving family who are able to see them through the bad times. While there is no systematic collection of data for failed adoptions, recent studies in the UK and US show that between a quarter and a third of all adoptions fail. Horrendous. And these figures rise with the age of the child, so that if a child is nine or over when placed for adoption there is a 60 per cent chance of it failing and the child being returned to care. The effect of this is devastating, both for the adoptive parents, who feel they've failed, and the child, who may never fully recover or come to terms with their feelings of rejection and abandonment. More needs to be done to prepare adoptive parents (Rosemary and Edward had unrealistic and naïve expectations of adoption), and if problems do arise then intensive practical support should be available for as long as necessary. As a society we have a duty to support and nurture our children, who will one day be raising the next generation, bringing with them their own childhood experiences. We need to make sure those experiences are good.

Well done, Alex, Gwen, Gareth and your wonderful family. Love to you all.

For the latest on Alex and the other children in my books, please visit www.cathyglass.co.uk

SUGGESTED TOPICS FOR
READING-GROUP DISCUSSION

———————

In Chapter Four, the reader senses that Cathy isn't completely bowled over by Rosemary and Edward. How is this conveyed in the narrative?

What legitimate reasons might there be for a foster carer asking for a child to be removed from their care?

Cathy says the timetable of introductions for adoption is standard. What are your thoughts on this?

How would you have handled Alex's return after the adoption failed?

Was the adoption disruption meeting useful?

Gwen and Gareth are very different from Rosemary and Edward. Discuss with reference to the text. What skills did Gwen and Gareth posses that Rosemary and Edward did not?

Why do you think so many young people from the care system end up in young offenders' institutions? What could be done to change this?

What aspects of the adoption system would you like to see changed and why?

How would you improve the care system generally? Would adoption still feature, and if so, in what circumstances?

With hindsight, how could Alex's case have been handled differently?

Cathy Glass

———

One remarkable woman, more
than **150** foster children cared for.

Cathy Glass has been a foster carer for
twenty-five years, during which time she has
looked after more than 150 children, as well
as raising three children of her own. She was
awarded a degree in education and psychology
as a mature student, and writes under a
pseudonym. To find out more about Cathy
and her story visit www.cathyglass.co.uk.

Can I Let You Go?

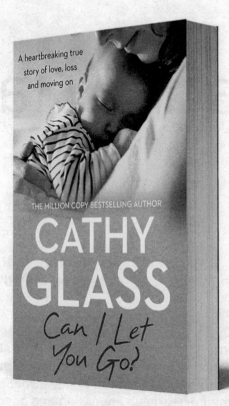

**Faye is 24 and pregnant, and
has learning difficulties as a result
of her mother's alcoholism**

Can Cathy help Faye learn enough
to parent her child?

The Silent Cry

———

A mother battling depression. A family in denial

Cathy is desperate to help before something terrible happens.

Girl Alone

———

An angry, traumatized young girl on a path to self-destruction

Can Cathy discover the truth behind Joss's dangerous behaviour before it's too late?

Saving Danny

———

Danny's parents can no longer cope with his challenging behaviour

Calling on all her expertise, Cathy discovers a frightened little boy who just wants to be loved.

The Child Bride

A girl blamed and abused for dishonouring her community

Cathy discovers the devastating truth.

Daddy's Little Princess

A sweet-natured girl with a complicated past

Cathy picks up the pieces after events take a dramatic turn.

Will You Love Me?

A broken child desperate for a loving home

The true story of Cathy's adopted daughter Lucy.

Please Don't Take My Baby

Seventeen-year-old Jade is pregnant, homeless and alone

Cathy has room in her heart for two.

Another Forgotten Child

Eight-year-old Aimee was on the child-protection register at birth

Cathy is determined to give her the happy home she deserves.

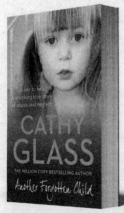

A Baby's Cry

A newborn, only hours old, taken into care

Cathy protects tiny Harrison from the potentially fatal secrets that surround his existence.

The Night the Angels Came

A little boy on the brink of bereavement

Cathy and her family make sure Michael is never alone.

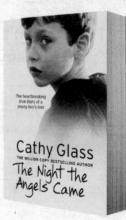

Mummy Told Me Not to Tell

A troubled boy sworn to secrecy

After his dark past has been revealed, Cathy helps Reece to rebuild his life.

I Miss Mummy

Four-year-old Alice doesn't understand why she's in care

Cathy fights for her to have the happy home she deserves.

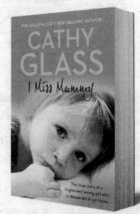

The Saddest Girl in the World

A haunted child who refuses to speak

Do Donna's scars run too deep for Cathy to help?

Cut

Dawn is desperate to be loved

Abused and abandoned, this vulnerable child pushes Cathy and her family to their limits.

Hidden

The boy with no past

Can Cathy help Tayo to feel like he belongs again?

Damaged

A forgotten child

Cathy is Jodie's last hope.
For the first time, this
abused young girl has
found someone
she can trust.

Inspired by Cathy's own experiences...

Run, Mummy, Run

The gripping story of a
woman caught in a horrific
cycle of abuse, and the
desperate measures she
must take to escape.

My Dad's a
Policeman

The dramatic short story
about a young boy's
desperate bid to keep his
family together.

The Girl in the Mirror

Trying to piece together her past, Mandy uncovers a dreadful family secret that has been blanked from her memory for years.

Sharing her expertise...

About Writing and How to Publish

A clear and concise, practical guide on writing and the best ways to get published.

Happy Mealtimes for Kids

A guide to healthy eating with simple recipes that children love.

Happy Adults

A practical guide to achieving lasting happiness, contentment and success. The essential manual for getting the best out of life.

Happy Kids

A clear and concise guide to raising confident, well-behaved and happy children.

Be amazed
Be moved
Be inspired

———